A Guide to Britai

David Clarke is a ne
has been investigating the legends, folklore
and strange phenomena of the British Isles
for many years. He graduated from
Sheffield University with a degree in
Archaeology and Medieval History in 1990
and is studying towards a PhD in British
Folklore at the University's Centre for
English Cultural Tradition and Language
(CECTAL). He is the author of three previ-
ous books including *Phantoms of the Sky:
UFO's – A Modern Myth?* (with Andy
Roberts) also published by Hale.

A Guide to Britain's Pagan Heritage

DAVID CLARKE

ROBERT HALE • LONDON

ISBN 0 7090 5405 X

Robert Hale Limited
Clerkenwell House
Clerkenwell Green
London EC1R 0HT

2 4 6 8 10 9 7 5 3 1

Printed in Great Britain by St Edmundsbury Press,
Bury St Edmunds, Suffolk and bound by
WBC Book Manufacturers Ltd., Bridgend, Glamorgan.

Contents

List of Illustrations

Illustration Credits

Christopher Hill Photographic, Navan at Armagh: 2. Paul Devereux: 3(a). Ben Stocker, Dover Archaeological Group: 4. Manchester Museum: 5. Joe Sheehan: 6(a). Estate of Sidney Jackson: 7, 11. Bob Trubshaw: 8. Derby Museum and Art Gallery: 9. Andy Roberts: 10, 14.

All other illustrations are from the collection of the author.

Acknowledgements

Special thanks to the following for practical help, advice and information which has helped in the preparation of this book: Andy Roberts, John Billingsley, Martin Petch and Manchester Museum, Dr Anne Ross, John Taylor Broadbent, Keith Parfitt, Bob Trubshaw, Andrew Dunwell, Claire Lawrence, Liz Linahan, Dr Miranda Green, Paul Devereux, and Peter Clarke for the cover illustration.

The author wishes to thank Penguin Books Ltd for kind permission to reproduce material from Bede's *Ecclesiastical History of the English People*, edited by Leo Sherley-Price.

Preface

Lonely circles of standing stones on remote moors, strange customs and ceremonies, the names of the days of the week, charms and superstitions, a grim stone head staring with sightless eyes ... these are all the relics of Britain's rich pagan heritage.

The word 'pagan' originated from a Latin term meaning a civilian, a countryman or villager, and has come to be used to describe people, beliefs or practices that do not belong to monotheistic religions of the modern world. Pagans, according to dictionary definitions, worshipped a number of gods and goddesses and the forces of the natural world, long before the appearance of organized religions centred upon a single God.

During the Middle Ages the word came to be used as a term of abuse to describe anyone who did not profess Christianity, and could therefore be equally applied to believers in Judaism and Islam as well as to those who continued to swear by the old gods. Today 'pagan' has many new connotations, for the revival of interest in prehistoric religion and the birth of the Earth Mysteries movement since the 1960s has seen the adoption of the name by a great number of different people, from latter-day witches to children of the New Age and green movements. They have attempted to reconstruct what they believe to be elements of the pagan tradition in a guise more suited to the social climate of the late twentieth-century, such as belief in the Mother Goddess on the part of some feminists and the use of the Green Man as a symbol of opposition to the destruction of forests.

However, despite the huge and self-perpetuating literature aimed at resurrecting 'the Celtic tradition' for modern pagans and Wiccans, few people who profess to be pagans today have any real idea of the true nature of the religion practised or the gods and goddesses worshipped in these islands before the arrival of Christianity. Until recently the nature of the evidence itself has remained obscure and, in the case of archaeology, much remains beneath ground waiting excavation.

Most works on the history of the British Isles tend to begin with the invasion of Rome or the arrival of the Anglo-Saxons, with Christianity seemingly delimiting everything we know of the civilization which flourished before. Our knowledge of the old religion and the pagan deities is of course limited because their followers did not commit their beliefs to writing, and what records there were from Roman Britain have not survived the ravages of time.

Archaeology and the study of ancient texts can take us so far, but the only way our pagan heritage can be effectively reconstructed is through a cross-disciplinary study which takes account of archaeology and the written word together with the more nebulous evidence provided by mythology, folk tradition and custom. Questions may be asked of folk traditions – whether they really are survivals of paganism, or if they are simply examples of magic or superstition aimed at giving comfort or security to people long after the beliefs which created them had lost their real meaning. However, the subject of alleged continuity of tradition from pagan times to the present in Britain is a vast and controversial topic in itself, and requires a book of its own.

This work was planned as a sourcebook for those who wish to make their own in-depth exploration of the magical landscape of the British Isles, to experience the traditions and customs themselves, and to draw their own conclusions at the end of their quest. Good luck.

David Clarke
Sheffield, May 1994

How to Use This Book

During the last twenty years many dozens of guidebooks to the ancient mysteries and legends of the British Isles have been published. All of these works have been produced in response to a growing upsurge of interest among the general public in that 'hidden past' which does not feature in the conventional history books we read at school. Some have focused upon specific regions or periods of prehistory and history, others have attempted to offer long lists of the more interesting and visible sites and monuments which can be visited by the seeker of the magical past.

This guide is not aimed at those with a superficial interest in Britain's pagan heritage. Instead of listing hundreds of places to visit with brief commentaries on each, I have confined myself to what I believe are fifty of the most important places in Britain and Ireland which retain some atmosphere from their pagan past. Each of the places I have selected are accompanied by essay-length descriptions, not just relating to what can be seen and visited, but also aimed at placing them in some wider geographical and historical context.

Whereas some of the entries concentrate upon a specific named site or monument, others focus upon a number of places set within a larger landscape including both the monuments and related legends, traditions and folklore. Some of these related sites can be visited as part of one itinerary.

The fifty 'Places to Visit' featured in this guidebook have been split into seven different zones in a classification which neatly divides the islands by geography rather than by modern political boundaries. These include the countries of Ireland, Scotland, Wales and England, which has been split into four areas: Northern England, Central England including East Anglia, Southern England (including Wessex) and South-west England.

Each of these seven zones contains within it approximately seven places which can be visited and a section follows at the end of each essay giving details of how to get there and what to see (including details of access by road and foot, ownership and on-site facilities like museums and visitor centres). England, Scotland, Wales and Northern Ireland are covered by the excellent Ordnance Survey 1.25 inch to 1 mile (2 cm to 1 km) Landranger maps, and the newer 2.5 inch to 1 mile Pathfinder series may also be useful for visitors who wish to explore landscapes in more detail.

Subject Definitions

The fifty entries in this guidebook feature a variety of sites stretching from 'silent' prehistoric monuments (standing stones, megalithic circles, henges and chambered tombs) to others where there is both archaeological and written evidence (holy wells, hill figures, stone carvings), and modern-day folk traditions and calendar customs. These can be grouped in the following rough categories:

Ritual Landscapes

This is a new term used by archaeologists and Earth Mysteries researchers alike to describe an area of land, such as a hill range, valley or plain, which encloses a number of ritual monuments linked to each other but not necessarily constructed at the same time. Landscapes like these can be said to have 'evolved' often from one early earthwork or ritual focus, like those at Avebury in Wessex and the Boyne Valley in Ireland. From recent work it seems these landscapes were laid out with particular emphasis upon integrating monuments with both the heavens and the human mind using subtle manipulations of topography along with stellar and lunar alignments.

Included within this definition are the landscapes surrounding mysterious hill figures like the Cerne Abbas Giant and the Giant of Penhill, which appear to be images of pagan deities created by the whole community as part of a ritual act. Celtic gods and goddesses always seem to have been visualized as giants in the ancient lore, their features being occasionally marked out by the rocks, hills and valleys themselves. In some cases these hill figures seem to have acted as tribal symbols, labelling land or territory, as in the case of the horses at Uffington and Middle Tysoe. Often this persistent 'folk memory' of earlier rituals and the names of the deities themselves survives in the form of place-names, traditions and legends to the present day.

Archaeological Sites And Remains

Archaeological sites of an important ritual nature are included in the guide, and visits to some of them, such as the museum at the large Bronze Age water shrine at Flag Fen in Cambridge-shire, can provide a unique insight into the nature of prehistoric religion.

Over the last twenty years many startling new archaeological discoveries have changed the way we interpret the past, often causing textbooks to be rewritten and dating sequences to be thrown out. Sometimes these discoveries have come about as a result of new building developments, which have by accident cut into 'lost' ritual landscapes, like that at Deal in Kent during the 1980s. In Britain, the discovery of the Lindow Man bog body has thrown new light on the very end of the Iron Age, just as the discovery of the 'roofbox' at New Grange in Ireland has thrown light upon the theory that movements of the sun and moon were studied and marked with great precision by prehis-toric man.

In addition, scientific archaeology now has at its disposal a wide range of technological expertise with which to investigate these new discoveries, including vastly improved radiocarbon and tree-ring dating techniques, geophysical surveys and aerial photography. But lurking behind the technology is the often ignored human factor – intuition, inspiration and vision, often springing from interaction with the landscape itself. It is here and only here where modern man can really feel a connection with his ancestors who created the monuments he is investigat-ing.

Customs And Traditions

For many historians and some folklorists, those who attempt to trace surviving calendar customs back to paganism are living in a fantasy world of 'past as wished for'. They argue that because there is no written evidence a custom or tradition existed before it was first recorded in print two or three hundred years ago, then we cannot assume it can be any older than that early date. True, many calendar customs are recent inventions or revivals and others, like the Castleton Garland in Derbyshire, have changed substantially within living memory. However, negative evidence is not evidence of absence nor an adequate excuse to dismiss the large amount of material from folk tradition and custom as having no relevance to the study of pre-Christian religion, as this book will demonstrate.

The customs and traditions included in the guide are those which the author feels appear to have genuine archaic roots, particularly where these are connected with one of the early seasonal festivals or standing monuments. Some of the more unique customs seem to embody a 'folk memory' of earlier rituals or 'lost' deities, particularly in the case of the Padstow Obby Oss, the Haxey Hood game and the Burning of Bartle.

Time Chart

The chart on page 20 should be used by the reader as a reference tool when reading the entries in this book. For those unfamiliar with the tradition whereby prehistoric and historical periods are broken into a chronological sequence (all of which overlap considerably), the following brief definitions may help:

Neolithic or **New Stone Age** (c. 5000–2200 BC) begins with the origins of agriculture around 4500 BC and its spread from Asia Minor westwards across Europe. The third millennium BC saw farming become the basis of settled and wealthy civilizations whose intellectual and engineering skill led to the construction of the great megalithic temples like the Avebury henge in Wessex and New Grange passage grave complex in Ireland.

Bronze Age (2200–1000 BC), saw introduction of the first metals, a time of great social change with an emphasis on individual wealth, land ownership and the development of hierarchies. These developments were accompanied by corresponding changes in religious ritual away from great megalithic monuments towards cults of water and idols, perhaps influenced also by rising sea levels and changes in weather patterns.

Iron Age (1000 BC–AD 55) in the British Isles often associated with the arrival of the Celts around 500 BC and was brought to an abrupt end in the first century AD with the Roman invasion of Britain. It is during the Celtic period when the evidence of the written word can be added to that of archaeological remains, with the accounts of the Classical historians throwing light upon the beliefs and practices of the tribes they found inhabiting the British Isles.

Romano-British period (AD 100–500), the period of the Romanization of Britain, which saw the construction of the first towns, villas and roads and fusion between Classical and native Celtic gods and goddesses. The arrival of Roman civilization also brought with it writing and Christianity. The legions conquered most of England and Wales, defeated the Caledonian (Scots) tribes, but never reached Ireland which remained a Celtic outpost.

The Dark Ages (c. AD 400–1000), followed the collapse of Roman administration in Britain in the middle of the fifth century AD. Germanic tribes of Anglo-Saxons migrated across the North Sea to settle in eastern England and set up their own kingdoms. They were followed in the ninth and tenth centuries by pagan Scandinavians, the Vikings.

Time Chart

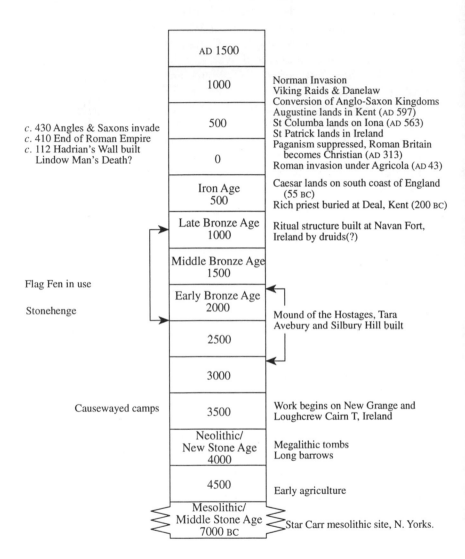

c. 430 Angles & Saxons invade
c. 410 End of Roman Empire
c. 112 Hadrian's Wall built
Lindow Man's Death?

AD 1500

1000

Norman Invasion
Viking Raids & Danelaw
Conversion of Anglo-Saxon Kingdoms
Augustine lands in Kent (AD 597)
St Columba lands on Iona (AD 563)
St Patrick lands in Ireland
Paganism suppressed, Roman Britain
    becomes Christian (AD 313)
Roman invasion under Agricola (AD 43)

500

0

Iron Age
500

Caesar lands on south coast of England
    (55 BC)
Rich priest buried at Deal, Kent (200 BC)

Late Bronze Age
1000

Ritual structure built at Navan Fort,
Ireland by druids(?)

Middle Bronze Age
1500

Flag Fen in use

Early Bronze Age
2000

Stonehenge

Mound of the Hostages, Tara
Avebury and Silbury Hill built

2500

3000

Causewayed camps

3500

Work begins on New Grange and
Loughcrew Cairn T, Ireland

Neolithic/
New Stone Age
4000

Megalithic tombs
Long barrows

4500

Early agriculture

Mesolithic/
Middle Stone Age
7000 BC

Star Carr mesolithic site, N. Yorks.

Introduction

Pagan and Christian in Anglo-Saxon England
Celtic Christianity and St Patrick
Holy Places and Temples
The Goddesses
Pagan Gods
The Festivals
The Pagan Year

I shall not speak of the ancient errors ... that bound the whole of humanity before the coming of Christ in the flesh ... I shall not name the mountains and hills and rivers, once so pernicious, now useful for human needs on which, in those days, a blind people heaped divine honours ...

Gildas, *The Ruin of the Britain*, sixth century AD

On a fateful day in AD 597 a small band of missionaries, said to be forty in number, led by a man called Augustine, landed with some trepidation on the Island of Thanet, off the eastern coast of a pagan kingdom. The group, sent by Pope Gregory, had brought with them interpreters from among the Gaulish Franks. They were dispatched to Canterbury, the capital and court of the Kentish King Aethelbert, saying they came from Rome bearing 'very glad news'.

Hearing about the landing of the missionaries, the pagan Anglo-Saxon king who traced his ancestry directly from the god Woden gave instructions that the foreign priests and the new god they brought with them should remain upon the island until he decided what course of action to take. The Northumbrian monk Bede, who told the story three hundred years later in his *Ecclesiastical History of the English People*, says Aethelbert

21

was already familiar with the Christian faith via his Frankish wife, whom he had married on condition that she could practise her faith unhindered in his realm.

Bede describes the meeting between the two cultures graphically: 'After some days, the king came to the island and, sitting down in the open air, summoned Augustine and his companions to an audience'. However, the king made sure he did not meet them inside a house 'for he held an ancient superstition that, if they were practisers of magical arts, they might have the opportunity to deceive and master him.' But, wrote Bede, 'the monks were endowed with the power from God, not from the Devil, and approached the king carrying a silver cross as their standard and the likeness of our Lord and Saviour painted on a board.'[1]

After singing a litany for the souls of those they had come to convert, the king allowed the monks to sit down and preach the new religion to his court. He told them after careful consideration: 'Your words and promises are fair indeed; but they are new and uncertain, and I cannot accept them and abandon the age-old beliefs that I have held together with the whole English nation. But since you have travelled far, and I can see that you are sincere in your desire to impart us what you believe to be true and excellent, we will not harm you. We will receive you hospitably and take care to supply you with all you need; nor will we forbid you to preach and win any people you can to your religion.'

Pagan and Christian in Anglo-Saxon England

How accurate the account of this meeting between pagan and Roman missionary actually is will never be known, for it was committed to history by a monk of the very religion which tried to squash those 'ancient errors' mentioned earlier by Gildas. What is clear is that it was from these shaky roots that the history books tell us Christianity once again took root on English soil.

The 'official version' of the Roman mission to England tells us how from these humble beginnings the kings and courts of the pagan Anglo-Saxon kingdoms were converted within a period of one hundred years, quickly followed by the mass of the common people. However the truth is more complex for it is clear these conversions were at the very best superficial, and for most people, especially those living in the countryside, the influence of Christianity upon entrenched traditions would have been superficial at best.

Aethelbert's baptism was followed by that of the king of the East Saxons (Essex), achieved as a result of Kent's political influence which was crucial for the spread of Christianity. For Aethelbert was not only the king of Kent but also the overlord (bretwalda) of the whole of southern England. Although this status had its advantages, in a tribal society governed by blood-feud it could be a double-edged sword. Upon the king's death in AD 616, the fragile toehold established by Augustine in Kent was lost, as Aethelbert's son was a pagan and so too were the three sons of King Saberht of Essex. They were quick to profess idolatry 'which they had pretended to abandon during the lifetime of their father' and encouraged their people to return to the old gods.

At this point the monk Lawrence, Augustine's successor, was all set to abandon the mission to England but was deterred by a vision of St Peter, which was luckily followed by the conversion of the new king of Kent. Another lucky break came with the conversion of Edwin, king of the Northumbrians, a tribe which seems to have been made up largely from Celts ruled by an Anglo-Saxon aristocracy. The hope enshrined in Edwin soon ended when he met with a common fate of his time and was slaughtered in battle against the fearsome Penda, pagan king of Mercia (the Middle Angles) in AD 633.

By the middle of the seventh century AD the new religion had made advances into the rich kingdom of East Anglia, whose king Redwald had accepted Christianity while visiting Kent at an early date. To Bede's great disgust this was to no good purpose 'for on his return home his wife and certain perverse advisors persuaded him to apostacise . . . so his last state was worse than his first for he tried to serve both Christ and the ancient gods, and he had in the same temple an altar for the Holy Sacrifice of Christ side by side with an altar on which victims were offered to devils.'[2]

Redwald came from a Swedish royal dynasty known as the Wuffingas, who arrived on the eastern coast in longboats and settled in Suffolk after the fall of Roman Britain. Experts now believe it was this great king whose cenotaph was contained within the great ship burial mound discovered at Sutton Hoo,

Suffolk, in 1939. He may have been the last king of his time to receive a pagan burial in the old style for his body, missing from the interior of the ship, was presumably burned upon a funeral pyre like the hero in the epic poem *Beowulf*. Afterwards, his splendid gold regalia, helmet and weapons were placed inside the longship which had been dragged from the River Deben nearby and covered by a great burial mound. Excavations here in recent years have uncovered many dozens of bizarre boat-burials alongside those of humans, some of whom appear to have been sacrificed in pagan rites.[3]

The impressive whetstone discovered inside the Sutton Hoo burial mound is carved with four faces which appear to represent divine ancestors, including the god Woden, and symbolises the authority of a pagan king upon whom Christianity had made little impression. The richness and elegance of the Sutton Hoo grave demonstrates how culturally sophisticated and intelligent the pagan rulers and their priests undoubtedly were, a far cry from the stories of bloodthirsty barbarians related by the Roman and Christian propagandists.

The deaths of Redwald and Edwin marked the beginning of the second generation of the Roman mission which saw the official conversion of most of the Anglo-Saxon kingdoms. In AD 640 King Eadbald of Kent was the first English king 'to give orders for the complete abandonment and destruction of idols throughout his realm'. In Northumbria, the sons of Edwin were converted while in exile at the court of the Irish kingdom of Dalriada in Western Scotland, and upon returning to the throne sent for Celtic monks to found a Christian monastery at the Holy Island, Lindisfarne.

The power of the Christian overlords continued to compel lesser, stubborn pagan kings to the baptismal pool, and soon the tribes of Wessex and Essex were converted. During this process, Christianity was itself shaped by the tribal culture which remained saturated with the ways of the old religion. The new faith had to adapt to the violent and uncertain lives of the tribal warriors, offering kings the new talisman of divine power and political advantage over pagan adversaries in the process. Missionaries often used the message that invoking the Christian god could deliver kings victory in battle. Bede describes how the last great stronghold of paganism, the kingdom of Mercia, finally received the word of God after its king Penda, heathen to his last breath, was killed in battle after the Northumbrian king bound himself with an oath to the Christian god, following an unsuccessful attempt to bribe his enemy with heathen gold.

By AD 664, when at the Synod of Whitby the Roman and Celtic Christian traditions met and merged leaving the Romans victorious, history tells us most of the Anglo-Saxon peoples had been converted. The extent of the religious change among the population as a whole is uncertain, for it is clear that it was the power of kings to compel their tribes to accept the new beliefs which was of vital importance. Paganism clearly survived in the countryside where native Celtic cults, often based upon agricultural rites and healing shrines, continued to worship the old gods.

The extent to which latent and underlying beliefs survived the Christianization of England was demonstrated when the invasion of the Scandinavian Vikings led to a revival of paganism during the ninth century AD. Anglo-Saxon kings were then forced to legislate against the old religion, and Pope Formosus wrote to the English bishops complaining 'the abominable rites of the pagans have sprouted again in your parts.'[4]

For the dwellers in the countryside, many of whom were native Celts, it is clear the acceptance of this new religion from the east by their Germanic rulers would have meant very little in practical terms. The arrival of Christianity would have meant firstly a change of the names and rites practised at the seasonal festivals, and a change in burial rites as is evident from the early eighth century AD when pagan burial rites came to an end.

Despite this change demonstrated by archaeology, it is clear the ordinary people continued to follow the old religion, resorting to the holy places of the natural world and utilizing the old charms and magical rites, as is evident from the edicts passed by successive kings against such pagan practices. The biographer of the Northumbrian St Cuthbert described how countryfolk refused to pray for the safety of monks who were in danger at sea: 'Nobody shall pray for them! May God spare none of them! for they have taken away from men the ancient rites and customs, and how the new ones are to be observed nobody knows.'[5]

Although there is some slight evidence of opposition, which may have been organized by the priests of the old religion who sometimes appear in the lives of the saints, it appears the real power of the pagan gods was weak and broken in England before the documentary evidence of Bede begins. The influence of the lesser gods and spirits lingered in the natural world and fireside hearth, as is clear from late Scandinavian myths and surviving charms which exhibit subtle Christian influences.

At the end of the seventh century AD King Wihtred, in the last surviving Kentish law code, forbade both freemen and slaves from making offerings to 'devils' (pagan gods). Over the next four centuries, the laws of Alfred, Edward the Elder, Aethelred the Redeless and Cnut continued to legislate in vain against paganism. Cnut specifically stated: 'namely, the worship of idols, heathen gods, and the sun or the moon, fire or water, springs or stones or any kind of forest trees, or indulgence in witchcraft, or the compassing of death in any way, either by sacrifice or by divination or by the practice of any such delusions.'[6]

Celtic Christianity and St Patrick

More than ten years before Augustine's mission to the English, the Irish priest and monk St Columba landed with a small group of holy men upon the tiny sacred island of Iona in the Inner Hebrides of Scotland. There he founded a monastery, and his followers helped to spread the missionary zeal of Celtic Christianity to England via northern and western routes. It was the power of this form of ascetic Celtic Christianity, rooted as it was in the native druidic tradition of the British Isles, which allowed it to meet paganism on equal terms and was the real driving force behind the conversion of Britain.

Most of what we know about the indigenous pagan religions of the British Isles we know only through the writings of the early Christians for both the Celtic and Germanic peoples had a culture which was wholly based upon oral tradition. Writing was unknown, and arrived in these islands only with the intro-duction of the Roman alphabet which often accompanied Christianity. Bede and other writers did not think there was anything to be achieved by preserving any useful record of the pagan religions, which he dismisses in one account by saying: 'Thanks be to you, O Jesus, who have turned us away from these vanities.'

Celtic enclaves survived centuries of Anglo-Saxon advances

in the west and north of Britain during the so-called Dark Ages. Some of the earliest writing in Western Europe originates from Ireland in this period, including the famous early mythological literature, the Book of Invasions, and the Fionn and Ulster Cycles. Preserved by Christian scribes from the oral tradition of the *fili* or poets, guardians of the ancient tradition of the land, they are written in the context of an earlier pagan Iron Age society and are rich with stories about earlier gods and goddesses, magical journeys to the Otherworld and supernatural happenings. A similar series of stories from medieval Wales have survived in the collection known as the Mabinogion from a slightly later period of the Middle Ages.

We are fortunate that Bede's account of the landing in Kent has survived, because the circumstances surrounding the first appearance of Christianity in the British Isles remain a mystery. It is important to remember that in the western Celtic regions of Britain an earlier form of Christianity predated the Roman mission to Kent by as much as 300 years. The first written evidence for the presence of Christians in Roman Britain dates from AD 313 when three British bishops attended the Council of Arles in France.

At this time Christianity was just one of many exotic Eastern religions competing for new followers as the death of the Empire drew nearer. Christianity, officially adopted by Rome early in the fourth century, was an urban-based religion dependent upon the existence of cities, but it failed to penetrate the countryside until after the fall of Rome, when the end of urban life forced it to adapt to new conditions.

At this crucial period, Christianity in Britain was almost overshadowed by the Eastern religion of Mithras, and by other strong native pagan cults whose adherents were still building temples to their gods. Early in the fourth century AD there seems to have been a pagan revival in Britain, for a governor in Cirencester set up a statue and column to the god Jupiter 'in honour of the old religion.' At the same time new shrines were being built in the countryside, and a temple to the hunting god Nodens was refurbished above the River Severn in Gloucestershire.[7]

Although it was Christianity's own identification with towns and cities which led to the definition of paganism, at the end of the day it was the new religion which proved to be the most successful and adaptable of the two, giving new hope of eternal salvation to people trapped in a rapidly changing and uncertain world.

One very early British folk tradition suggests the first Christian church was actually founded at Glastonbury in Somerset by Joseph of Arimathea, who visited the Severn estuary as a result of his involvement in the tin trade. It was also said that Christ himself visited Glastonbury during the mysterious early part of his ministry. Whatever the truth, there is evidence for a wood and wattle church at Glastonbury as early as the sixth century AD, but all we know of this time of fable is from the pen of monks in later centuries who were trying to make sense of their own beginnings, often it seems by falsifying records and rewriting what scraps of history had survived the fall of Rome.[8]

This early, primitive form of Christianity identified with St Columba and his Celtic contemporaries, was strongly influenced by pagan beliefs and it is distinctly possible that some of the early monks were originally pagan priests, priestesses, poets *(fili)* and druids whose status in society had become discredited. Many seem to have switched allegiance to the new religion, preserving the mysteries and secrets of the old religion in the process. For example, in one of the lives of the early Welsh saints it is said St Illtyd came from a family of pagan priests and seers and he was 'the most learned of all Britons in all the arts of philosophy and the wisest magician in his tribe and knowledgeable about the future.'[9]

Perhaps the most important early Christian saint associated with the period of conversion is the fascinating St Patrick, the apostle of Ireland. Strongly associated with Ulster, Patrick was actually born in Britain, possibly in Glastonbury or Brigantia (northern Britain). He was captured by pirates early in the fifth century AD at the age of sixteen and taken to Ireland as a slave, but escaped back to Britain. Patrick returned to Ireland by his own will and, without imperial authority, following 'a vision', set about the conversion of a pagan nation which was still living in an heroic Iron Age society untouched by the Roman legions.

There is very little evidence to show how pagan Ireland came to adopt Christianity, or the true nature of the process of conversion but we can be sure that as in England, it was a long and tortuous process with very fragile beginnings. We know there were

Christians living perhaps as slaves in southern Ireland as early as the mid-fifth century, but it remains a mystery what happened between this early period and AD 575, when at the Convention of Drum Ceatt the power of the *fili* or bards (who had inherited much of the druidical lore), was seen to be in terminal retreat. We can guess the most important factor in the christianization of Ireland was the conversion of the guardians of the native religion itself – the *fili*.[10]

As there were no towns in existence in Ireland until the Viking age, Patrick was unable to establish his church upon the traditional Roman urban pattern and was forced to take his message directly to the pagan cult centres themselves, and by establishing new ones centred upon the burial places of saints. His main centre of operation seems to have been Ulster, where his cathedral of Armagh was located in direct opposition to the pagan centre at Emain Macha (Navan fort). The college of druids or poets there seems at some stage to have switched from worship of the sun god and become priests of the new religion. A similar process occurred in the province of Leinster, where a college of priestesses of the triple goddess Brigid ('The Great Queen'), became nuns led by St Brigid during the sixth century AD. They continued to tend a sacred flame in their temple until it was snuffed out by the Normans.

Another pagan sanctuary has been identified as Clogher in County Louth, where Patrick founded a church in AD 443 upon the site of a temple containing an oracular stone encased in gold.[11] The early Irish life of St Patrick describes how he then moved south to convert the kings of Tara, one of the centres of Irish paganism and a final druid stronghold. His followers, often isolated ascetics, pressed the Christian message further by establishing monastic settlements in isolated and inhospitable places proving their god as more powerful than those of the old religion.

In this way, the cult of saints took root in Ireland by a subtle takeover of the functions of the pagan deities they replaced, and today it is difficult to locate any purely pagan cult sites in Ireland, for they were all transformed into churches, monasteries or the burial places of their particular new saint or guardian. Although later texts try to emphasize 'continuity' in Irish history at this time, it is clear the fifth and sixth centuries were a period of great religious and social change, exacerbated by the attack of the great plague and the decline in the reputation of the druids, which proved fruitful ground for the establishment of Christianity.

What became of the pagan priesthood of the British and Irish people is a mystery, of which there is but scant evidence in the records left by Christian scribes. A king never changed his religion without very careful consultation with his chief advisors, which in Ireland at least would have been druids. Writing of the British king Vortigern who ruled in the mid-fifth century AD, the monk Nennius tells us his religious advisors were not bishops but magi (magicians) and there is mention of druids active, but discredited, in Ireland and Pictland as late as the medieval period.

Bede has left us with one tantalizing account of the conversion of the Northumbrian royal court under King Edwin, which may well be fictitious but serves to show how in times of change, pagan priests were wont to switch religious allegiance. The account describes how Edwin, as overlord, extended the boundaries of his kingdom as far as Anglesey and the Isle of Man. During his campaigns and through alliance with the kingdom of Kent he was married to Ethelberga, the Christian daughter of the Kentish king Eadbald, on condition that she was allowed to practise her faith. Like Aethelbert before him, he professed his will to accept the new religion if his advisors decided that it appeared 'more holy and acceptable to God than their own'.

The missionary Paulinus was consecrated bishop and travelled north with the princess in AD 625. The account implies the king spent many years in turmoil unable to decide which religion to follow despite the many miracles and temptations offered to him by Paulinus. In the end, King Edwin summoned his court, composed of his principal advisors and friends, asking each of them in turn his opinion of 'this strange doctrine and new way of worshipping'.

One of the king's thanes or chief men presented his view of the new religion in a beautiful passage which retains its strength today. He said:

> . . . when we compare the present life of man on earth with that time of which we have no knowledge, it seems to me like the swift flight of a single sparrow through the banqueting-hall

where you are sitting at dinner on a winter's day with your thanes and counsellors. In the midst there is a comforting fire to warm the hall; outside, the storms of winter rain or snow are raging. This sparrow flies swiftly in through one door of the hall, and out through another. While he is inside, he is safe from the winter storms; but after a few moments of comfort, he vanishes from sight into the wintry world from which he came. Even so, man appears on earth for a little while; but of what went before this life or of what follows, we know nothing. Therefore, if this new teaching has brought any certain knowledge, it seems only right that we should follow it.[12]

This argument proved too much for a man named Coifi, 'the chief priest', who dismissed his own religion as 'valueless and powerless' and, using a very materialistic argument, urged his king to accept the new one. According to Bede, Coifi formally renounced the old religion and asked the king for a horse and a spear, an act which was in itself taboo for priests were forbidden to carry weapons. Riding to the kingdom's central pagan temple at Goodmanham, near York, he cast the spear at the idols inside and told his companions to set fire 'to the temple and its enclosure and destroy them'.

There is no direct Irish equivalent of Bede's detailed account, and we know nothing of what happened afterwards but it is certain something similar must have occurred there too. One of the few accounts of a direct encounter between St Patrick and pagan gods is an episode in his *Life* which describes his visit to northwest Cavan, the centre of a cult landscape known as Meg Slecht or the 'Plain of Prostrations'. Here, seemingly on an island in a loch, for Patrick approached it by boat, stood a megalithic stone circle at the middle of which towered 'the chief idol of Ireland' Cenn or Crom Cruaich, a name which has survived in Irish folklore as Crom Dubh, 'the black crooked one', a harvest god.

The account describes how the idol was covered with gold and silver and had 'twelve other idols covered with brass about him.' When Patrick drew near the idol, he raised his hand to put his crozier upon it, whereupon it 'bowed westwards to Tara . . . and the earth swallowed the twelve other images as far as their heads, and they are thus in sign of the miracle, and he cursed the demon and banished him to hell.'[13]

Ij,olp Plarcs and Temples

And there were many
Dark springs running there, and
grim-faced figures of gods
Uncouthly hewn by axe from the untrimmed tree-trunk,
Rotted to whiteness.

Lucan, Pharsalia III (first century BC)

To the Celtic and Germanic peoples who settled in the British Isles at the beginning of recorded history, we know the supernatural world pervaded every aspect of daily life. To them the entire landscape was alive and numinous ('holy, awe-inspiring and mysterious'); the natural world was possessed of spirits that were everywhere – on mountains and crags, in rivers, pools and water, in gnarled and ancient trees, and other open air places where ritual was practised. The early Celtic tales and folk tradition make clear how the veil between this world and the Otherworld was thin at these places, particularly at certain times of the year, especially Samhain (1 November), the end of the year when spirits were loose and mankind could interact with the gods.

So few remains of pagan temples have been identified by archaeology precisely because of their fragile and ambiguous nature. From the early literature we know that trees, foliage and sacred groves performed a central role in Celtic religion, and Lucan's famous description (above) of a temple near Marseilles gives us some idea of the horror Mediterranean travellers may have experienced when they encountered pagan cults with their idols, carved wooden totem poles and severed human heads.

The second Lindow Man exhibition held at Manchester Museum in 1991 set out to recreate just such a Celtic shrine, with a gallery of wooden staves leading to a sacred grove at the centre of which was a holy pool into which offerings were thrown. This was surrounded by grim stone heads and carved idols, and the eerie atmosphere was increased by the noise of dripping water and enhanced by subdued lighting. It was in forest and watery sanctuaries like this that Classical writers tell us the pagan priests or druids practised their mysterious rites.

Celtic religion was radically different to the imperial religion of Rome with its urban temples, and because it was based in

natural shrines few unambiguous examples have been identified. However, many Celtic cult sites have evidence of a long
continuity in use from as early as the Neolithic and Bronze Age,
and were often replaced by larger stone or wooden structures
during the later Romano-British period. One of the best known
examples was uncovered when Heathrow Airport was built at
Middlesex, and found to contain a fourth century BC wooden
prototype of the simple square enclosure which was developed
in later Romano-British temples.[14]

One way of identifying the sites of former forest shrines and
sacred groves is by the use of folk tradition and place-names.
The Celtic word nemeton (sacred grove) can be compared with
the Greek temenos, and is found widely distributed across western Europe and Britain. It appears in the name of the Peak
District healing waters at Buxton, known to the Romans as
Aquae Arnemetiae (meaning the goddess 'who dwelt over
against the sacred grove'); at Vernemeton ('the especially sacred
grove') in Nottinghamshire; and again in Medionemeton ('the
middle sanctuary') in Scotland, thought to be the Neolithic
henge monument on Cairnapple Hill, near Edinburgh, which
had continuous ritual use through the Bronze and Iron Ages.
These places probably all functioned as centres of tribal gatherings, like those known at Tara and Navan Fort in Ireland.

Another important cluster of 'nemet' placenames occurs in
central Devon, and archaeologists have suggested this was the
same sacred grove or forest mentioned in the Ravenna
Cosmography (second century AD) as 'Nemetostatio', west of
Exeter.[15] Many villages in this region contain the words nymet
or nymph in their names, and there are also an 'exceptional
number' of depictions of the Green Man with their connotations
of tree worship to be found in these very same parish churches.

Images or idols like the later medieval Green Man and
Sheela-na-gig, depicting localized nature gods and divine
female deities were in all probability the centrepiece of these
open air Celtic shrines focused upon groves, springs and wells
and the sources of rivers, and may have been exhibited at tribal
gatherings. At a number of excavated sites post-holes have been
found. These apparently contained huge wooden poles which
may have been carved or painted with images of pagan deities,
of a tribal or totemic nature.

Many damaged stone idols have survived in Britain particularly carved stone heads, but many more made of wood have perished. It is clear from historical sources that worship of idols continued beyond the fall of Roman Britain, was revived by the pagan Anglo-Saxons and probably continued even after the Norman Conquest. Gildas, the British monk, mentions idols surviving in the ruined Roman cities during the sixth century AD, and Pope Boniface, writing to the newly converted King Edwin of Northumbria one hundred years later, attacks continuing idol-worship in his still wholly pagan kingdom, enjoining him to 'reject the mummery of temples and the deceitful flattery of omens'.

His letter to the king, who was then torn between the traditions of his ancestors and the political advantages of the new religion, describes the idols' resemblance to 'living shapes' but says they have no intelligence, and have no power to hurt or help anyone. This passage resembles Caesar's description 600 years before of the 'simulacra' images worshipped by the Celtic tribes in Gaul. Describing the Anglo-Saxon idols, Boniface's account says they had eyes but could not see, ears but could not hear, and feet but could not walk, and he adds: 'They that make them are like unto them; so is everyone that trusteth in them.'[16]

The Symbol of the Severed Head

It has been said that to the pagan Celtic tribes the human head was as important a religious symbol as the Cross to the Christians. Although notions of a specific 'Celtic head cult' have been questioned, there is plentiful evidence to suggest that to the pagan tribes of Britain and Gaul, the human head appears to have been seen as the centre of the personality and the seat of the soul, and as such was capable of independent being. Early stories like that of the prophetic head of the god-king Bran, found in the fourth branch of the Welsh Mabinogion, contains very archaic elements concerning the power of the head in pagan tradition.

Because of these magico-religious connotations the head in certain pagan religious contexts became the subject of great veneration and reverence, a significance which was not exclusive to the Celtic lands or any one period in history. Many of the idols worshipped in pagan temples appear to have been representations of the head of the god or goddess alone, as this was believed to be the centre of the deity's power.

The power of the head as a sacred symbol pervades many aspects both of Celtic and Anglo-Saxon religion and mythology, and its use in cult contexts has been confirmed by the findings of archaeology.[17] Archaic beliefs about the severed human head remain today in certain parts of the North of England, where recent surveys have recorded up to 2,000 surviving examples of carved stone heads of the Celtic tradition of varying date in a variety of contexts, built into the gables of farm buildings and houses, acting as guardians at healing springs and wells, and even performing modern duty in garden rockeries.

Some may date from Iron Age or Romano-British times, but most experts agree the vast majority were carved in or since the medieval period, with a large number made within living memory with all the hallmarks of the Celtic tradition.[18] This apparent unique continuity of ritual function and placing may well provide evidence for lingering traces of religious instincts with their roots in prehistory surviving in certain upland areas of northern England. Here traditional carving techniques are still both consciously and unconsciously practised today in many forms, with stone heads still employed to bring luck to the household, and deflect evil.

In addition to heads of stone, real human skulls were sometimes taken as trophies in tribal skirmishes in Celtic times and used to adorn houses and forts. Also the preserved heads of ancestors were kept as portable oracles or to bring luck or fertility to the household. Guardian skulls (see Bettiscombe and Burton Agnes in the guide) are a very important motif in British folk-tales and seem to be an example of genuine continuity from pagan times into the present.

Water Cults

The sanctity of water in all its aspects, but particularly in the form of rivers, springs and wells, lakes and marshes, has been a central religious instinct of man since the earliest times. In the Stone Age, megalithic standing stones and wooden pagan temples appear to have been constructed near sacred watersources, including a new example recently discovered from the air at Avebury in Wiltshire. During the Bronze Age, people in Britain began to cast precious metal objects into sacred pools and rivers, both military items specially 'killed' in dedication to the gods, and small personal objects for 'luck' perhaps as people today toss coins into wishing wells.

As rising water levels flooded large areas of low-lying land in eastern England offerings to the watery gods reached their height upon a huge artificial platform built across shallow waters at Flag Fen in Cambridgeshire. This platform was made of thousands of oak posts and was of a purely ritual nature, judging from the many hundreds of weapons and small personal objects found by the excavators.

As the Bronze Age gave way to the age of Iron, it seems the places of offering and sacrifice to water evolved into centres of healing cults connected with a female deity – the mother goddess – and with Roman patronage these were developed into large stone built temples like that of Sulis-Minerva at Bath. Others existed on the Roman Wall, and at Lydney and Nettleton in the New Forest, and some seem to have been centred upon displays of cult objects, often stone carvings or statues of gods or human heads.

Holy Wells and Springs

The evidence of archaeology and folk tradition provides clear evidence that springs and wells, particularly those at the sources of rivers or underground caves, continued to be venerated wihin living memory as entrances to the Otherworld. At certain special places offerings have been made to wells and springs from time immemorial by those in search of healing or favours from the water gods or goddesses. These offerings could be of rags and pins, garlands of flowers or other small gifts to the spirits which people believed continued to preside over the water sources, often in direct opposition to the teachings of the Church.

When Christianity arrived in Britain, the early missionaries found that suppressing the worship of water was impossible. In the seventh century AD, the Penitentials of Theodore commanded that 'no one shall go to trees, or wells, or stones, or enclosures, or anywhere else except to god's church, and there make vows or release himself from them.'[19] Despite many prohibitions, water worship continued in the more remote parts of the countryside often under the nose of the church authorities. Six hundred years after Theodore's laws, the Bishop of Hereford was still trying to forbid 'the superstitious worship of wells and meetings of folk at Cerney ... and in other places of a like nature.'[20]

Many of the early Celtic and Anglo-Saxon saints are associated with holy wells and springs, and their stories often involve miracle cures and fertility, connected with the healing powers which were believed to be latent in springwater blessed by pagan deities. The goddess Brigid, the patron of many 'Bride wells' in the west and north of the British Isles, became the Christian St Brigid; similarly, the names of two other goddesses associated with water, Anu and Elen were Christianized as St Anne and St Helen.

This demonstrates how many early saints, of whom little is known, exchanged places with the guardian deities of these sacred springs and wells, taking over the functions of many minor pagan deities. The pagan spirit or deity in question was often granted a saintly 'prefix' to render him or her respectable and make them a fitting medium of powers now represented as divine rather than demonic – then the time honoured rituals could continue without interruption.

In addition to wells and springs, many British rivers were objects of worship by the pagan tribes and their sanctity is proven by the fact that the names of many of the most important rivers have retained their original Celtic meaning. Tales are still told around some of them which appear to have descended from a time when rivers were thought of as the habitations of gods and spirits possessing definite characteristics, occasionally benevolent, to whom in some cases offerings and 'sacrifices' continued to be made until a time within living memory, if they have stopped.

The gods and goddesses of water have left their mark upon folklore and legend as well as place-name evidence. Lakes, lochs and wells in many parts of Britain are frequently said to be haunted by spirits described as 'white ladies' or 'green ladies'. Such localized deities were very frequently found as the inhabitants of lakes in Wales, where they became integrated into fairylore. Superstition relating to water still lie within us – in the twentieth century wishing wells are often incorporated into the plans for new buildings. However, few people realize when they toss a coin into the waters and make a wish they are making an offering to a spirit in much the same way as their far-off ancestors.

Sacred Trees

Like wells, trees venerated by the pagans were often singled out for attack by the early Christians. In Germany, Charlemagne led the destruction of the Saxon pagan shrine at Marsberg on the River Diemel in AD 772. This was a giant oak tree known as the Irminsul, a symbol of the 'world tree' known in Norse mythology as the Yggdrasil. The oak tree in particular was sacred to the Celtic gods, and to the German god of Thunder, Thor, whose great oak at Geismar in Hesse was struck down by the Anglo-Saxon missionary St Boniface.

In Irish tradition, sacred trees were known as *bile* and Navan Fort (Emain Macha) in Ulster, had the bole of a huge sacred tree as its cult-focus. In mythology, the oak, yew, ash and hazel were particularly sacred, with their longevity symbolizing divine wisdom and, with deciduous trees, their seasonal renewal being symbolic of death and rebirth.

Maypoles, still the central feature of most village celebrations on May Day, are perhaps the most obvious survival of tree worship in British folk tradition. The tall posts, with their flowers and ribbons, are symbolic of the living tree and fertility rites, and became objects of particular hatred for the Puritans. Although the first written reference to the maypole comes from fourteenth-century Wales, the earliest examples were not permanent structures like the ones which survive today, but were young trees brought from the woods. In some places the more archaic form of tree worship has survived, perpetuating the old reverence for single or guardian trees which were believed to harbour spirits, like the famous Major Oak in Sherwood Forest. The best known tree ceremony is held at Aston-on-Clun, Shropshire, on Oak Apple Day, 29 May, where a black poplar tree is decorated with ribbons and flags.

Worship of trees and forests continued in the more remote regions of the British Isles where some isolated examples are still believed to be capable of raising storms, granting wishes and healing the sick.

In 1968 the editor of the archaeological journal *Antiquity* described a visit he made to just such a 'holy rag tree' in southern Denmark, which could well have been a native shrine in any part of medieval Britain. He said the trees closed in above as the group of archaeologists walked further into the wood, and soon they had an overpowering feeling of being 'surrounded and out of this world'.

After taking a side path the group suddenly found themselves inside a clearing where they saw a very tall tree distinguished by a hole through its centre. Surrounding the tree, hanging from branches, were coloured rags including everything from dirty handkerchiefs to silk stockings.

Glancing nervously around the eerie circle of dripping fir trees the writer realized that he was standing within a sacred shrine still in active use in twentieth-century Denmark, though its exact location remains a closely guarded secret. He concluded:

'We were, it might be said, in the presence of a mystery. We were actually in the presence of heathendom, of pre-Christian religion and magic.' [21]

The Goddesses

Erce, Erce, Erce, Earth Mother
may the Almighty Eternal Lord
grant you fields to increase and flourish,
fields fruitful and healthy,
shining harvests and shafts of millet,
broad harvests of barley . . .
Hail to thee, Earth, Mother of Men;
bring forth now in God's embrace,
filled with good for the use of man. [22]

The Anglo-Saxon charm above preserves the universal pagan belief in the Earth Mother or mother goddess, known by many different names, but shared equally between the Celtic and Germanic tribes who settled in the British Isles. Here, the fertility charm aimed at bewitched land is clearly influenced by Christianity, but even then the all-pervading influence of belief in a female deity continued in a new form with the veneration paid to the Virgin Mary, the mother of God, and at a more local level in folk tradition as divine female saints like St Brigid, St Ann and St Helen, all of whom were alter-egos of earlier pagan goddesses.

The Mother Goddess
Divine female goddesses in many hybrid forms, both Celtic,

Roman-Celtic and Christian – play a large and important part in the mythology of the Gaelic portions of the British Isles. The goddess is often in triple form, as in the three Irish war goddesses Morrigan, Macha and Badb, and represent fertility and abundance. The goddess Brigid (from whom Brigantia takes its tribal name), also appears in a triple form which survived into the Christian tradition as three sisters or nuns. In Romano-British art the three goddesses are often depicted as seated along with symbols such as bread, babies and fruit, with the three deities representing the different stages of womanhood – virgin, mother and hag, who also symbolize the changing seasons of spring, summer and winter.

The Mother Goddess in her Hag form (known as the Cailliche or Cailliagh), is found throughout the Gaelic lands, but in Ireland she is infinitely old. Folklorist Eleanor Hull wrote in 1927: 'In Ireland the goddesses are held to be both more numerous and more powerful than the gods and still regarded as the builders of mountains, the impersonators of winter, and the harbingers of spring.[23]

In Scotland, the same mountain-building traditions are found, but in the Emerald Isle she is associated in particular with the province of Munster, where are the Da Chich Anainne, or the Paps of Anu, two great breast-shaped hills with twin summits in County Kerry.

In Irish tradition, the territorial goddess is described as offering a cup to the man who is destined to be king, with the king representing human society and the goddess representing the divine power which is manifested in nature. The Celtic king was often described as having a symbolic marriage to the land, in effect a mating with the territorial goddess, in whose womb – the burial mound – he would return to in death.

After the Christianization of Britain, the female deity survived in the form of a variety of local divinities often, like banshees, attached to a particular house or family, and as water nymphs, ghostly White Ladies or Washers-at-the-Ford, like Shakespeare's Three Weird Sisters, warning of death and destruction. In Wales the fairies or departed spirits as they are thought to be are known as 'Y Mamau', the Mothers. Behind these shadowy forms are dimly seen the figures of the Mothers or Mother Goddesses, from whom all the gods derive their origin.

The Sheela-na-gig

These medieval carvings are found throughout the British Isles and Europe but in particularly large numbers in central Ireland, where belief in a territorial goddess was very strong. They portray a hideous hag-like being, its features often displaying a repulsive leer, with a naked body often in a crouched position, with grossly exaggerated sexual organs indicated by the hands. The oldest known examples date from Norman times, but the motif has clear origins in the Celtic Iron Age, and Dr Anne Ross has also suggested that 'in their earliest iconographic form they portray the territorial or war goddess in her hag-like aspect, with all the strongly sexual characteristics which accompany this guise in the tales.' [24]

The term 'Sheela-na-gig' itself comes from the Irish *Sighe na gCioch* or 'old hag of the paps', and was first recorded by antiquarians in the nineteenth century, but because breasts are not a feature emphasized upon these carvings an alternative derivation is Sile-ina-Giob, or Sheela on her hunkers, a better description of their crouched or squatting posture.

Several hundred Sheela-na-gig carvings have been recorded by experts, who are fiercely divided as to their age and function. Recently, Jerman and Weir in *Images of Lust*[25] have ascribed a Romanesque origin for all these carvings, which they regard as only one type of a variety of sexual exhibitionist figures carved by pilgrims on the European pilgrim routes during the Middle Ages, who imported their ideas into the British Isles. They argue that all sexual carvings were vehicles for Christian teachings on the evils of lust, temptation and the sins of the flesh.

Although it appears probable that pilgrims may have carved some of the Romanesque exhibitionist figures, Irish scholar Etienne Rynne has argued that their prototypes existed in the pagan Celtic Iron Age and he suggests that when the Romanesque Sheela concept reached Ireland in the twelfth century AD 'it found a prepared and fertile soil'. [26]

Describing the large number of Sheelas discovered hidden away in English parish churches from the Isle of Wight to Yorkshire and from East Anglia to the Welsh Border, Norse scholar Brian Branston has called them 'the actual representation of the Great Goddess Earth Mother on English soil'. He relates them to the Norse mother goddess Freya or Frig, known as Nerthus to the Anglo-Saxons, for there are accounts of temples containing richly-adorned goddess images in Scandinavia as late as the tenth century AD.[27]

There is nothing Christian about these carvings, and a mystery lies in why so many of them are found inside Christian churches, often hidden away near the altar or in some special niche. Their presence, along with those of the Green Man and other blatantly pagan objects in the fabric of many pre-Reformation churches, suggests they must be part of an attempt to channel their evil-averting power for the benefit of the new religion, with the people continuing to worship old and new gods side by side in the place they were accustomed to. Pope Gregory the Great gave his missionary Mellitus clear instructions early in the sixth century AD that pagan temples he found in England should on no account be destroyed. Instead, they should be cleaned with holy water and 'purified from the worship of demons and dedicated to the service of the true god.'[28]

Pagan Gods

One survey has noted more than 400 names of Celtic deities are recorded in Roman Gaul, with three-quarters of them appearing only once and appear to be have been purely local interpretations of the greater Celtic gods, goddesses and nature spirits.[29] The Romans added to the confusion by giving their own interpretation of the Celtic deities, for Julius Caesar wrote of the Celtic gods he saw worshipped in Gaul as if they were deities from the Roman pantheon, describing them as Jupiter, Mercury, Apollo and Minerva. When the Romans invaded Britain, the Roman deities were often equated with native ones, as in the case of Sulis-Minerva at Bath, and this process has become known as *Interpretatio Romana*.

Despite the confusing multitude of deities known from the Roman period and the early Celtic literature, it is possible to group them roughly into male and female categories.The female deities all appear to be manifestations of the Earth Mother, while their male counterparts despite their wide variety of attributes, all seem to function as gods of the tribe, of warriors and of the sky or sun.

The Tribal God

In early Irish literature the major god upon whom all the male deities were based was In Dagda ('the Good God'), who was the representation of all the skills of the tribe. Second in importance was the god Lugh or Lud, a father god whose name is widespread across the British Isles and Gaul, being found at cities like Carlisle (Luguvalium) and Lyon (Lugdunum). His importance for farming and agriculture is reflected in the naming of one of the Celtic quarter days, the harvest festival celebrated at the beginning of August known as Lughnasa. This was also the date the Romans celebrated the feast of the divine emperor Augustus. Another guise of this god is that of Finn ('the Fair Haired One'), Fionn McCummail in Irish and Scots legend. His equivalent among the Anglo-Saxon tribes is undoubtedly the tribal god Woden/Odin, from whom six of the eight royal houses traced their descent and who gave his name to Wednesday.

The gods and goddesses of the Celtic pantheon quite clearly had their equivalents in Germanic and Norse mythology. The Greek poet Lucan, writing of religion in the second century AD in Gaul, mentions three Celtic tribal deities – Esus, Taranis and Teutades – all of whom have equivalents in the western Celtic lands. The second of these, the hammer-god Taranis comes from a Celtic root word meaning 'thunder' and he is clearly the same deity as the Scandinavian Thor.

The Horned God

This important god in Celtic tradition and iconography is clearly a tribal deity of great antiquity, and perhaps originated as a god of the hunter-gathering peoples in the remote past. At the Mesolithic site at Star Carr in North Yorkshire, evidence was found of antler headdresses made from the skulls of stags which may have been worn by shamen in hunting rituals 10,000 years ago. The god's long pedigree is reflected in his depiction in the Celtic tradition in a semi-zoomorphic form, as a hybrid between humanity and the animal world. Metamorphosis or shape-shifting is a common element in the early Irish and Welsh stories, with the gods often taking on the attributes of animals, and in the case of the horned god he was perceived to be so close to the natural world that he appears as 'Lord of the Animals'.

The earliest depiction of the horned god in Celtic art is the fourth century BC rock carving in the Carmonica Valley of northern Italy depicting a ram-horned figure. A similar deity appears on one plate of the famous Gundestrup cauldron depicting him seated cross-legged, with torcs (neck ornaments) hanging from each antler, and a ram-horned serpent below him. On one carving only, from Paris in the first century AD, does this image have a name, Cernunnos, which means 'the horned one'. This name has been applied to images of the horned god across the whole Celtic world but it is likely he had many other names specific to the tribes which depicted him.

Other versions of the horned god, particularly popular in Britain, depict him with bull or ram-horns, and in this form he appears as a god of war. Many dozens of carvings of this nature, often depicting his head alone, have been found in Britain particularly on the Roman frontier regions of Brigantia where he seems to have been invoked by the northern tribes as a symbol of war and sexuality (he is often depicted as phallic).[30]

Magical Animals
The Celtic gods had the ability to transform themselves into animals, and for this reason certain animals were regarded as possessing magical powers. These could have functioned as totems for certain tribes, signifying their identity or territory, as may have been the case with the strange white horse depicted below the Iron Age hillfort at Uffington, Berkshire. Archaeology has also produced evidence that certain special animals, dogs, horses and oxen, were selected for sacrifice as offerings to deities or to dedicate temples, particularly in the Romano-British period.

In Celtic and Germanic religion one of the most important animals was the boar, which was used as a symbol of martial power. Depictions of the boar have been found on a Celtic shield dredged from the River Witham, and upon grave goods found inside the Sutton Hoo ship burial. A fine representation of a boar crowns the top of an Anglo-Saxon warrior's helmet, of sixth-century AD date, found at Benty Grange in Derbyshire, and now on display in Sheffield Museum.

To the Germanic peoples the symbol of the dragon played a very important role in the religious imagery of their heroic warrior society, but appears to have had less prominence with the Celtic tribes. To the Anglo-Saxons, the dragon was clearly a metaphor for the powers of nature, these creatures were located in the landscape where they functioned as protectors of treasure and guarded royal burial mounds, as depicted in the epic *Beowulf.*

Of important cult significance was the dog, an animal which features strongly as an Otherworld beast in folk tradition in every region in Britain, particularly in Norfolk where the Anglo-Saxon word scucca ('demon') is used to describe the ghost dog known as 'Old Shuck'. Images of dogs are found associated with the horse goddess and there even appear to have been pagan temples devoted to some kind of dog god, at the late Roman-Celtic temple at Lydney in Gloucestershire where the mysterious deity Nodens was worshipped.

As well as stags, bulls and certain birds, the horse was a particularly sacred animal to the pagan cults. The horse seems to have been associated with a Gaulish goddess known as Epona, who gained popularity throughout the Celtic world including Britain during the Romano-British period. In the British Isles, Epona already had native equivalents, the Irish Macha and the Welsh Rhiannon, and the sacred nature of the animal has survived in folk tradition in the strange midwinter 'horsing' ceremonies which survive in South Wales, Kent and elsewhere.

The Green Man

This symbol of many meanings has been described as 'one of the most pagan and archaic concepts in the imagery of the christian church.'[31] The Green Man (a very recent catch-all term) docs have archaic roots in pagan times, but the original symbol has resurfaced many times in different contexts throughout history, most recently in the twentieth century on pub signs, novels, and latterly as a symbol of the environmental movement.[32]

Half-man, half-tree, he is a frightening image of a severed human head, almost always male, with leaves and foliage intertwined around it and often sprouting from mouth and nostrils. The image is found hidden away in Christian churches, carved upon roof bosses, capitals, rood screens and misericords. The purpose of the carvings is unknown but early folklorists tended to view them as representations of a pagan fertility spirit. The oldest appear to date from the period after the Norman Conquest with a great upsurge in carving during the fourteenth and fifteenth centuries, the same period that the poem *Sir Gawain and the Green Knight* was produced in north-west England.

In an influential article 'The Green Man in Church Architecture' published in the *Folklore Journal* in 1939, Lady Raglan suggested the Green Man (a name she gave to these carvings herself) was the identical character who danced, covered in foliage, in May Day processions and was paraded on horseback covered in a garland of leaves and flowers in the isolated village of Castleton in Derbyshire. She made another connection with James Frazer's theory in *The Golden Bough*, relating to the sacrifice of the sacred king, a personification of the god, at the beginning of spring, in a ritual to fertilize the earth. The first academic study of the symbol was published by Kathleen Basford,[33] who said her personal quest for the Green Man began when she saw a striking carving upon the apex of one of the tall windows at twelfth-century Fountains Abbey in North Yorkshire. It was 'a head with vegetation coming from its mouth, coiled around its brow and twisted over its throat.' The stone catches attention because of the total lack of any other imagery or sculpture at Fountains Abbey, and it remains a mystery how the Green Man survived here in a strict Cistercian establishment, where even statues of angels are rare.

Kathleen Basford saw the image of the Green Man not as a representative of May Day revels or Jack-in-the-Green, but as a symbol of death or ruin – 'a thing of sorrow'.[34] Her study showed that these heads are also found in French and Romanesque churches, and the ancient prototype for the carvings appeared to have been masks sprouting vegetation in Roman sites in the Rhineland and Rome itself. Faces emerging from a leafy background also appear in Iron Age La Tene art and Jupiter columns of the Romano-British age. Those found in medieval churches had a more 'menacing' or 'demonic' appearance than the more ancient examples and one folklore authority says 'some of the better carved specimens have such a mysterious intensity of expression which makes it difficult to believe that they have no cult significance.'[35]

The association of the Green Man with the mythological aspects of the Robin Hood legend and the Greenwood have yet to be fully investigated, but good examples can be found within Sherwood Forest itself at the fourteenth-century chapter house at Southwell Minster in Nottinghamshire (which sits on top of a

Roman villa). Here there are twelve green men, each highly individual, depicting heads emerging, peeping out of, or merging with various sacred plants including the hawthorn, maple and ivy, highly suggestive of May Day and the Jack-in-the-Green figure.

Good examples of Green Men can be found carved upon wooden roof bosses in many medieval English cathedrals, including those at Exeter, Norwich and Canterbury. Some of the best but least known examples are found in Sheffield Cathedral where, in the Lady chapel there is a complete suite of pagan carvings upon the wooden roof, embossed in gold paint. They date from the fifteenth-century and are clearly not medieval fancies; they appear to have some religious meaning which is not of the Christian tradition.

The centrepiece of the carvings in Sheffield is the figure of the Mother Goddess herself, depicted as a Sheela-na-gig, sitting upon tree roots which gush from the mouth of a head on the apex of the great stained-glass window. No less than seven carved bosses depicting the Green Man appear in the Lady chapel, all arranged geometrically and surrounded by stylized foliage. It appears the medieval masons were trying to bring into this holy space pictures of the forests and trees outside, and perhaps also memories of idols which once adorned the pagan temple which the Church replaced.[36]

The Festivals

Much work has been done by archaeologists and Earth Mysteries researchers into the astronomical significance of henges, stone circles and other megalithic monuments whose stones, axes and entrances seem to have been aligned on the rising and setting of the sun, the complicated movements of the moon and other celestial bodies at important times of the year. Some theories have also claimed the prehistoric farming people were also concerned with plotting the movements of the stars, but this argument is less convincing.

Despite the once fiercely divided nature of the fields of study, there is now plentiful evidence that the rising of the sun at the festivals was marked in the layout and orientation of ritual monuments in the Neolithic and Bronze Age, but there seems to have been much diversity both between different regions and within them, as found later with the Celtic festivals.

The great pagan festivals and feast days of the Celtic period probably evolved from the earlier solar and lunar observations of tribal astronomer-priests in the Neolithic and Bronze Ages. How their knowledge was transmitted in an age before the invention of writing remains a mystery, but we do know the druids were skilled in the transmission of sacred knowledge by complex methods of oral recitation. Caesar described how in Gaul the druids forbade the writing down of their tradition, and instead pupils had to memorize a great number of verses. He wrote: 'they hold long discussions about the heavenly bodies and their movements, the size of the universe and the earth, the physical constitution of the world, and the powers and properties of the gods.'

To the Celtic tribes, the year was divided by four great 'fire festivals' or quarter days, 1 February, 1 May, 1 August and 1 November, all of which were observed with differing intensity across the British Isles. These important dates were also greatly influenced and adapted by festivals and feast days imported by the Romans (themselves a mixture of many different races), the Anglo-Saxons and Danes, and finally by the Christians. All these dates were transposed upon more ancient dates marking the rising and setting of the sun during the course of the year, observed by the prehistoric peoples.

The following table attempts to place all the main dates of the pagan calendar into a context for use alongside the places to visit detailed in this book:

The Pagan Year

1 February (Imbolc)

Also known as Oimelg; one of the quarter days of the Celtic calendar about which least is known. This pastoral festival was celebrated in Ireland and Wales with the lighting of bonfires, and appears to have been connected with the beginning of lambing. Imbolc was the feast day of the triple goddess Brigid, and the festival was connected with Candlemas on 2 February in the Christian calendar, also known as the Feast of the Purification of the Virgin Mary.

21 March (The Spring Equinox)
The first of two occasions in the year when the day and night are of equal length. The rising of the sun on this day was marked at various Neolithic sites, including Loughcrew in Ireland.

Easter/Spring Festival
Bede's account of the religious festivals of the Anglo-Saxons makes no mention of May Day, but he does mention a festival for victory, a time of sacrifice to Woden at the beginning of summer. The nearest equivalent to the Celtic festival appears to have been the feast of the spring goddess Eostre, a time of tremendous rejoicing at the return of the summer.

1 May (Beltane – 'bright' or 'goodly fire')
Also known as Cetsamhain in Ireland; Calan Mai in Wales. The epithet 'Bel' refers to a light, and some authorities believe it refers directly to a Celtic god of Light, Belenos. The festival we all know as May Day has very ancient roots in the prehistoric past, in the past 1 May was associated with the start of open pasturing, the beginning of summer and the welcoming of the sun's heat to promote the growth of crops. At one time on May Eve great bonfires were kindled in sympathetic magic to welcome back the sun, carols and songs were sung on high places, and even more archaic was the Bringing in of the Summer – spending of the night in the woods and the bringing back of green branches in the morning to celebrate the return of fertility to the land.

21 June (The Summer Solstice – Midsummer Day)
The first of two occasions in the year when the sun is farthest away from the equator, in this case the longest day. Marked in the Neolithic by the builders of Stonehenge whose primary alignment was to the midsummer sunrise over the famous Heel Stone. Midsummer was not a feature of the Celtic calendar, but appears to have been marked by the lighting of bonfires, which still continues in Cornwall.

1 August (Lughnasa – the festival of the god Lugh/Lud)
The beginning of Lammas-tide, marking the start of the harvest in the rural calendar, a period of hard agricultural work which ended with the feast of the Harvest Home and agricultural fairs and gatherings. In Ireland, the Festival of Lughnasa was of great importance as demonstrated by surviving folklore, with gatherings of people at places sacred to the gods and goddesses like

Teltown, in County Meath and Navan (Emain Macha) in Ulster. In the Christian calendar, Lughnasa was the Festival of First Fruits, when the first bread was made and dedicated to Christ. To the Anglo-Saxons, the festival was known as 'Loaf-mass', a name which evolved into Lammas.

21 September (The Autumn Equinox)

Followed on 29 September by Michaelmas, which marked the end of the harvest when the amount of fodder available for winter animals was calculated. A time of great fairs, the collection of rents and the sale of animals.

1 November (Samhain – 'Summer's End')

The most important fire festival which marked the end of the Celtic year, a time of great danger when spirits walked amongst mankind. In a first-century BC Celtic calendar found in Gaul it is identified as 'Samonios'. Samhain was a quarter day and fire festival celebrated across the pan-Celtic world but was of particular importance in Ireland, where it marked the end of the pastoral year when animals were slaughtered for the winter. Great assemblies took place in the five provinces of the country, with the Feast of Tara hosting the ritual mating of the tribal god with the goddess of war and fertility. In mythology, it was a strange time when humans were susceptible to divine and supernatural influences – when the border with the Otherworld was down and gods and goddesses were manifest.

The supreme importance of this feast was acknowledged just as strongly by the Anglo-Saxons, for whom the beginning of November was blodmonath, the month of sacrifice, when surplus cattle were slaughtered 'for plenty and peace'. Samhain survives in modern folk tradition as Hallowe'en, with the fires of Bonfire Night following on 5 November. The 1 November festival was Christianized as the Feast of All Saints in AD 837, with the Feast of All Souls following the next day.

21 December (The Midwinter Solstice)

An important pagan festival celebrated by the Germanic people, including the Norse who gave the name Yule to the festival. Festivals connected with fire and light were held around this time to mark the rebirth of the sun, and to the Romans 25 December was *Dies Natalis Invicti Solis* – the birthday of the Unconquered Sun. The twelve days which followed were the pagan midwinter festival known to the Romans as the Saturnalia. In the fourth century the Pope gave the church's backing to the belief that 25 December was also the birthday of Christ, although the real date is unknown, but this enabled the church to incorporate a number of powerful pagan festivals into its own most important day.

ꓠorthern ꓰngland

Burton Agnes, Humberside
Hadrian's Wall, Northumberland
Halifax, West Yorkshire
High Peak, Derbyshire
Lastingham, North Yorkshire
Penhill, North Yorkshire
Ribble Valley, Lancashire

Burton ꓭgnes, ꓧumberside

Guardian skulls credited with magical powers are a little-known aspect of British folk tradition; they have on the whole been neglected both by students of folklore and archaeologists and have been left to populate the pages of ghost-hunting manuals.[1] The west and northern regions of the British Isles are particularly rich sources of skull superstitions, with the majority of the stories originating from the hills of the Peak District, Lancashire and Cumbria. Here ancient and mysterious skulls are the foci of various phantom events, bad luck and strange phenomena if they are moved from their place of residence in old halls, manor houses and farms. Some of the stories are better known than others, and some skulls have 'pet' names, like 'Dicky O'Tunstead' in the Derbyshire High Peak. A particularly good example is the well-known tradition connected with Burton Agnes Hall in East Yorkshire, where the skull of an Elizabethan woman was bricked up in the walls a century ago specifically to prevent its removal from the house.[2]

The Burton Agnes estate was passed in the reign of Edward I

to the Griffith family, and when Sir Henry Griffith died in the early seventeenth century he left his three daughters as co-heiresses. They decided to rebuild the hall into a splendid mansion house and Anne Griffith, the youngest girl, was passionately involved in this work. In 1628 it was completed, but before the sisters could move in Anne was attacked by a gang of beggars whilst visiting nearby and left unconscious by the roadside.

On her deathbed she made her sisters promise that her head should be severed and kept in the house she loved so much, and threatened to make it uninhabitable if the promise was broken. Of course the promise was broken and within days things started to happen. In the middle of the night the household was woken by violent slamming of doors, groaning and screaming noises. On the advice of the vicar, Anne's grave was opened and her head brought back into the house.

So long as it remains in the house, says local legend, nothing untoward will happen. All the attempts to remove the skull or bury it have failed and at some point in recent history it was bricked it up in a secret location inside the house. Anne's spirit still haunts the old mansion, and is known locally as 'Awd Nance', a guardian spirit of the household, linked to the prosperity of the land.

Despite the colourful legend attached to Burton Agnes, there appears to be no record that Anne Griffiths, the owner of the skull, ever existed. The family tomb in the church nearby, makes no reference to her despite her appearance on a famous painting in the hall where the ghost still walks. So whose is the skull, and where did the elaborate story attributing it to the ancestor of an ancient family originate?

There is a very similar story of a skull at Threlkeld Place, near Keswick in the Lake District. It was discovered by a new tenant of the farm who was horrified to find it grinning at him from a wall niche in a small dark room that had not been used by his predecessor. Historian Gerald Findler[3] writes how the skull was buried with great reverence by the tenant, but soon afterwards when his wife went to the small room she was frightened to find the object in the same niche in the wall where it was first discovered. The farmer, alarmed and afraid, carried the gruesome object to St Bees Head and cast it into the sea, only to find on his return home that the skull had travelled quicker than he had, for it was sitting grinning in its niche when he returned home.

The story ends: 'Friends came to assist the farmer in his dilemma, and the menfolk made several attempts to dispose of the skull, but it was always back again in that small room. Finally it was bricked up in the wall, and the farmer and his wife quickly found another farm to work without any eerie companion.'

There are obvious links between the functions of these skulls and the ubiquitous archaic-style stone heads, for they perform a similar function. Many of the skulls preserved in farms and manor houses are said to originate in the Civil War period and folktales say they are the heads of Catholic priests decapitated by Parliamentarians. One, kept in a niche at the Catholic bishop of Manchester's residence at Wardley Hall, is protected by a clause in the deeds which stipulates that the skull must be kept in the house if it is sold. However, careful examination of the literature and the skulls themselves provide clues which suggest they may be older than the legends which seek to explain them.

Burton Agnes Hall can be reached by the A166 between Great Driffield and Bridlington. The building is privately owned, but opens to the public six months of the year, and visitors should consult Historic Houses, Castles & Gardens *guide. An admission fee is charged, and guided tours are available.*

Ḥadrian's Ⱳall, Ⱨorthumberland

Although the Roman invasion of Britain began with Caesar's incursion on the south coast in 55 BC, the conquest did not begin until AD 43 when 40,000 troops landed in eastern Kent. As the legions moved north and west under the Governor Gnaeus Julius Agricola, they encountered bitter resistance from the tribes in the Pennines and Scottish lowlands who were never entirely subdued. When the Emperor Hadrian visited the new province of Britannia in AD 112, the Romans had already pulled back from their conquests in Scotland to a border line between the Solway and the Tyne in Northumberland. It was here that he ordered his soldiers and engineers to build a wall not only 'to divide the Romans from the barbarians', but as a clever means of frontier control.

Substantial sections of this 80-mile wall, built entirely of stone and running from the coast near Newcastle west across spectacular crags and beautiful countryside towards the River Irthing in northern Cumbria, can still be seen today. Hadrian's Wall has been called 'the most important monument built by the Romans in Britain', and its impact upon the tribal culture of the north cannot be underestimated. The presence of soldiers would have imposed peace on the warlike Brigantes and Votadini, but great changes in settlement patterns and agriculture must have occurred. Foreign soldiers also brought with them new and exotic religions including the imperial cults and Eastern mysteries like the cult of Mithras, which merged with and influenced the local religious traditions.

The Romans were tolerant of native deities who were often equated with those in the imperial pantheon. In this frontier region, the majority of native deities appear to have been male, and depicted as horned warrior gods, but the Brigantes took their name from the tutelary goddess of the land, Brigantia (the High One), whose image is carved upon a stone found at the outpost fort at Birrens. Often depicted in triple form, Brigantia is equated with the Roman Victory on several altars from the Wall and she appears as guardian of sacred springs and wells.

One Celtic god found in this region is Maponus (Divine Son), a god of poetry, music and hunting equated by the Romans with Apollo whose cult appears to have been centred in Dumfriesshire. Another deity linked with hunting is Cocidius, a name which has so far defied explanation. He is found most often in Northern Cumbria (linked with Mars), where the Ravenna Cosmography identifies the god's shrine in the Irthing Valley at the very edge of the Wall.

There is evidence of dozens of other lesser gods, showing the vitality and variety of native religious belief found among the tribes of the wall. There are depictions of wheel and sky gods at Corbridge, and carvings of three mysterious hooded figures, named Genii Cucullati, at Birdoswald (the hood or cochull appears frequently in Irish mythology).

The best evidence for native and exotic cults on the Wall are a group of sites situated beside the Roman fort of Procolitia at windswept Carrawburgh, built around AD 130. Three separate shrines have been located by archaeologists in this small region, including a mithraeum, a temple to the mysterious Eastern God Mithras ('Lord of Light') built by soldiers from the First Cohort of Batavians, drawn from an area at the mouth of the Rhine.

Mithraism, a mystery religion which at one time rivalled Christianity, was a military cult whose followers were exclusively male. Its temples were dark and gloomy places meant to reflect the primordial cave where the god captured and killed a sacred bull, whose fertilizing blood brought life to the earth and mankind. The mithraeum at Carrawburgh, whose focus was a sculpture of Mithras killing the bull, was discovered beneath peat in 1949. Today visitors can see the remains of shrine and copies of three altars dedicated by commanding officers of the fort, along with a small statue of a native mother goddess. A scale reconstruction of how the temple would have looked 1600 years ago can be seen in the Museum of Antiquities at Newcastle-upon-Tyne.

The Well of the Nymphs at Carrawburgh was excavated by Dr David Smith of Newcastle University in 1960. Here there was an altar dedicated to the local nymphs and 'the god of the place', which stood upon a low pedestal within a small building. Into this spring, which appears to have been demolished around AD 300, pilgrims had cast coins, pottery and a small bronze figure of a deity. A short distance away is another better-known sacred well fed by three springs running south and flowing into the Tyne, dedicated to the native water goddess or nymph Coventina. The well occupied a central position within a forty-foot square Romano-British temple. When it was excavated in 1876 it was found to contain an amazing cache of votive objects including 13,490 coins dating from AD 41 to AD 383. The well also contained inscriptions, pottery vessels, pins, shrine bells, a bronze horse and dog, incense burners and brooches which the guide says were 'all thrown in to honour, or to help win favours from the goddess.'[4]

A number of large carved statues were also recovered from the well, including a number of altars dedicated to the goddess herself, one of which depicts her floating on the leaf of a water lily. Another has an iron ring attached, which suggests they may have been suspended above or immersed in the spring waters. Objects cast into the waters as offerings included three masks or heads in bronze, the head of a male statue and a stylized 'Celtic head' carved in stone on the front of a stone altar. The most intriguing find was the top part of a human skull, which may have been used as a cult object in the temple. These finds (on display at the Roman museum in Chester) suggested to experts that 'the human head was not without significance to worshippers to Coventina.'[5]

It appears all three of these temples were destroyed during the fourth century, after the Emperor Theodosius passed an edict against paganism. Ironically, experts believe the Mithraeum at Carrawburgh may have been attacked not by 'pagan barbarians' but by Christians who had a particular hatred for this cult because they saw its ritual of taking bread and water as a mockery of the Holy Sacrament.

The emphasis on the human head as a cult object at Carrawburgh is found elsewhere along the Wall, where dozens of carvings of horned heads have been unearthed during the last three hundred years. The best known is the 'harsh and angular' head of a horned god found at the outpost fort at Netherby in 1794, and now on display at the excellent Tullie House Museum in Carlisle. The god has a flat head with a heavy forehead, narrow deep-set eyes and a slit mouth. Large ram's horns curl round the ears down towards the base of the neck. One account describes it as: 'a crude but highly effective piece of sculpture executed wholly in the Celtic style. It ranks as one of the most expressive pieces of Celtic sculpture found in Britain. The ram's horns and the fierce scowling expression make it likely that the head represents a native warrior god.'[6] Horned heads are also found at Carvoran and Chesters, and it is possible these represented the local military god known as Belatucadros (Bright Shining One), linked with the Roman Mars.

Belatucadros is also found at the fort and town in Maryport (Alauna), on the coast of western Cumbria, which has the largest number of dedications to the Horned God in the north.The fort here was built on a headland above the River Ellen in the first century AD as a base for Agricola's planned attack on the Solway. Maryport was garrisoned for 280 years by soldiers from three different European cohorts who left evidence of a thriving and wealthy culture. A large number of carvings depicting native Celtic, Roman and Eastern deities have been unearthed in the ruins and are on view in the Senhouse Roman Museum, the oldest private collection in

Britain, which was first noted by Camden in 1599.

One plaque depicting the Horned God shows him in stylized form, phallic, with a rectangular shield and club reminiscent of the Cerne Giant hill figure in Dorset. Phallic rites are also suggested by the extraordinary Serpent Stone, which the museum guide describes as combining 'all the occult Celtic symbols of supernatural power with the phallus – a Roman symbol of good fortune.'[7] The stone depicts a severed head with closed eyes and half-open mouth on one side, with a 45-inch-long phallic serpent on the opposite.

From the same site are a number of crude Celtic-style heads, a radiate figure with sun rays surrounding his head, altars dedicated to Setlocenia ('goddess of long life') and a plaque depicting three naked goddesses. Most puzzling of all is the strange 'shadow god', an elongated figure with no facial features other than eyes, similar to some of the Celtic-influenced carved stones found in the Peak District.

Sections of the Roman Wall can be visited along the main A69 road which runs from the city of Newcastle-upon-Tyne on the Northumbrian coast to Carlisle in Cumbria. Forts and visitors' centres are cared for mainly by English Heritage, and opening times should be obtained from local Tourist Information Centres. Archaeological displays can be seen both at museums on the wall at Chesters, Corbridge, Housesteads, Carvoran, South Shields and Vindolanda, as well as the excellent Tullie House Border Museum in Carlisle and the Museum of Antiquities in Newcastle.

Halifax, West Yorkshire

Archaeology has shown that during the Iron Age and Romano-British period the human head was a religious symbol as important as the Cross, and in the Pennines it remained an object of superstition and ritual into modern times. The Celtic warriors were head hunters who used their grisly trophies as testimony of their military prowess. They also believed that severed heads, later replaced by carvings in stone and wood, had magical powers which could deflect evil and promote good luck.

Hundreds of archaic carved stone heads have survived in the Calder and Aire valley of West Yorkshire. Some are carved on boulders and rock outcrops, others are incorporated into field-walls and and farmhouses, barns and other buildings. The concentration of heads in this region was first noted by the late Sidney Jackson, curator of Bradford Museum, who recorded hundreds of specimens in West Yorkshire during the 1960s. These included two three-faced heads carved in yellow sandstone which were found buried at Greetland, near Halifax in 1967, in the same area which produced a Roman altar dedicated to the tribal goddess Brigantia in the nineteenth century. A number of other archaic heads of early date have since been found in the same area, suggesting this was a cult centre where native carving traditions were stimulated by the presence of Roman auxiliary troops. [8]

The Upper Calder Valley was the subject of a special study by Earth Mysteries expert John Billingsley,[9] who has documented over 200 stone heads there. John first noticed these strange crude sculptures built into the gable ends of farmhouses and barns when walking on hillside footpaths along the Calderdale Way in 1978. In the foothill village of Mytholmroyd alone there are said to be eighteen heads incorporated into houses and field-walls.

The oldest stone heads in the valley seem to be those which have been found in dry stone walls or dug out of topsoil; these could have functioned as portable 'field gods' to promote fertility and watch over the flocks, and some may be of Iron Age origin. Those on buildings appear to have been carved by masons employed by wealthy yeoman farmers who grew rich from the woollen trade. Stone heads appear on the earliest domestic stone secular buildings and churches in Calderdale, dating from the sixteenth century onwards, where they perform a 'guardian' role as protective talismen.

Peter Brears, of Leeds Museum, in his book on North Country folk art, [10] says heads such as these are found only in a limited number of architectural locations, including gables and doorways on houses and medieval churches, beside springs and wells, and surprisingly on mill-chimneys. This suggests an active tradition of carving surviving until recent times as part of the repertoire of stone masons in Calderdale and elsewhere in West Yorkshire.

As in other regions where a head cult survived, the motif features prominently in the folk tradition of the area. The wool town of Halifax, the urban capital of Calderdale, is said to take its name from a legend regarding a 'Holy Face', with the severed head acting almost as a symbol for the town. The most arresting manifestation of this obsession with decapitation is the infamous 'Halifax Gibbet'. Despite its title, the gibbet was not a scaffold but a guillotine which was used to decapitate criminals during the Middle Ages, all but unique in England and of special importance because of the tradition of carving archaic Celtic-style heads which survived particularly strongly in this valley.

The Halifax Gibbet was at one time universally feared, and became part of the thieves' litany: 'From Hell, Hull and Halifax, may the Good Lord deliver us.' The gibbet began life as a deterrent to cattle rustling and cloth stealing, for during the sixteenth and seventeenth centuries the domestic woollen industry was the main livelihood of people in these Pennine valleys. Harsh treatment was given for minor offences in those days, with the law stating that anyone found guilty of stealing cloth to the value of thirteen pence halfpenny (less than 6p today) would 'be taken to the gibbet, and there have his head cut off from his body.'[11]

There are a number of conflicting theories surrounding the meaning of the name Halifax, all of which surround the existence of an earlier shrine or hermitage dedicated to St John, the patron saint of the church, associated with water and heads. Two of the legends concern the motif of the severed head. A representation of 'the face of St John the Baptist' appears on the coat of arms of the town, displayed prominently over the entrance to the Piece Hall. This relates to a legend that the town was in the Middle Ages a centre of pilgrimage and 'within the hermitage chapel of St John there was preserved, as a most sacred relic, the face of that saint. This gave peculiar sanctity to the spot as a place of pilgrimage, and so attracted great concourses of people from every direction.'[12]

The antiquarian William Camden recorded a very similar tradition when he visited Halifax at the end of the sixteenth century. In his work *Britannia*, published in 1586, he tells a story of how a monk from Whitby once arrived in the Calder valley after searching for 'a wild and solitary spot' in which to practise greater austerities. He erected a hermitage or cell on the spot where the town now stands which attracted many pilgrims, one of whom was a young nun who aroused such desire in the hermit that he became deranged and was convinced 'the fair penitent was none other than the Devil himself, who had taken this fair form to allure him to mortal sin.'

In a fit of madness, he decapitated the nun and fixed her head in a yew tree 'as a warning to others', after which he flung himself from a rock face. Camden describes how the head was hung on a yew tree, where it became an object of pilgrimage, with visitors plucking off branches from the tree as holy relics. Eventually the tree was reduced to a mere trunk, but retained its reputation of sanctity among the people 'who believed that those little veins, which are spread out like hair in the rind between the bark and the body of the tree, were indeed the very hair of the virgin ... thus the little village which was previous called Horton, or sometimes "the Chapel in the Grove" grew up to a large town, assuming the new name of Halig-fax or Halifax, which signifies "Holy Hair".'[13]

These strange and patently pagan legends hark back to earlier beliefs connected with the worship of stone heads and sacred trees, both of which are found in Celtic religion. It is interesting that the Christians thought it fit to dedicate their church at Halifax to St John the Baptist as the severed head of this saint figures strongly in the cult of relics during the Middle Ages. Pieces of the head or skull of the saint were preserved as holy relics in a least three separate Christian shrines on the Continent.

St John was also the adopted patron saint of the order of Crusader monks known as the Knights Templar who were disbanded by the Pope in 1308 after they were accused of heresy and idol worship. One of the accusations levelled against them was the worship of the human head and among the allegations it was said that in each province they kept idol heads 'of which some had three faces and some one, and others had a human skull'. It was said the Templars worshipped these heads in their chapters and assemblies, believing the heads 'could save them, that it could make riches, that it made the trees flower, and the land germinate.' [14]

Amongst the records of the dissolution of the Templar order in England, one priest was recorded as saying that he had been told by an old renegade Templar that in England there were four mysterious heads belonging to the Order, one of which was in the North of England beyond the Humber; was this the head of St John the Baptist, preserved in a shrine at Halifax?

Although the original gibbet does not now exist, replicas can be seen in the Piece Hall and on Gibbet Street in the town centre. Halifax is easily accessible by road via the M62 trans-Pennine motorway between Manchester and Bradford. Heads of the Celtic tradition can be seen at the Cliffe Castle Museum in Keighley and the Manor House Museum in Ilkley.

High Peak, Derbyshire

The River Etherow, a tributary of the Mersey, begins life on the high moorlands at the head of Longdendale, a valley which was once part of the Royal Forest of the Peak. The Etherow is a Celtic name, and it is thought the river acted as a boundary between two tribes, the Cornovii of Cheshire and the northern Brigantes, long before the Romans arrived in this area. Today, the valley remains in a boundary position, a meeting place of three counties, a mixture of both urban and rural scenery. At Gamesley, now a western suburb of the Derbyshire town of Glossop, are the remains of the Roman military base of Ardotalia, known as Melandra Castle. The fort was established on the banks of the Etherow around AD 155, and garrisoned by a cohort of Frisian auxiliary troops. It was one of a number of military bases set up by the general Agricola to bring order to the warlike Pennine tribes.

One of the earliest traditions of the area tells of a great battle which took place between the advancing Roman armies and the native tribes. Before the battle the druids are said to have sacrificed the daughter of the British chief to the gods on a rough altar on the rugged moors, but to no avail.[15] Historians believe the defeated Britons retreated to strongholds in the more remote parts of the Pennines following their defeat. In Poole's Cavern, a huge cave in the hillside above the spa town of Buxton, archaeologists have found evidence of water worship dating back 2000 years. Bones, skulls, coins, pottery and Roman jewellery have been found in parts of the entrance chamber, where it is believed both native Celts and Romans worshipped their water gods, leaving small groups of bent pins and bronze brooches as offerings.

Roman coins were also discovered in the pool at the source of natural mineral waters called St Anne's Well in Buxton during a council excavation in 1975. The two healing springs here, at the bottom of the valley, were the focus of a Celtic shrine to the mother goddess Anu in the Celtic Iron Age. When the Romans arrived they named Buxton 'Aquae Arnemetiae' referring to the goddess and the sacred grove. A stone carving of the goddess, Christianized as St Anne, is said to have appeared miraculously in the waters, and was preserved here until the sixteenth century.

The healing shrine in Buxton remained in good repair, lined with lead and surrounded by Roman brick and cement, until 1709 when a Cheshire man, Sir Thomas Delves, was cured and built a new stone porch around the water. The old shrine had become a centre of pilgrimage and was visited by as many as 12,000 people per year, the best known being Mary Queen of Scots during her imprisonment at Sheffield. But the pilgrimage was brought to a crude end during the reign of Henry VIII when his agent, Sir William Bassett, closed the well chapel and destroyed the statue of St Anne.

The worship of water, well dressings and other archaic practices, including the keeping of human skulls and many curious seasonal customs are still carried on in the villages in this north-west corner of Derbyshire, on the border with Cheshire, which has a concentration of Celtic place-names. This is a region where old beliefs have lingered from the remote past to a remarkable degree. Many dozens of carved stone heads, some of medieval origin, others dating back to the Celtic Iron Age have been found in the valleys of the High Peak. Often they are built into fieldwalls and houses, or have been dug out of topsoil in gardens, and a collection of strange carved stones including a horned head from Glossop can be seen arranged in an archway at Buxton Museum.

In a wall behind the vicarage at All Saints Church, in Old Glossop, are two carvings which survived from the medieval church of which nothing remains. They are male and female half-figures with upraised arms, and the distinctive Celtic 'spectacle eyes'. Similar grotesque-style carvings of human heads and faces adorn the north wall and tower of the 'mother church'

Mystical spiral patterns on the impressive entrance stone at the opening of the 62-foot-long entrance passage at New Grange or Brugh na Boinne, County Meath, Ireland. This huge mound or temple was built around 3000 BC on a ridge above the River Boyne, its entrance aligned directly upon the rising of the sun at the midwinter solstice

The Iron Age ritual site at Navan Fort (Emain Macha), near Armagh in Northern Ireland, which appears in the early Irish tales as Emain Macha, the tribal centre of the people of Ulster. Archaeological excavation has found evidence of a huge wooden roundhouse and a central totem pole as the focus of a huge ritual complex

Part of the great Neolithic stone circle at Avebury in Wiltshire, showing one of the entrances to the henge. Avebury was described by John Aubrey in the seventeenth century as 'exceeding in greatness the so renowned Stonehenge as a cathedral does a parish church.'

Silbury Hill, Wiltshire. Built around the same time as the Avebury henge, at 130 foot in height it is the largest man-made mound in Europe, and may have been the centre of the whole Avebury ritual complex

The Deal Man. A small pagan idol from Kent, discovered by archaeologists in 1984 inside an underground chamber or shrine dating to the first or second century AD. Excavators believe the figure may represent a guardian deity or god of the underworld

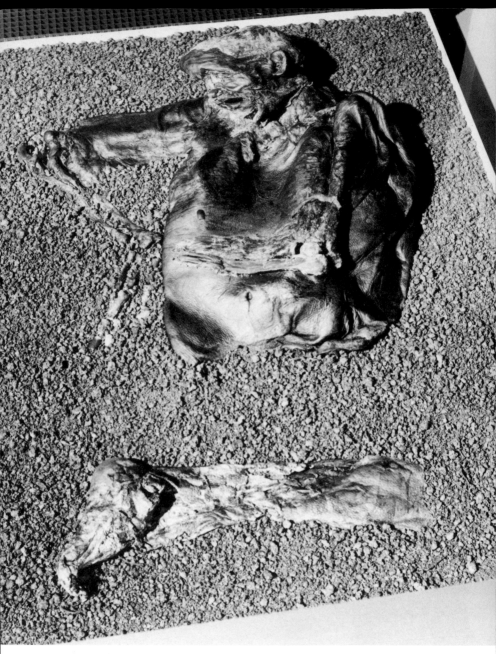

Lindow Man. 'The body in the bog', found in a Cheshire peat bog near the village of Mobberley in 1985 and now preserved in the British Museum. Scientists have dated the body tentatively to the first century AD. He had suffered a brutal 'triple death' as a human sacrifice to the Celtic gods, and experts believe he may have been a member of the pagan Celtic druid priesthood

The Mother Goddess, carving on roofboss in Sheffield Cathedral, Yorkshire. A wooden carving of fifteenth-century date found in the Lady chapel of the cathedral, depicting the goddess as a Sheela-na-gig alongside Christian symbols. Elsewhere in the suite of carvings are seven Green Men

The Paps of Anu (Da Chich Anainn), two breast-shaped mountains in County Kerry, Ireland. Anu or Danu was one name for the pagan goddess of Munster. In Celtic tradition, the goddess was often depicted in the landscape in the form of landscape features, mountains and stones

Sheela-na-gig carving from Hellifield, North Yorkshire. One of hundreds of similar medieval carvings found throughout England, Wales and Ireland, depicting a hideous hag-like figure displaying her sexual organs. The earliest appear to date from Norman times, but the prototypes for the figures seem to date back to the pagan Celtic period.

Pagan goddess, stone carving from Braunston, Rutland. This puzzling medieval carving was unearthed beneath the floor of the porch at All Saints Church in the nineteenth century, where it had presumably been buried by Christian priests. It may represent a territorial goddess, perhaps the Black Annis found in Leicestershire folklore

Carving of the pagan horned god, found near the walls of the Roman fort at Littlechester, Derby, in 1894. Like many other depictions of Celtic deities carved in stone after the Roman invasion, the native god – perhaps Cernunnos, the Horned One – is combined with the attributes of Mercury

above Carving of the Green Man, Chapel of the Nine Altars, in the twelfth-century Fountains Abbey, North Yorkshire. A strange image to find in an austere Cistercian abbey, the green man is half man, half tree and has been described as 'one of the most pagan and archaic concepts in the imagery of the Christian church' (Anne Ross, *Grotesques & Gargoyles*, 1975). The late Sidney Jackson, curator of the Cartwright Hall Museum, Bradford in West Yorkshire, exhibiting archaic carved heads of the Celtic tradition. Hundreds of these carvings have been found in Brigantia, some of them ancient, others carved within living memory as part of a continuing tradition. They can be found in guardian positions at thresholds, doorways, wells and springs

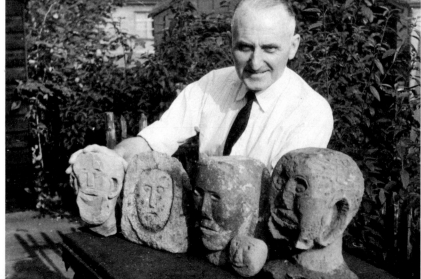

in the valley, at Mottram-in-Longdendale. The church here, dedicated to the dragon-slaying St Michael, stands on a prominent hilltop, which also functioned as a meeting place or crossroads in antiquity.

Another cult head, carved in sandstone, was found in the vicinity of Russet Well, an underground spring which emerges from the mouth of Peak Cavern at Castleton across the high moors to the south-east. This head, now in Sheffield's Weston Park Museum, has one purposefully closed or winking eye, which suggests it may be an image of a one-eyed god or the Norse god Odin.

Castleton village nestles below the famous 'Shivering Mountain' of Mam Tor at the head of the Hope Valley. The mountain takes its name from the mother goddess of the Brigantes, who built the Bronze Age hillfort, the remains of which can be seen upon its summit. Visitors to the village can see a strange and archaic ceremony take place every year on 29 May (unless this falls on a Sunday) which has echoes of both fertility and the sacrificial rites of the Celts.

The Castleton Garland Day is a unique and powerful calendar custom which involves the whole village and attracts hundreds of visitors from around the world every year. The Garland King is a man in Stuart costume who rides through the streets of the village with his consort, and is covered by a garland of flowers gathered by the villagers. At the end of the ceremony the Garland is hoisted onto the tower of the parish church, which is decorated with oak boughs. The earliest record of the garland dates from the eighteenth century, and experts are divided about the age and origins of the custom, but the *Peakland Post* continues to tell visitors the Garland 'is a surviving form of the Green Man which represents the growth of crops and all living things in the new season.'

Melandra Castle fort is found on a minor road running south off the A57 Glossop to Manchester road, after the junction with the A626 and carved heads and figures from the region can be seen in Buxton Museum on Terrace Road. St Ann's Well can be visited beside the Micrarium on the Crescent and Poole's Cavern is signposted from the A54 road west of the town.

Lastingham, North Yorkshire

The village of Lastingham lies on the southern flanks of the North York Moors and is dominated by the church of St Mary. Most of the building dates from the thirteenth century, but inside are the remains of a Norman church which was itself built upon the site of an early Anglo-Saxon monastery founded by the brothers St Cedd and St Chad, of Lindisfarne in AD 659.

The eerie crypt of the church is certainly its oldest part, and is in fact built into the side of what is believed to be a Bronze Age mound upon which the monastery and church were originally founded. The crypt appears to have been built in the late eleventh century AD, when Abbot Stephen of Whitby built a new monastery on the site. It has remained virtually unchanged since that time and still retains a strange and powerful atmosphere.

The monk Bede first mentions Lastingham in the eighth century AD, describing how the Northumbrian king Ethelwald, the son of King Oswald, asked St Cedd to accept a grant of land upon which to build a monastery where he might be buried, perhaps following the ancient custom, in a sacred mound. According to Bede, St Chad chose the site among high and remote hills which he said seemed more suitable for 'the dens of robbers and haunts of wild beasts' than for human habitation.[16]

It seems he knew of some ancient, pre-Christian power here for his first wish was to purify the site of the monastery from 'earlier crimes' by prayer and fasting, before laying the foundations. St Cedd asked permission to stay at Lastingham throughout Lent, fasting until evening every day except Sunday in order to dedicate his chosen spot. Years later an attack of plague wiped out the entire brethren of the monastery including St Chad, except for one little boy 'who was preserved from death by the prayers of his Father Chad.' Chad himself was originally buried in the open, and it was not until a stone church was built sometime later that his body was reinterred beside the altar in the crypt. Strangely, the church was dedicated to 'the blessed Mother of God' rather than St Chad himself as was usually the custom in early foundations of this kind.

Chad's body probably lies in the crypt of the church, and as the guide states 'if you walk down the stairs to the crypt, you are stepping back in time ... In this holy place the spirits of Cedd and Chad move on the stones of the floor and in the air you breathe ....'[17] To add to the sanctity of this dark underground chamber are the remains of a number of early Anglo-Saxon stones, including an eighth century AD carving of a 'dragon's head' which once formed part of the decoration of a large throne, perhaps that of the abbot.

Dragon power is also evident from other stones depicting sinuous serpent motifs in the crypt, which also contains the remains of a Danish tombstone and parts of a large crosshead dating from the time of the Vikings, who are said to have destroyed the monastery in the ninth century. Several people have had strange experiences whilst visiting the crypt, including a blind former vicar, the late Canon Gordon Thompson, who told one writer he had met a 'discarnate spirit' on several occasions at the door between the vestry and the sanctuary.[18] Authors Janet and Colin Bord have told how they experienced 'overwhelming energy emanations' whilst in the crypt,[19] and Paul Devereux noticed a great strength of 'earth force'. He describes the eratic behaviour of a compass inside the crypt, with the needle making 'a rhythmic jigging motion perhaps only noticeable in the magnifying system of a prismatic type of compass. This may be due to some perfectly explicable factor . . . but we could find no obvious answer at the time or since.'

It is intriguing that we should find such powerful feelings at this holy place with its mixture of pagan and Christian sanctity, as we know from Bede's account that it had some special power or attraction to the Anglo-Saxon kings and monks. This kind of continuity of use of sacred sites is found throughout the country, but is particularly explicit in the north of England, so much so that Guy Ragland Phillips concludes that 'virtually every old church in Brigantia seems to be built on what was formerly a pagan cult site'.

Possibly the most unambiguous evidence of this kind of Christianization can be found only 30 miles south-east of Lastingham, and 5 miles from the coastal resort of Bridlington on the edge of the Yorkshire Wolds. Here, in the churchyard at Rudston is the largest standing stone in the British Isles, towering above the graveyard at more than 25 feet in height. The Rudston Monolith is a roughly cut block of gritstone whose source is found 10 miles away in the North Riding, from where it appears to have been moved and erected on this hill sometime between 2200 and 1400 BC, for unknown ritual purposes.

The stone may have been only one of a group, which may have been the focus of a vast ritual landscape which features burial mounds and cursus. These are mysterious earthworks, only visible today on aerial photographs as crop marks, which were built in the Late Neolithic period perhaps as processional ways or avenues. As elsewhere, the sacred landscape at Rudston is connected with a sacred watersource. In this case it is known as the Gypsey Race, a stream fed by a spring which flows irregularly through the valley. It was used locally as a means of predicting unhappy local events, including storms and wars. In one tradition, the stone was erected in gratitude for the supply of water from the spring,

Christian missionaries appear to have built the first church, dedicated to All Saints, directly beside the pagan standing stone after the Norman Conquest for there is no mention of a church here in the Domesday Survey of 1086. In medieval legend it was hurled at the new church by the devil, but he was thwarted and the huge missile landed in its present position. Today, we know the stone was here almost three thousand years before the church, but the legend may be a memory of past struggles between the church and followers of the old religion. As the church guide so clearly states: 'the stone and nearby church thus occupy a site which has been sacred from prehistoric days to the present.'

Lastingham can be reached via a minor road north of the A170 from Thirsk to Pickering. Rudston is found on the B1253 north of the main A166 road between York and Bridlington.

Penhill, North Yorkshire

Throughout history the dales and moorland of North Yorkshire have remained remote from the changes in culture and religion which have taken root in the lowlands further south. Nowhere is this more evident than in the valley of Wensleyside, north of Whernside, one of the famous Three Peaks in Yorkshire Dales National Park.

The village of West Witton lies at the foot of Penhill, 1,792 feet in height and topped by a beacon which is said to cover the grave of an Iron Age chieftain. Not far away is a natural spring of water named, like many others in the region, Robin Hood's Well. From the hilltop there is a clear view north and west towards the Cleveland Hills and the Lake District, and south and east towards the North Sea and York Minster.

Penhill has a folktale which appears to link it indirectly with an annual ritual which takes place in the village below, of a very archaic and powerful nature, known as the 'Burning of Bartle'. Today it takes place on one night during the 'Witton Feast' which lasts three days, but originally the whole event lasted more than one week and may have ended with the burning of an effigy to mark the end of a key point in the agricultural cycle.

The 'Legend of Penhill' tells of a giant named Bartle who once lived in a castle or fortress on the hilltop where he kept a herd of swine guarded by a huge hound named Wolfhead. From here he terrorized the whole of the district. On one occasion, he set his hound to attack a herd of sheep, and when the beautiful shepherdess begged for mercy he tried to violate her. The girl resisted and struggled free, whereupon Bartle set Wolfhead after her. She bravely fought off the hound with a stone, but was slain by a blow from the club of the giant. Not long after this, the hound itself also died at the hand of its cruel master.

Later that year, Bartle found one of his young boars had been killed by an arrow, and he threatened to kill the first-born of all the tenants in the valley unless the guilty party owned up. Despite a warning from a hermit that if one drop of blood was spilled the giant would never enter his castle again, Bartle attempted to carry out his threat. He was struck speechless when he set out the next day to confront his tenants, for he came across nine boars dead on his path every three strides he took. Meanwhile, his steward had set fire to his fortress and as the giant caught sight of the flames he was shocked to the ghosts of the shepherdess and Wolfhead, who leapt at his throat, sending the two of them toppling over a precipice. [20]

That is the legend, a story which is difficult to date but which does seem to contain some archaic elements similar to those found in the old Welsh and Irish tales. There are for instance the magical pigs, special numbers, fires burning upon the hilltop and the figures of the girl or goddess and the wolfhound who may represent Fenris, wolf of Norse mythology.

Earth Mysteries researcher Ian Taylor has made connections between the legend and the ritual which takes place on St Bartholomew's Day (24 August, or the Saturday following this date), in the village of West Witton below the hill. The parish church is dedicated to the saint, and the effigy which is carried through the village street and then burnt with some ceremony is known as 'owd Bartle'. The name is similar to that of the Celtic god known as Bel or Belinus, which means 'bright' or 'shining one'.

The grotesque figure or effigy of Bartle, similar to the traditional Bonfire Night guy, is made in secret during the day by a local family from old clothes stuffed with straw. Bartle's special mask and eyes – formed by battery-operated lightbulbs – are kept and re-used every year, while the rest of the figure is burned.

The event starts at around 9 p.m. just as darkness falls, when the streets of the village are deserted. Bartle is carried shoulder-high between two men who march down the road stopping outside each of the three pubs where landlords offer refreshments. The group also calls at cottages and houses whose inhabitants await his call with expectation, looking upon the figure not with fright but with great affection and awe. Householders welcome Bartle as if he brings good luck and others who are too ill or infirm to venture out gaze out of upstairs windows while the figure is held up for them to see.

Most important of all is the special verse which is shouted, with great seriousness on every occasion the group stops by the 'chanter', a local man called John Spence:

> At Penhill Crags he tore his rags,
> At Hunter's Thorn he blew his horn.
> At Capplebank Stee he brak his knee,
> At Grassgill Beck he brak his neck,
> At Waddam's End he couldn't fend,
> At Grissgill End he made his end.
> Shout, lads, shout (Hooray!) .

The whole event is complete in just over one hour, when the procession arrives at Grass Gill (Grissgill in the rhyme). Here Bartle is placed on a small stone by the road, his clothes are covered in paraffin and he is set alight. As the effigy burns, the villagers sing a collection of popular modern songs. The Bartle ceremony is carried out with little frivolity and a striking air of solemnity pervades the scene, which like other archaic customs has a special atmosphere all of its own.

The tradition has been passed down in the oral tradition of the valley from one generation to the next by a community which is determined it will continue. Writing at the beginning of this century, historian Edmund Bogg said the vicar of West Witton believed the origins of the ritual were 'lost in the mists of time', but he thought the figure represented St Bartholemew himself. Another version says that until the time of the First World War the effigy was paraded through the village on a cart 'pulled by six strong local lads'.[21] Today, the people who organize and take part in the ceremony believe it commemorates the chase, capture and execution of a thief who stole pigs and sheep belonging to the monks of Jervaulx Abbey, to whom the manor of Witton was leased in the sixteenth century. They lay in wait for the thief, who was pursued through the various places mentioned in the rhyme until he was burned at the stake on Grassgill End.

Jervaulx Abbey was founded in 1156, and it seems the composite legend and ritual may be the result of a complex mixture of pagan and Christian mythology. The fearsome effigy of Bartle was quite possibly the figure of a pagan god associated with the harvest, who has been transformed in the intervening years into a swine thief and less convincingly into a Christian saint.

Ian Taylor takes the story further with a chronicle of the author's quest to rediscover not only the real figure of the giant, but what he believes is a 'real terrestrial effigy hidden in the landscape around Penhill'.[22] Taylor believes, with good reason, that the Bartle ceremony in West Witton originates in the renactment of a far earlier Celtic ritual connected with the hillside giant. His search, helped along by personal intuition like that which led T.C. Lethbridge to the vanished Wandlebury giants thirty years before, retraced the course of the St Bartholomew's Day communal fell race which once formed part of the festival activites. As he approached the eastern end of Penhill, he suddenly 'saw' the image of an enormous giant on a hillside at an angle of 36 degrees on a slope covered with bilberries.

It seems the three-dimensional giant figure (the highest effigy of its kind in the British Isles) is best observed in the evening sunlight of midsummer when deep shadows mark the outlines of its torso, waist and right arm. Part of the left arm and the giant's legs appear to be missing, but the head of the figure is made up of the cairn and beacon fire on Penhill ('pen' being a Celtic word meaning 'head').

West Witton can be reached via the A1 Great North Road, where the A684 runs west towards Kendal and the Lakes. The village is three miles south-west of Leyburn, and Penhill is accessible by footpath.

Ribble Valley, Lancashire

Until recently the beautiful River Ribble in Lancashire was regarded as the haunt of Peg O'Nell, a malignant spirit who once in seven years claimed a human life. Unless a small animal or bird was offered to her at the end of this period she would, it was said locally, demand a human victim. Today, a spring in the grounds of Waddow Hall bears the name of the water goddess and a headless stone statue on its banks is thought to represent her. Stories tell how at one time servants of the house would not remain under the same roof as the statue, so at some stage it was removed to the grounds.

The legend runs that Peg O'Nell was a servant at the mansion of Waddow, which stands beside the river. She was victimized by a tyrannical mistress who one day wished she might slip and break her neck as she performed her duty fetching water from the well which today bears her name. Sure enough, Peg slipped on ice and drowned in the waters of the river. Soon afterwards, Waddow Hall was in chaos, the farm stock fell sick and the children grew sickly. Local people said the misfortune was all due to the vengeance of Peg and when 'Peg's Night', the septennary of her demise, came round unless a cat, a dog or a bird were drowned in the river, some human being was certain to lose his or her life there in its place.

Accidents and deaths in the locality have long been ascribed to the water goddess represented in folk tradition by the figure of Peg. When in 1908 a man was drowned in the Ribble near Brungerley, a writer in the *Lancashire Evening Post* said: 'It is curious that the last fatality in the Ribble took place exactly seven years ago, and the one before that was fourteen years ago.' [23]

The legend of Peg O'Nell seems to be a distant memory of sacrifices offered to a water goddess who, if she could not be appeased with an animal, demanded a human victim, in return for her power to influence irrigation and the harvest. A Roman geographer mentions a 'Belisama Estuarium' on the north-west coast in the second century AD, and it is possible the River Ribble was known in Romano-British times as 'Belisama'. An altar dedicated to the British war god Belatucadros was found at Ribchester nearby, which makes it apparent that in Roman times Celtic deities dwelt in the Ribble Valley.

In Yorkshire there is evidence of a similar water goddess connected with the River Wharfe at Ilkley, where there is a carving (now inside the parish church) found in the seventeenth century beside an ancient spring on the moor. The figure depicted upon the stone has a large head and wears a long dress which reaches almost to her feet; in her hands she holds long sinuous serpents, further linking her with the cult of sacred waters. From an inscription on an altar found with the carving it appears her name was Verbeia, which may mean 'She of the Cattle'.

Following the river upstream from Ilkley, Bolton Abbey is reached, and at a place called the Strid (from Stryth, meaning the rush of water) the youthful river is rapidly channelled from a width of 50 to just 4 feet, crushed between massive gritstone rocks for nearly a quarter of a mile. At one point a long pointed rock slopes down from the bank, called the Strid jump, the scene of many fatal accidents where the river has claimed the lives of those who were not content to regard the river with respect and awe. It was a drowning of a son of the King of Scotland here in the twelfth century which led to the foundation of the Priory by the banks of the Wharfe.

The Celtic goddess of the Wharfe is said to appear in the form of a horse, and in the late nineteenth century the Revd Thomas Parkinson recorded a tradition of how 'on the morning of the May Day preceding any fatal accident in the Wharfe a spectral white horse, the steed of the queen of the fairies, is to be seen rising from the spray and mist around the Strid.' [24]

Further south another vengeful river deity, this time connected with a tree, haunts the River Derwent as it runs through the central Peak District, where water worship is still very much in evidence today. This river can at times be very dangerous, as it is fast-flowing and full of pot holes in places which have contributed to its reputation. In the medieval period a chapel was built on a bridge crossing over the river at Cromford to provide safety for travellers, possibly on the site of an early shrine to the god or goddess of the river. Nearby was a huge and menacing ash tree nick-named 'Crooker'.

An account by a local woman in 1904 reads:

> There has been a man drowned in the Derwent and great excitement about finding his body. I tell you this because I was so struck with the way Mrs Dale, a washerwoman, talked of the river, as if it was a living personage, or deity. I could almost imagine the next step would be to take it offerings! 'He didna know Darrant' (a kind of triumph in her voice) – 'he said it were nought but a brook. But Darrant got 'im. They never saw his head, he threw his arms up, but Darrant wouldna let him go. Aye, it's a sad pity, seven children! but he shouldna ha' made so light of Darrant. He knows now! Nought but a brook! he knows now!' It sounded as if Darrant [Derwent] had punished him for blaspheming and he had now been summoned before Darrant his judge![25]

Peggy's Well can be seen beside the river in the grounds of Waddow Hall, at Brungerley Bridge, north-west of Clitheroe on the B6478 to Waddington. The hall is owned by the Girl Guide Movement, from whom permission to visit should be sought.

Central England
including East Anglia

Flag Fen, Cambridgeshire
Gogmagog Hills, Cambridgeshire
Hallaton, Leicestershire
Isle of Axholme, Lincolnshire
Lindow Moss, Cheshire
Ludchurch, Staffordshire
Middle Tysoe, Warwickshire

Flag Fen, Cambridgeshire

This site is the subject of an exciting on-going archaeological excavation at the time of writing, and the dig and adjoining visitors' centre are open to the public. The large wetland ritual landscape, excavated by a team led by Francis Pryor, has been billed as the largest Bronze Age ritual site in Europe, and deserves a mention here. In the guide to the site Mr Pryor describes how it was discovered in 1982 as part of an archaeological survey of freshly cleared dykes in the fens. 'When asked why was the site discovered, we often reply "because we were looking for it". . . Did we know it was there? No . . . but hunches are strange things.'[1]

Flag Fen lies in a low-lying basin east of the city of Peterborough, which began to flood around 2000 BC as sea-levels rose. The farming people who lived on higher ground to the west at Fengate had laid out fields, paddocks and droveways during the Neolithic period and grazed their livestock on lush floodplains watered by the River Nene. As water-levels rose in the Late Bronze Age flooding neighbouring communities, the

Fenland folk began to build a defensive barrier or palisade of wood to limit access to their land.

The building of this half-mile-long barrier was 'a major feat of engineering', and it was made so well it remained in place for 400 years until around 950 BC. It was along the line of the barrier that archaeologists first found what appeared to be the remains of an artificial island, which in the Bronze Age would have stood in the middle of an area of shallow water. The island, covering 3.5 acres, was constructed from more than a million pieces of timber in the wettest part of the fen, and it was surmised that, like the Swiss lake villages, this was a place where people lived and worked. However, as the excavation progressed, this idea was discarded and today the real function of the island remains a mystery.

In 1989 the dig moved 400 yards from the original site for a rescue excavation in advance of the building of a new power station. Here a thousand oak posts were discovered running in an alignment straight out into the fen from the end of one of the farming settlements on the edge of the wetland on to the artificial island. Under the lowest timbers of the platform, the archaeologists found four complete and virtually untouched quernstones, perhaps placed there as offerings to water deities.

More astonishing, among the remains of the posts and laid alongside what may have been a sacred boundary wall were found more than 300 bronze implements, some of which appeared to have been broken and 'deliberately damaged' in some way. These were valuable military objects including swords, rapiers, daggers and spears, and the earliest date from the Middle Bronze Age around 1400 BC. There is a distinct lack of functional tools among the collection of weapons, and there are also a number of smaller objects, including small bronze pins, rings and brooches, all of which appeared to have been 'carefully placed or dropped into shallow water'.

These early metal objects were found alongside animal bones and pottery including shale objects, which appear to have been cast or carefully placed in the water in a fashion that has been compared to the legend of Excalibur. Francis Pryor has concluded that 'the vast majority of the material was deposited in religious or ritual circumstances.'[2]

In 1992 the excavation moved to a third site, on the other end of the post alignment, at a place called Northey. Here there was evidence of more Bronze Age fields and droveways, and in addition a number of archaeological discoveries had been made here in the past. Here a building is being erected to cover part of the post structure, so the site can be placed on permanent display to visitors from the spring of 1994. Hundreds of Bronze Age posts have been uncovered by the excavators, and many more lie below the modern visitors' centre which floats upon an artificial lake. The posts, all of oak brought from dry land to the west, have been preserved by the marsh water and examples can be seen in situ today. It seems the post alignment, made up of four rows, ran from dry land on Fengate to the north-west, in a straight line south-east across the fen to Northey

From the point of view of ritual, one of the most interesting aspects of Flag Fen is its apparent longevity, with religious activity beginning in the Late Neolithic and continuing through the Bronze Age when ritual deposition of weapons began, until 950 BC when the site was abandoned to the rising water. After this time, the site continued to be regarded as sacred, with swords, ornaments and jewellery being smashed and dropped into the water during the Iron Age.

Use of the site stops only with the construction of a Roman road through the fen late in the first century AD – Flag Fen was therefore in continuous use as a ritual site for between 1000 and 1500 years. Francis Pryor has dismissed earlier theories attributing the island and post alignments as defensive structures as too simplistic, and sees the whole monumental landscape at Flag Fen as ritual in function.[3] Archaeologists have seen this practice as evidence of a major change in religious practice in the Bronze Age, possibly as a result of changes in climate which may have led to a movement away from the great communal megalithic monuments in the uplands to new centres in the lowland river valleys.

At other Bronze Age 'ritual landscapes', elaborate items of metalwork also appear to have been deliberately dropped or thrown as offerings in pools, bogs and rivers to propitiate the powers of the Underworld in times of change or disaster. Ironwork and decorated bronze appears to have been particularly favoured for votive deposition, perhaps by virtue of the magical aura surrounding the craft of the blacksmith, whom we know from the Anglo-Saxon period was often depicted as a god. In Celtic mythology, weapons were often the dwelling places of gods and spirits, and daggers and swords seem to have been decorated with faces of those to whom they were dedicated.

Flag Fen is situated three miles east of the city centre of Peterborough, and is signposted from the A47 and A1139 roads. The visitors' centre is open from 11 a.m. to 5 p.m. every day except 25 and 26 December, with guided tours from Easter to the end of October. For more information ring (01733) 313414.

Gogmagog Hills, Cambridgeshire

The Iron Age hillfort of Wandlebury, south-east of Cambridge, was of strategic importance to the tribe known as the Iceni who once held the surrounding tracts of flat fenland before the arrival of the Romans. It appears the earthworks here, at one time two external banks with external ditches and a bank, were occupied from the third century BC onwards, and on a clear day, a visitor standing on the grass-covered ramparts of the fort can see up to twenty miles across the fens towards the cathedral town of Ely.

The name Wandlebury is Anglo-Saxon and means Wendles-biri or the fort of Waendel, a name which folklorist Jacqueline Simpson has argued is that of 'a superhuman being, almost certainly a Germanic war-god'. The same god is depicted in the form of a huge landscape figure at Wilmington in Sussex, where the same name is found as a Domesday hundred.[4] At Wandlebury, the 'giant' is lost, but traditions collected in the 1950s by the late T.C. Lethbridge, a Cambridge archaeologist, led him to rediscover an elaborate group of hill figures on the hillslope below the fort, which seem to include not only a Germanic god but also earlier figures representing a Celtic moon goddess and her chariot.

Folk tales recorded by Lethbridge include one about the burial of two giants or gods, 'Gog and Magog' on these hills which today bear their names. Gogmagog, or Gog and Magog are mythological figures, described as 'the last of the British giants' by Geoffrey of Monmouth in the twelfth century. Geoffrey said they were the leaders of the original race of giants conquered by Brutus and his Trojan warriors in his semi-mythical history of Britain, and a later legend tells how they were captured by

Brutus and made prisoners in his palace on the site of London's Guildhall, where statues of Gogmagog and Corineus, ruler of Cornwall, were erected in the fifteenth century. After destruction in the Fire of London in 1666, the statues were replaced with new ones depicting 'Gog and Magog', which can still be seen today.

Lethbridge attempted to connect the names of these giants with the figures he had found on the slopes of Wandlebury, and his theory was supported by the former existence at Plymouth Hoe of two huge giants carrying clubs which were cut in the turf below the Citadel. They are clearly described in the sixteenth century as 'Gog Magog', which seems to have been a generic term used at that time to describe hill-figures (another, also lost, were recorded in the eighteenth century upon Shotover Hill, near Oxford). At Wandlebury, the figures cut in the turf were still visible in 1724 when the antiquary William Cole wrote: 'I remember [on] the road from Babraham there lying through the camp ... [they] always used to stop to show me the figure of the Giant carved in the turf; concerning whom there were many traditions now worn away.'[5]

Cole does not describe the nature of these traditions, but William Camden mentioned one of them in 1610, describing a 'Martiall spectre' – a ghostly black knight on horseback who was connected with Wandlebury Fort. This tale was originally recorded by Gervase of Tilbury in 1211, when it was still 'current in his day' that if one went to the entrance of the Iron Age camp by moonlight and shouted a challenge, a knight 'or what looked like a knight' would come out and fight. Horses clearly figure prominently in Wandlebury's folklore, which is not surprising as the Iceni tribe are thought to have taken their name from the horse, a sacred totem animal for the Celtic tribes. There is even a tradition of a buried horse, often confused with the famous Godolphin stallion, on Little Trees Hill, half a mile to the west of Wandlebury – a hill connected with the breeding of champion racehorses for more than 300 years!

Intrigued by this collection of tales, Lethbridge set out in 1954, with the permission of the Cambridge Preservation Society, to examine the slope below the hillfort which had been half-planted with a belt of birch trees 300 years earlier. Using a traditional method of employing a long bar to probe for hidden features in the chalk beneath the ground, he plotted the outlines of the weathered figures after taking up to 50,000 soundings during an exhaustive 8-month search. Large numbers of sticks were used to mark the edges of hollows found in the chalk, and these were carefully plotted by tape triangulation.

Lethbridge found that a legible picture began to be formed only when the locations were marked on a plan, and an excavation revealed that his picture was, in fact, beneath the turf. The figures revealed by the survey were three, one smaller than the two which flanked it, along with a horse, the moon and a figure of a warrior waving a sword above his head. Their finder soon became convinced the hillside picture was meant to represent an entire 'ritual picture' which was formed around a figure of a moon goddess and her horse of earlier origin.[6]

If the figures are of Celtic date then the goggle-eyed moon goddess might be a depiction of Epona or Andraste to whom Boudicca, the Queen of the Iceni sacrificed her captives. Lethbridge interpreted the whole picture as an image of the moon goddess following her horse and chariot while behind her poses an unknown figure brandishing a sword. 'Before the goddess, and of larger size and greater importance, a sun figure is about to unfold his wings and rise into the sky,' he wrote.[7]

Clearly the sun and moon were of importance to the people who constructed this ritual landscape, and it is possible the pantheon of deities was the site of a religious festival to ensure the triumph of light over darkness at a festival which marked the beginning of the summer. Lethbridge believed the figures were ancient, and were the site of fertility rites as there are accounts of gatherings of people there during the sixteenth century. He published the results of his investigation in 1957, but the world of academic archaeology poured scorn upon his ideas and dismissed the hill figures as the results of 'frost action in glacial times'.

In more recent times, folklorists have re-examined some of the arguments and now accept there is evidence for at least one lost hill figure at Wandlebury. Further archaeological excavation would be necessary to discover if the Gogmagog Hills do indeed hide a lost pantheon of giants, perhaps a composite picture containing both a Celtic goddess and Anglo-Saxon war god or hero who may be 'Waendal' himself.

In 1956, *The Countryman* published a letter by a correspondent, T.A. Ryder, which describes an oral tradition about this same Waendel/Wandil which the writer heard in Gloucestershire.

He said an old man had said to him that Wandil took away the spring, in order that winter would persist. Winter persisted relentlessly until it seemed that the world would surely die. After a time Wandil was forced by the gods to relinquish the spring. He was, in common with the gods, immortal and there-fore indestructible. However, they threw him upwards into the sky and he was transformed into the constellation of Gemini. 'When his eyes (Castor and Pollux) glare down, as on the night of our encounter, there will be a keen frost; and there was ... then a friend told me of the Scandinavian legend that Thor fought the giant Orwandel and threw one of his toes into the sky, where it became a star ... If that is the origin of the story, it appears to be a remarkable example of folk memory.'[8]

The Gogmagog Hills, owned by the Cambridge Preservation Society, are situated in a country park north of the A1307 road, south-east of the town. There is a public car park nearby.

Hallaton, Leicestershire

Julius Caesar wrote that the British tribes had a number of animals they regarded with religious sanctity, and he noted in particular the cockerel, goose and hare. Another classical writer describes how the Queen of the Iceni, Boudicca, released a hare as she invoked the war goddess Andraste before her attack on the Roman army in AD 60. Although the archaeo-logical evidence for hares in ritual contexts is scanty, these agile creatures are linked in folk tradition with witchcraft and shape-shifting.

The peculiar sanctity of the hare was shared by the Anglo-Saxon people, and we know from Bede that at Easter time the pagan English had a festival for a spring goddess called Eostre or Hretha, who may well have had connections with fertility rit-uals. Easter Monday was a time for traditional games, one of the most important of which is the bizarre 'Hare Pie Scramble' and 'Bottle-kicking' which takes place in the East Leicestershire vil-lage of Hallaton. The game is just one of a number of seemingly ritual battles between neighbouring villages which have at their core the belief that gaining possession of a piece of a sacrificed or dedicated animal would bring luck and perhaps a fruitful harvest in the year ahead.

At the Haxey Hood and Shrovetide Football customs it seems it is the possession of a severed head, whether human or animal, which lies at the core of the ritual, but at Hallaton it seems it was the image of the whole animal (the hare) as a totem or symbol of the spring was important. An account from the *Daily News* of 1929 describes the scramble in graphic terms:

> Hallaton Hare Pie plays an important part of an old custom known as Hallaton Bottle-kicking, which dates back for some hundreds of years. The story goes that one of the ladies from the manor house was saved from death by a hare running across the path of a mad bull which was attacking her. To celebrate her escape she gave a sum of money to provide a hare pie each Easter Monday, also four bottles of beer. The bottles are small wooden casks such as were used to hold beer in olden days.
>
> The pie is scrambled for on Hare Pie Bank and a tussle takes place between Hallaton men and Medbourne – the next village – for the bottles, each village having certain boundaries over which their men must get two out of three of the bottles to be winners. Later the beer is drunk at the old Market Cross . . . another correspondent states that two hare pies were formerly provided and also two dozen penny loaves, as well as the bottles. Now there is one large pie which is cut up into portions to be scrambled for, and still another says the hare pie has now been replaced by pies of veal and bacon.

The account adds: 'Some years ago a former rector of Hallaton tried to divert the money to an annual dinner for the old people of the village, but feelings ran high, the walls of the houses and church porch were plastered with various devices and threats of "No Pie, No Parson" and the attempt to interfere with this Easter performance was abandoned.'[9]

Some writers have suggested the symbolism of this rough and tumble game may represent the scattering of the sacrificial animal across the land to promote its fertility, and we know that at one time an image of a hare was displayed on a pole and carried in procession to Hare Pie Bank before the scramble began. The identification of the whole community with the ritual animal they eat or chase on an annual feast day has connotations of totemism, with the animal selected being appropriate to the worship of a locally important god or goddess.

A ritual 'hare hunt' also took place until the end of the eighteenth century on the outskirts of the city of Leicester, also on Easter Monday. It seems there was an annual fair on the Dane Hills, west of the city, which culminated in a hare hunt led by the Mayor and Corporation of the city, with the huntsmen and hounds riding at full cry through the streets to the Mayor's door at the end of the day.

In this case the hare may have been associated with a mother goddess or crone known in Midlands folklore as Black Annis. She was said to live in the Dane Hills in a cave on a hillside clawed out by her own talons, known as Black Annis's Bower. The spectre of this hideous, witch-like hag was used by parents within living memory as a bogey to terrify misbehaved children, who were told that if they played too long or late on the hills at night she would seize and eat them, scattering their remains around her cave and hang their skins on an old oak tree nearby.[10]

The name Annis has clear associations with the goddess known to the Irish Celts as Anu or Danu, a being identified with the landscape, the changing seasons and the waxing and waning of the moon. She may be the same goddess remembered at the village of Braunston in Rutland, eight miles north-east of Hallaton, at the Norman church of All Saints. A unique pillar-like stone carving, now leaning against the west end of the tower in the churchyard, depicts a hideous hag-like creature, with staring eyes and prominent breasts at the top of a truncated body. The carving, described as a Sheela-na-gig in the church guide, was found in the nineteenth century buried face downwards and acting as a doorstep. Although historians have suggested it may be of recent origin, its appearance suggests it could well represent a pagan goddess who retained her power here as late as the Norman Conquest.

The village of Hallaton can be found on a minor road south of the main A47 which links Leicester and Peterborough.

Isle of Axholme, Lincolnshire

In the eighth century AD the people of Hatfield are mentioned in an Anglo-Saxon document as a tribe living in a remote area of marshland where three rivers, the Don, Idle and Torne, meander towards the sea. Today, Hatfield Chase and the neighbouring Isle of Axholme mark the border between the modern counties of South Yorkshire and Humberside. The tribe were probably the descendants of the Celtic people, whom air photography and archaeology have revealed lived in this area in prehistoric times, before rising sea-levels caused flooding in the Humber Estuary.

Although only ten miles east of the Roman settlement at Danum (Doncaster), before the seventeenth century when Dutch engineers began to drain the fens, the people of Hatfield Chase, Lindholme and the Isle of Axholme lived in geographical isolation on islands in the middle of vast wetlands. Because of its isolation, the Isle and surrounding moors have long been regarded a strange area where old customs and beliefs have lingered.

One curious folk-tale from this region concerns a medieval hermit, William of Lindholme. He is described in some stories as a giant or wizard who was fond of throwing great stones, and it seems he lived in a hermitage made up of two large megalithic standing stones on an island in the middle of a peat morass. When antiquarians visited the remains of this 'hermitage' in 1727 they found an ancient cottage which resembled a small chapel, complete with an altar at one end and a stretch of causeway running away towards Thorne Moss. The account says the men caused a huge slab of stone known as the hermit's grave to be lifted 'and digging under found a tooth, a skull, the thigh and shin bones of a human body, all of very large size ... in the grave was a peck of hemp seed and beaten piece of copper.'[11]

Near this 'chapel' was a well of clear water, blessed it was said by the wizard, who seems to have been a marshland spirit or deity in disguise. One tale describes how once he planned to build a causeway across the marshes for a farmer 'on condition that the rider should not look behind him'. When the farmer summoned the courage to look over his shoulder he saw the hermit 'in the midst of hundreds of little demons in red jackets macadamising as fast as possible ... the terrified horseman exclaimed "God speed your work" which put a stop to the whole business and left the good people who had to pass and repass from Lindholme to Hatfield, to wade through the bog for two hundred years longer.'[12]

The village of Haxey, the natural centre of the Isle of Axholme, appears in the Domesday Book as Acheseia (Haxa), a name made up of Celtic, English and Danish elements which some antiquarians believe originally came from an old German word meaning 'Druidess'. It lies in the middle of what archaeologists have described as 'the most important area in England for bog bodies', these being the remains of prehistoric and early historic people who seem to have met a sudden, perhaps sacrificial death in the marshy waters as executions or ritual offerings to the marsh spirits.

It was during the seventeenth and eighteenth centuries, when the Isle of Axholme was first systematically drained, that many prehistoric remains were discovered. These included prehistoric forests, ploughs, coins, a Bronze Age trackway and in 1805, between Haxey and Misson, 'a statue of oak, black as ebony, about two yards high and carved in the habit of a Roman warrior ... one hand held an arrow, and a bow was slung over the shoulder.'[13] This figure, with an inscription identifying it as the god Mars, has since been lost along with the many important finds of crouched human bodies. Some of these appear to have met a sacrificial death similar to that which befell the Iron Age man found at Lindow Moss, Cheshire, in 1985.

Around 1645 the naked body of a man was found in the bogs near Doncaster 'lying at his length with his head upon his arm as if asleep ... his skin hair and nails preserved his shape intire'. One hundred years later a woman was found, naked except for a pair of sandals, lying 'upon one side bended with her head and feet almost together.'[14] There have been at least three other similar bodies found in similar circumstances, but none has survived for examination today, and the manner in which they met their watery end must remain an insoluble mystery.

The grim deities of marsh and bog to whom these people may have been offered are known by a number of different names in these parts, boggard and barghast being one common term. The little beings in red jackets mentioned in the legend of William of Lindholme may have a curious connection with the thirteen villagers from Haxey nicknamed the Boggans who take part in the curious Hood Game, held every year on 6 January, Twelfth Day or Old Christmas-Day, traditionally the heart of the pagan mid-winter festival.

The Haxey Hood is an ancient contest which resembles a rugby scrum. In actuality it is a fierce ritual battle with few rules between opposing villagers for ownership of a curious object which may originally have been either an animal or a human head, possession of which brought good luck to the community. One expert has written the game 'has every appearance of being the folk survival of a ritual combat between local groups, and there can be little doubt that originally the hood was the sacrificial victim.'[15] The 'hood' is in fact a 25-inch-long piece of thick rope encased in leather, which may in the past have been taken from the hide of the sacrificed animal.

In local legend the Haxey Hood game dates back to the thirteenth century, when the lady of the manor had her hood taken by a gust of wind. Thirteen men ran to catch it, but the man who retrieved it (the village fool) lacked the courage to return it to the noble lady. She was so amused by this quaint sport she promised each of the men a piece of land if they would play the same game again every year. The man who eventually returned the hood became known as the Lord, and today his descendant wears a floral headdress and carries an elaborate ritual 'wand' made of thirteen willow saplings, held together with thirteen willow bands. A new wand is carefully made each year, and all twelve Boggans who serve the Lord dress in scarlet jackets.

The ceremony always begins with a procession headed by the 'Fool', a man with a blackened face, who is 'smoked' above a fire which is lit below his feet as he stands on a low stone outside the churchyard wall. He exhorts them to take part in the struggle, calling:

> Hoose agen hoose, toone agen toone,
> If tho meets at man, knock 'im doone
> But don't 'ut im!

The fool then leads the crowd of villagers to a half-acre field, the Hoodland, where legend says the lady's hood was lost. After a short struggle for 'sham hoods' by children, the Sway Hood is thrown into the air and the serious battle commences, formed by rival gangs from Haxey and neighbouring Westwoodside. The aim of those participating is to seize the hood and carry it to their village pub, and the battle can last several hours and often results in injuries, usually broken limbs. When the hood finally reaches the successful hostelry, the inn remains the proud owner until next 6 January.

The role of the scarlet-clad Boggans, who try to prevent the hood leaving Haxey, remains a mystery but their name clearly links them with the spirits of the bogs found in the same region. The battle between neighbouring communities for the possession of a ritual object resembles the rough and often violent traditional football games which took place elsewhere in Britain at Shrovetide and are believed to be of pagan origin. Some, like the street game still held at Kirkwall in the Orkney Islands, known as the *ba*, retain an old tradition which asserts the football was originally a severed human head. As in other calendar customs the real age and origins of the Haxey Hood are a matter of debate, but most experts believe the story of the lost hood is apocryphal. As one participant told a writer in 1993: 'It's more important than Christmas round here, it's in your blood. If you're brought up local, if you grow up with the Hood, it's part of your whole make-up. Keeping the tradition going is everything.'[16]

Haxey is six miles north-west of Gainsborough on the B1396, and can be reached either from Bessacarr in Doncaster or from the A161 road between Goole and East Retford.

Lindow Moss, Cheshire

Two thousand years ago a young man, whose name we will never know, was sacrificed to a shadowy god or goddess of the Underworld. His body was cast into a pool of dark water, which later became a raised peat bog near the village of Mobberley in present-day Cheshire. Unearthed from his watery grave in August 1984 during peat cutting, the preserved body of Lindow Man has become a unique window upon the shadowy practice of human sacrifice in the late Iron Age immediately before the Roman invasion. Indeed, the reconstruction of Lindow Man's short life and savage death, using the latest techniques at the disposal of archaeologists in the twentieth century, has helped to bring into focus as never before the religion of the pagan Celtic tribes and the priests of that religion, the druids.

Following the discovery the landowner donated the find as a national treasure to the British Museum where the body is now freeze-dried and on permanent display. Lindow Man was carefully extracted from its watery grave by archaeologists and has been subjected to an intensive investigation by a team from the British Museum led by Dr Ian Stead. Since the body had been preserved so well by immersion in the acidic marsh water, even the contents of the stomach, including the last meal survived for study. Scientists found the last food Lindow Man had eaten had been a portion of burnt bread (probably a kind of coarsely ground barley bread or bannock, baked on a heather fire) in which traces of mistletoe pollen were found. Mistletoe was, according to the Roman historians, a sacred plant and central to the secret rituals of the druids which probably included human sacrifice.

Forensic examination revealed Lindow Man was aged between twenty-five and thirty years, he was around five foot six inches tall and weighed ten stone, had a powerful unblemished body complete with carefully manicured fingernails and trimmed beard. This suggests he was an individual of high status, certainly not a farmer, and from his muscle development it appeared unlikely he was a warrior. The only other option was that he was a member of the Celtic aristocracy or priesthood, which in this context can only mean the druids.

He had undergone a brutal 'Triple Death', first stunned by an axe blow to his head, then a garotte fashioned from sinew was twisted from behind with a stick, breaking his neck. The young man's throat was cut before the body, naked except for a tiny armband made of fox-fur, was dumped in a shallow pool of water. The date when the death occurred is still the subject of controversy due to a number of conflicting radiocarbon dates from two laboratories, but it seems most likely it happened during the first century AD, at roughly the time of the Roman conquest of Britain and the foundation of the legionary fortress at Chester.

There remains a mystery over who the subject of such an elaborate overkill could have been, but experts now agree that Lindow Man was certainly a human sacrifice rather than a victim of crime or execution. Dr Anne Ross believes Lindow Man was a druid priest, and cites the triple death as evidence he was sacrificed to the Celtic gods Taranis, Esus and Teuttades at a time when the Romans were advancing on the north.[17] Roman writers describe how human offerings to these gods had their throats cut, and were hung and drowned respectively. In addition there are a number of late medieval references to this kind of ritual death both from Ireland and northern Europe.

The 'body in the bog' from Lindow Moss is by no means the first of its kind found in the British Isles. A study in 1986 recorded over 80 similar discoveries in Britain over the last 500 years, with clusters of finds in the north-west and the Isle of Axholme between South Yorkshire and Humberside. Over one thousand bog bodies are known from Denmark and Northern Germany, the majority of whom met a violent death presumably as human offerings to deities in bogs and water. Some of the continental examples made famous in Professor Glob's book *The Bog People*[18] had been hung or strangled and a number were decapitated, with the head sometimes buried alone.

There is some evidence of this pagan cult practice in north-west England, including a severed human head found buried in a peat bog at Worsley in Greater Manchester in 1958. This was examined by the Department of Pathology at Manchester University who found it was that of a man aged twenty to thirty. He appears to have suffered a triple death in the same way as Lindow Man met his end, by the knife, noose and pool. Worsley Man had been decapitated and the head buried separately in a ritual clearly linked with the Celtic cult of the head.

The head of Worsley Man has been compared with others from Red Moss near Horwich in 1942 and Pilling Moss in 1824, where female severed heads were buried. Some have suggested this was an act to prevent the spirits of witches or other undesirable members of a tribe from walking. The Pilling head was found along with a necklace of jet beads, which suggests the burial dates from the late Bronze Age, and the practice of burying the head separate from the body is so well-known in British prehistory that it even has its own name – cephalatophy.[19]

Dr Ian Stead of the British Museum has suggested Lindow Moss itself may have been a ritual area where offerings were made to water gods in the Late Iron Age and early Roman period, when Lindow lay on the boundary between tribal territories.

Shortly before the discovery of Lindow Man peat-cutters unearthed a single human skull in the same area of peat. The skull was first thought to be that of a woman murdered in a nearby town whose body was never found. Although her husband subsequently confessed to the murder, when the skull was carbon dated by an Oxford laboratory it was found to belong to the second century AD! Experts now believe the skull is male, part of the body of a second sacrificial offering to the bog.

In 1987 the fragmentary remains of what was at first thought to be a third body were turned up by a peat-cutting machine at Lindow. The radiocarbon date obtained was so close to that of the skull it is now believed they belong to the same individual, who may have been decapitated. Analysis by X-ray of skin from the shoulder revealed the presence of high levels of minerals, and it appears this body (and probably that of Lindow Man) was adorned with designs painted with a bright pigment before death.[20]

An account by Julius Caesar, contemporary with the Lindow dates, describes how the British tribes often went into battle naked and 'stain themselves with vitrum, which gives a blue colour and a more fearsome appearance in battle'. Vitrum has been translated as 'woad', a blue dye obtained from wood, but it appears more likely it means a clay-based mineral pigment containing copper and zinc which would provide a basic stock of colours including red and bright green.

Experts agree the practice of colouring the skin for ritual or martial purposes survived longest in the north of Britain, where the Picts of Scotland took their name from a Latin phrase meaning 'the painted men'. The presence of copper and zinc in the skin colourings could be explained if Lindow Man lived near Alderley Edge, an imposing escarpment which towers above the Cheshire plain near Lindow Moss. The Edge appears to have been an important centre of ritual activity in the Iron Age, and there is evidence that a number of minerals, particularly copper, have been mined there from as early as the Bronze Age. This mineral wealth may have made Alderley one of the cult centres of the Cornovii tribe, whose name has been connected with that of the horned god, Cernunnos.

Alderley Edge itself is a site with mystical and occult associations dating back many centuries. It is especially famous for its connection with a mysterious wizard, commemorated in a pub of the same name on the Edge, not far from a holy well at the base of the sandstone outcrop. Here the face of the wizard is carved along with an inscription which reads:

> Drink of this and take thy fill,
> For the water falls by the wizard's will.

The legend of the wizard, the elemental forces of the Old Magic, along with the witches, elves and phantom horsemen from the folklore of Alderley Edge are all woven into twentieth century fiction in the prizewinning works of author Alan Garner, who was born and brought up nearby. The eerie woods and stones on the rock escarpment, provide the setting for Garner's first two novels *The Weirdstone of Brisingamen* and its sequel *The Moon of Gomrath*, which entwine the legend of the wizard with an adventure story setting two youngsters in a time-less battle of good against evil.

The preserved body of Lindow Man is on display in the archaeo-logical gallery of the British Museum in Central London. Lindow Moss itself can be found on the western outskirts of Wilmslow on a minor road off the A538. Alderley Edge and the Wizard's Well can be found on the B5087 road between Wilmslow and Macclesfield.

Ludchurch, Staffordshire

The valley of the River Dane is a magical and mystical place. The river appears to be named after the goddess Danu/Anu, who in Ireland is the mother of the divine race called the Tuatha De Danann. It is born on Featherbed Moss and is surrounded on much of its course by high moor-lands which rise on the boundary between the three counties of Cheshire, Derbyshire and Staffordshire. The current gathers strength as it rushes beneath an old packhorse bridge at Three Shires Head before heading west towards the Back Forest where it is joined by the Black Brook.

This remote region is redolent with folk tradition and custom which points to the old religion, from place-names identifying landscape features with the goddess to the acknowledgement of the spirit of the waters and high places. This is the landscape which provided the inspiration for the author of the greatest medieval English poem outside the works of Chaucer, the fourteenth-century masterpiece called *Sir Gawain and the Green Knight.*

Following the course of the Dane, near Wincle, the visitor must seek out Ludchurch, the chapel of the god Lud, a breathtaking rocky chasm hidden within the wooded Back Forest on the slopes of the Dane Valley. It appears to have been created as the result of a geological fault in the millstone rock and in the seventeenth century, Dr Robert Plot wrote of it: 'the stupendous cleft in the rock between Swythamley and Wharnford commonly call'd Lud-Church, which I found by measure 208 yards long, and at different places 30, 40 or 50 foot deep; the sides steeped and so hanging over, that it sometimes preserves snow all the summer.'[21] The dramatic cavern extends 200 foot into the hillside and is 50 foot deep and 9 foot wide. In places the walls of the chasm are vertical, and the early name suggests this place had a reputation as a chapel of demonic forces well before Plot's time.

The area is rich in legends about secret religious meetings held in Ludchurch during the fifteenth century, when the cavern appears to have become a remote sanctuary for the Lollards, followers of an heretical preacher John Wyclif. It is from the name of a follower of Wyclif, Walter de Lud-Auk, that history books attribute the strange name. The story, as told to Sir William de Lacy who visited the region during the reign of Henry VIII was that over a century before, the hiding place of Lud-Auk and his followers had been betrayed to the soldiers of the king who stormed the entrance to the cavern. During the struggle, a shot was fired killing the beautiful granddaughter of Lud-Auk, who was buried at the entrance.

This tale was at one time promoted by a local landowner who organized day trips for people from Buxton who travelled to Ludchurch in pony and trap and were charged an entrance fee. Research by author Doug Pickford has ascertained that Walter de Lud-Auk actually took his name from Lud Church itself, not the other way around, and hidden beneath the layers of romantic Victorian invention lie much earlier beliefs.[22] The name Ludchurch clearly refers to the Celtic sun and sky god Lud, Lugh of the Long Hand to the Irish tribes, whose name survives in the harvest festival known as Lughnasa or Lammas.

The Celtic Lud can be compared with the thunder god Thor found in Germanic mythology, and here we have an interesting connection between the name and a strange natural phenomena connected with Ludchurch. The ravine terminates in a deep hole descending far below the roof, and a number of explorers descending into this chasm have reported hearing a great loud rushing noise perhaps from the River Dane below, which has been described as 'a loud crowing' and 'a terrible clap as of thunder'. Perhaps the tribes who regarded this place as sacred believed these natural sounds to be the voice of the sky god they worshipped. The sanctity of Ludchurch survived in folk tradition as the entrance to fairyland, and special stones taken from outcrops here and the nearby Roaches were carved into amulets and worn, attached to string around the neck, as a protection against witchcraft and evil.

Of prime importance in the identification of the Dane Valley and Ludchurch as temple of a pre-Christian god is its connection with the mythological landscape featured in *Sir Gawain and the Green Knight*.[23] The tale opens at Arthur's court in Camelot where the knights are celebrating New Year with a great feast. The door bursts open and in rides the Green Knight, who is depicted as a fairy warrior, a denizen of the Otherworld, for the man and all his clothes are green – the colour of nature. He challenges the knights to strike him one blow with an axe, on condition that he may return the blow exactly one year and one day later. Only Gawain, who sits next to Guinevere at the table, comes forth to take up the challenge and strikes off the head of the Green Knight, which rolls on to the floor.

As the astonished court looks on, the headless horseman picks up the severed head by the hair and holds it up. The eyes open and the mouth says menacingly: 'Be prepared to perform what you promised, Gawain; Seek faithfully till you find me ... Go to the Green Chapel ... And gladly will it be given in the gleaming New Year. Such a stroke as you have struck.'[24] He departs with a roar and flash, as you would expect of a thunder god.

Heeding the challenge, Gawain sets out with his steed Gringolet at Samhain travelling through the mythical winter landscape of Logres, across many marshes and mires, 'unto North Wales and then over by the Holy Head to high land ... in

93

the wilderness of the Wirrall.' Finally at Christmas Eve he reaches a castle where a temptation episode takes place. Afterwards, the poem graphically describes Gawain's approach to the Green Chapel itself, 'a chapel of mischance', along a rocky path to the bottom of a valley where there are rocky crags. The chapel is clearly depicted as a prehistoric mound, 'a smooth-surfaced barrow beside a stream'. It has holes in either end 'and was overgrown with grass in great patches ... it was hollow, nothing more than an old cave or a fissure in some ancient crag it was within.' Here he hears the sound of the Green Knight sharpening his axe and the second phase of the beheading game begins – the final test which leads to Gawain's symbolic 'rebirth'.

Although set in a chivalric Christian court, the cyclical story contains many archaic elements, most notably the beheading game which can be traced directly to an eighth-century AD Irish tale known as Bricriu's Feast. The Green Knight is an embodiment of the power of nature and the old religion, a trickster who is capable of shape-shifting and whose colour identifies him with the foliate heads or Green Men which were being carved enthusiastically in the parish churches and cathedrals in the same period the poem was committed to writing.

Sir Gawain and the Green Knight was written by an unknown author whose style and dialect have allowed experts to conclude that he lived in a small area of land on the border between south-east Cheshire and north-east Staffordshire and it seems possible he was actually a monk living at Dieulacres Abbey, near Leek. This abbey was transplanted into wild moorland country of the Staffordshire Peak District in 1214 from a site nearer Chester by Ranulph, Earl of that city. His family owned a hunting lodge at Swythamley Hall within the abbey grounds, which has been identified as the castle of Bercilak de Hautdesert, where Gawain stays and is told the Green Chapel is 'not two miles hence'.

Professor Ralph Elliott, an expert on the poem, has identified the Green Chapel directly with Ludchurch itself, writing how 'the poet was obviously at home in the wild, hilly country he describes', the topography of which directly relates to the valley of the Black Brook and the River Dane.[25] Others have suggested a strange cave on a knoll at Wetton Mill in northeast Staffordshire, which stands in the valley of the River Manifold, was the

Green Chapel. Nearby is another deep cave in a hill called 'Thurshouse' ('house of the fiend'), known today as Thor's Cave. A less plausible theory connects it with the remains of a Bronze Age chambered tomb known as the Bridestones, at Congleton in Cheshire. John Matthews, in his book *Gawain: Knight of the Goddess*, weighs up the evidence and concludes 'even if neither site actually inspired the Green Chapel, the association of the names Thor and Lud suggest that the area was rich in associations with the Otherworld.'[26]

Ludchurch is best approached from the Youth Hostel at Gradbach, reached from the A53 road between Buxton and Leek. A footpath runs beside the River Dane towards Swythamley, and the path forks left through the woods, signposted to Lud's Church.

Middle Tysoe, Warwickshire

The name of the Anglo-Saxon god of battles and war – Tiw or Tig – is preserved most notably in a day of the week, Tuesday. In England, it seems a hillside shrine to this Germanic god was associated with what historian Sir Frank Stenton has called 'one of the most striking natural features of the southern Midlands'. His name occurs close to the site of one of the greatest battles in the English Civil War, that at Edgehill in 1642, a decisive turning point in the fortunes of King Charles I.

The village of Middle Tysoe (Tiw's-Hoh) stands at the foot of a large escarpment which sits upon the border of the flat Warwickshire plain. Spurs project from the line of the ridge, and the settlement which bears the name of the war god sprang up beneath one of them. In 1765 Sir William Dugdale, wrote of this valley:

> Within the Precinct of that mannour in Tishoe, now belonging to the Earl of Northampton..there is cut upon the side of Edg-Hill the Proportion of a Horse in a very large Forme; which by reason of the ruddy Colour of the Earth is called The Red Horse, and giveth Denomination to that fruitfull and pleasant Countrey thereabouts, commonly called The Vale of the Red Horse.[27]

This is the earliest reference to the hill figure, also known as 'the Nag of Renown', which once stood prominently above the vale which took its name. The horse was red because it was cut in the loamy Warwickshire soil, and although entirely lost today, it is known that certain lands within the parish were held by the service of annually scouring the outline, and up until 1800 this obligation was carried out by farmworkers. Furthermore, folklore and subsequent investigations have revealed there was not one horse but five, although two of these were recent creations.

The annual scouring of what seems to have been the original horse took place on Palm Sunday, when cakes and ale were provided by the landlord of the Sunrising Inn, a name which suggests a connection with the movements of the sun and other heavenly bodies, often marked in prehistory. When Simon Nicholls bought Sunrising Farm from the Marquess of Northampton in 1800 he ploughed up the horse, which brought an end to the annual festivity. A new landlord of the inn tried to revive the custom and cut a new horse, but this was only seventeen feet long, and he was followed by a farmer who cut another horse on Spring Hill at the turn of the century. Both have since disappeared.

In the 1960s, two retired schoolteachers, Kenneth Carrdus and Graham Miller, researched the history of the area and found a map drawn in 1796 with the symbol of the horse marked on a hillslope known as the Hangings. The hill was partly covered by young larches and Scots pines, but the two men took several photos over a number of years and during a dry summer, and one picked out a patch of discoloured vegetation which turned out to be the head, neck and back of the original horse.[28]

They also commissioned aerial photographs of the hillslope and a resistivity survey of the top soil which seemed to confirm their theory and revealed the outlines of two other horses, presumably the remains of a succession of figures cut at different times. Pictures from above seemed to show the ears, legs and tail of the the first horse, an enormous galloping figure, measuring 200 foot long and 250 foot high, with the second horse two thirds of its size immediately in front of it. The third horse – probably the last one ploughed up in 1800 – was much smaller with short legs, and faced in the opposite direction.

Carrdus and Miller believe the Vale of the Red Horse was the largest work of Anglo-Saxon art in England, but like T.C.

Lethbridge a decade before them, they were unable to generate any interest in their finding among archaeologists, and their theory remains unproven today. The most obvious reason for the presence of the horse is to commemorate a battle, and one piece of folklore suggests it was cut for Richard Nevil, Earl of Warwick, after victory in the Battle of Towton Field during the War of the Roses on Palm Sunday, 1461. He was said to have killed his own horse during a crucial part of the battle so as to face the enemy on equal terms to that of his infantry. One of his retainers is said to have returned to Tysoe where he cut the horse to commemorate the victory. If this story is true it more likely refers to a revival of the custom of scouring a more ancient horse which may have been cut on the Hangings during the Saxon period, perhaps to honour the god of war following a victory over British forces.

Many English place-names have survived which preserve the names of the Anglo-Saxon and Scandinavian gods and centres of pagan English worship before the arrival of Christianity. In 1941 Stenton identified between fifty and sixty sites mostly in southern England, and he divided these into two main groups, those which contain the words *weoh* and *hearg* meaning 'a pagan sanctuary', and those which contain the name of the god himself.[29] In south-eastern England, the name of the thunder god Thunor or Thor, who gave his name to Thursday, is found in six names associated with a sacred grove, and in Essex was associated with a pillar and a mound. The Germanic mother goddess Frig or Freya, from whom Friday takes its name, is found in place-names like Fridaythorpe and Fryupdale in the Yorkshire Dales.

The most popular name is that of Woden, a god of war and lord of all the dead, who survives in the weekday Wednesday. Most of the Anglo-Saxon royal houses traced their ancestry to him, and in the tenth century, Ethelward in his description of that of Wessex states: '. . . the pagans worshipped Woden as a god with sacrilegious honour and offered him sacrifice for the acquisition of victory or valour.' His name is found at the hilltop fort at Wednesbury in the West Midlands, an area where the old religion held out under the pagan Mercian king Penda in the seventh century AD. The former forest temple is now crowned by a church, for Woden was made a demon to be crushed by the Christians.

Woden survived in folk tradition and became associated with earthworks like the Wansdyke, the greatest linear fortification in southern England, of which Aubrey wrote 'the local people say it was made by the Devil on a Wednesday.' A burial mound in the vale of Pewsey upon the Wansdyke, was known as 'Wodnes beorg' in the tenth century, but today is 'Adam's Grave', and this may represent a late attempt to Christianize a place with stubborn pagan connotations. Woden is also found in place-names as Grim or grima (a word meaning 'mask' and 'spectre'), and his worship was revived by the Scandinavian Vikings who knew him as Odin. In the Danelaw, there are two large conical hills in East Yorkshire known as Roseberry Topping, a name meaning 'Odin's Mound.'

Middle Tysoe can be found on a minor road south of the main A422 between Stratford-upon-Avon and Banbury. Nearby is the site of the Edgehill battlefield, and at Burton Dassett to the north is an ancient beacon, Saxon church and holy well.

Southern England and Wessex including Guernsey

Avebury and Silbury Hill, Wiltshire
Central London (St Paul's Cathedral and the Tower)
Deal, Kent
Guernsey, Channel Islands
Hornchurch, Essex
Vale of the White Horse, Berkshire
Wilmington, Sussex
Windsor, Berkshire

Avebury and Silbury Hill, Wiltshire

Describing the great Neolithic temple at Avebury, the poet Sir John Betjeman remarked in the 1950s that it was: 'a haunting place to see in all weathers, but most impressive of all on a still moonlit night, when it seems to be peopled with ghosts and the old church and cottages of the village seem quite new and insignificant.'[1]

Avebury should always be the first point of pilgrimage for those on a quest into Britain's pagan heritage. The henge itself is surrounded by dozens of other Stone Age ritual sites most important of which is Silbury Hill, the largest artificial mound in Western Europe. Twentieth-century visitors to Avebury are following in the footsteps of pilgrims more than 4,000 years ago who came here to take part in religious assemblies, probably at the festivals which later became the Celtic quarter days.

The huge henge monument at Avebury alone covers almost 30 acres and encircles the medieval village, the parish church of the new religion standing just outside the ring of giant stones.

The bank itself is 1,400 foot in diameter and 25 foot high, with the ditch inside it being a staggering 33 foot deep. It is a sobering thought that in the Stone Age (a time we are told when society was barbaric and rent with disease and low life expectancy) people could be motivated to dig 10,000 tons of chalk from the ground using tools as basic as antler picks, long before the invention of metal tools. Visitors should note that the ditch, now silted up, is actually *inside* the bank, which had no defensive function and may have been built as a 'grandstand' for observers of rituals taking place inside the henge.

Our knowledge of how Avebury looked in antiquity has been greatly assisted by writings and drawings made by the antiquarians who first 'discovered' the henge and circle in the seventeenth century. The first of these was John Aubrey who was responsible for the famous description of Avebury that 'it does as much exceed in greatness the so renowned Stonehenge as a Cathedral does a parish church.' His work recording the layout of the temple was continued later by William Stukeley, who watched helplessly as local people destroyed the stones as he drew up his plans of the remains.

The breaking up of the stones for use in local buildings in Stukeley's time was only the latest phase in the destruction of the temple which seems to have begun early in the fourteenth century. This attack on the stones was probably encouraged by the first Christian priests to settle in the village, who may have been alarmed at the continuing power of paganism (there was no record of a church at Avebury in the Domesday Book). Dozens of stones in the inner and outer circles and the two avenues were toppled and buried in chalk-cut pits, while others were broken into pieces. This process seems to have come to an abrupt end when a thirteen-ton sarsen fell upon a barber surgeon as he was helping to move it, crushing him to death. His skeleton was found in 1938 when the stone was replaced near the south entrance of the henge by a team led by Alexander Keiler. It is quite possible that a superstitious reaction followed this accident which, combined with the arrival of the Black Death in 1349, seems to have halted further destruction of the stones.

Keiler's enthusiastic restoration work during the 1930s reconstructed lost parts of the henge circle and West Kennet Avenue, and with great effort many of the buried stones were re-erected. Where evidence of destroyed stones was found, these were marked by small concrete posts, which can be seen interspersed with the remaining standing stones.

Today experts agree the henge and circle dates from between 2600 and 1600 BC, and it seems that in its heyday the whole structure would have been a stunning sight, with the banks and ditch a dazzling white from the exposed chalk. There were 4 entrances to the henge through the bank and ditch, around the circumference of which was a circle of 100 gigantic sarsen stones, some of them weighing as much as 40 tons, all dragged here from the downlands to the east of Avebury. Only 31 of these stones can be seen today.[2]

Inside this main circle were two smaller inner rings, each of these more than 300 foot in diameter. The north circle contained a 'cove' made up of three stones facing north-east, while the south circle featured the tallest standing stone, the Obelisk, which appears to have been the central ritual focus of the henge. Stukeley sketched the fallen Obelisk shortly before it was destroyed in the eighteenth century, but its importance may have survived in folk tradition for villagers still danced around a maypole set up in the south circle one hundred years later.

From the south entrance of the henge begins an avenue of standing stones known as the West Kennet Avenue, which may have functioned as a processional way for those taking part in the rituals at the henge. Originally there were around 100 separate pairs of stones, arranged so that slender upright pillars faced diamond-shaped companions, perhaps as male and female symbols. Twenty-seven stones remain today, with 37 concrete posts marking absent friends. It has been suggested there was a second avenue of stones running from the eastern entrance to the henge. Stukeley, who saw Avebury as a giant serpent-shaped temple, recorded stones here in the eighteenth century, but so far no definitive proof of its existence has been found, and all that can be seen today are two large standing stones known as Adam and Eve, to the north of Beckhampton Crossroads.

The West Kennet Avenue runs one-and-a-half miles to a site known as 'the Sanctuary' on Overton Hill near the River Kennet. Although there is little to be seen here today, we know it was originally made up of two rings of stone and six concentric timber rings – the remains of a large wooden roundhouse. Evidence of feasting and mortuary rituals have been found, but the function of the structure remains a mystery.

Avebury henge, stone circle and the avenue are the most visible and attractive parts of the ritual landscape for visitors, but the remains of the temple itself are only one part of a group of inter-related sites, the oldest of which appears to be Windmill Hill, a mile to the north-west. This hilltop was settled very early in the Neolithic and appears to have functioned as a meeting place or 'fairground' for over a thousand years. The hill is encircled by the ditches of a causewayed camp which dates back to 3400 BC and remains of animals and humans, including skulls have been found in them.

Many barrows cluster on the hillsides above Avebury and the River Kennet, the most impressive and famous of which is the West Kennet Long Barrow, of similar age to Windmill Hill in a field just south of the A4 road. West Kennet is one of the largest of its kind in England, 330 foot long and orientated east–west, with a façade of huge stones blocking the entrance at the eastern end. In 5 side chambers inside, the disarticulated remains of around 50 people were discovered, and it seems to have been used for ritual purposes over a long period of time. Of the skeletons found, there was a marked lack of skulls and long-bones – these may have been removed and taken elsewhere for rituals, perhaps to Windmill Hill itself.

From the entrance of West Kennet Long Barrow the visitor is treated to an impressive view of Silbury Hill nestling in the lowest part of the Kennet valley below, with the ridge of Waden's Hill (the hill of the god Woden) behind it. Silbury appears to have been the real focus of the entire Avebury ritual landscape, and is a unique and staggering piece of prehistoric landscape engineering. This 130 foot high gigantic man-made mound has been likened to a 'giant Christmas pudding' in shape and is truly a monument to the ingenuity of its Neolithic architects.

For many hundreds of years, people believed Silbury was the burial mound of a rich king or warrior, and folklore told of a man buried here on horseback or in a golden coffin. We now know the mound was not a burial place, but the product of community effort, pieced together over a period of 50 years like a giant birthday cake from blocks of chalk covered with turf, at around the same time as the Avebury henge was under construction. It was probably the crowning achievement of the pagan priests who planned Avebury. A high-profile excavation, sponsored by the BBC in the 1960s, cut a tunnel deep into the heart of the mound, but no evidence of a grave of any kind was found. What was discovered were the original turves used in the construction of the hill in the Stone Age, with the grass and insects miraculously preserved inside! Analysis showed they were cut at the beginning of the harvest, perhaps early in August at the time of the festival of Lughnasa.

The failure of archaeology to fully explain *why* Silbury was built with such an investment of time and effort by the Neolithic people has been compensated for by the theories of Earth Mysteries experts. Artist and author Michael Dames believes Silbury was a great 'harvest hill', a large-scale version of the Lammas towers built at Lughnasa in Ireland and Scotland within living memory. He argues that the sacred mound was built as an abstract image of the Neolithic Earth Mother or fertility goddess, visualized as a squatting figure in the landscape giving birth. Dames has traced the form of the goddess in the landscape around Avebury, with natural and man-made features marking the figure itself. His theory is enhanced by the presence below the hill of a spring, one of the sources of the River Kennet, which had healing powers.[3]

He compared the 'Sil' element of the word Silbury with Sul, the name of the Celtic goddess who presided over the healing springs at Bath. Sul or Sulis was also an eye goddess, linked with the sun. Silbury remained an important centre for gatherings of villagers until the eighteenth century when Stukeley wrote of a Palm Sunday feast held every year on the top of the hill. Another account of 1736 describes a race around the base of the hill, followed by wrestling and dancing which ended with a bull being baited on the summit, killed and roasted whole. All these customs suggest the hill was associated with ritual activity over a long period of time.

More recently Paul Devereux[4] has taken Dames' ideas and the evidence of archaeology and personal intuition one step further, making some startling new insights into the function of Silbury and its relationship with Avebury and the surrounding ritual landscape. These insights came to Devereux as a result of observations made from each of the sites over many years, at different calendar dates, and with the help of 'inspiration' the secrets of the landscape were revealed. Full details of Devereux's observations have been published in the archaeological journal *Antiquity* and in his book *Symbolic Landscapes*

(1992). They involve subtle visual connections, including harvest-dependent sight-lines, between Silbury and its surrounding barrows and stone circles. The most spectacular of these is a unique 'double sunrise' effect which can be observed from the terrace of Silbury Hill at Beltane and Lughnasa.

This kind of subtle interplay between astronomy, earth and horizon has been found at other megalithic sites and shows that geometry and landscape sculpture on a vast scale was designed and utilized by the prehistoric priests. The effect at Silbury can be seen on two important festivals in the pagan calendar, the beginning of May at Beltane (sowing of crops) and Lughnasa in early August (the harvest). Similar alignments based upon the Beltane sunrise have recently been uncovered at the site of an important Bronze Age temple excavated at Godmanchester, near Cambridge[5]. Devereux shares Dames' view of Silbury itself as a joyous harvest hill whose position, height and shape 'monumentalises the relevant elements of land and sky within the sacred landscape of the Avebury complex.' Silbury Hill was, he said: 'the expression of sacred geography par excellence.'

Avebury is well signposted and can be reached from Swindon to the north along the A4361, or along the A4 west of Marlborough. There are good parking facilities in the village, along with museums, shops and a restaurant.

Central London, (St Paul's Cathedral and the Tower)

In the heart of England's capital city one would perhaps not expect to find traces of pre-Christian belief or custom, but some tantalizing pieces of evidence have survived to suggest that in the Celtic period London was, in the words of Ralph Merrifield 'a city of contrasts, a curious mingling of civilisation and barbarism, of the exotic and the native.'[6]

It appears the city took its name from the Celtic father/sky god Lugh, and means 'the Fortress of Lud'. Ludgate Hill, a 'holy hill' near St Paul's is the burial place of the god in one story, and the White Mount (now covered by the Tower of London) is said to be the final resting place of the prophetic head of Bran the Blessed, another British god. The present cathedral at St Paul's was built by Christopher Wren, but stands on the site of four earlier churches. Tessellated pavements dating to the Roman occupation of Britain have been unearthed in the foundations of the cathedral and a number of medieval writers suggested the church originally stood upon a pagan temple in Romano-Celtic times.

Stow, in his *Survey of London* (1316) tells how, when the foundations were being dug for a chapel on the south side of St Paul's, 'there were found more than a hundred scalpes of Oxen or kine . . . which thing they say confirmed greatly the opinion of those which have reported that of old times there had been a Temple of Jupiter, and that there was a dayly sacrifice of beastes'.[7] Belief in the existence of this temple was of long standing, and may stem from the fact that London was the capital or metropolis of the Anglo-Saxon tribe of the East Saxons. St Paul's became the kingdom's first cathedral when the missionary Mellitus arrived in their territory early in the seventh century AD. Mellitus may have set up his church in the ruins of an earlier temple, as we know happened at Canterbury in the territory of King Aethelbert of Kent.

Ritual deposits of animal skulls and bones have been found at other pagan English sites, including the Anglo-Saxon royal court excavated at Yeavering Bell in Northumbria, and Harrow Hill at Angmering in Sussex where over a thousand ox skulls were found in association with a pagan shrine. Indeed, Pope Gregory the Great wrote specifically to Mellitus, who he sent to convert the pagan English, saying that since the pagans had a custom of sacrificing many oxen to 'demons', a more acceptable Christian festival should be substituted in its place, so they were 'no longer to sacrifice beasts to the Devil, but kill them for food to the praise of God.'[8]

Bearing Gregory's advice in mind 'a strange ceremony' observed by priests in St Paul's Cathedral in the Middle Ages, described by Stow, takes on great significance. He tells how during the reign of Edward I at Candlemass 1274, it was agreed between the Dean of St Paul's and an Essex knight, Sir William Baud, that in return for a grant of land in the Manor of West Lee he would present the canons with a doe at the Feast of the Conversion of St Paul (25 January) and also 'a fat buck' on the feast of the Commemoration of St Paul (28 June), roughly the dates of the summer and winter solstices.

This strange rite involved the carrying in procession through the cathedral the head of a sacrificed animal on a pole before the cross, by priests adorned in special vestments and carrying garlands on their heads. Stow, who witnessed the rite as a boy, said it 'savours more of the worship of Diana and heathenism than of Christianity.' Describing the scene in June 1557, he wrote in *The Survey of London*:

> The buck being brought up to the high altar... the dean and chapter... with garlands of roses on their heads ... sent the body of the buck to baking and had the head fixed on a pole, borne before the cross in their procession until they issued out of the west door, where the keeper that brought it blowed the death of the buck and then the horners that were about the city answered him in a like manner.

The carrying, or wearing of horns is found elsewhere in folklore and appears to be an echo of the cult of the Celtic horned or antlered god, Cernunnos. It is probable the Anglo-Saxon and Norse peoples worshipped a similar god, and certainly used the heads of sacred animals in their religious rites.

Elsewhere in central London the magical head of the god Bendigeidfran or Bran the Blessed, a mythological god king of Britain is said to be buried. The story gives its location as the White Mount or Hill in London, which has been identified as the mound beside the River Thames upon which the Tower of London was built by William the Conqueror. Today, the Tower is a powerful symbol of the sovereignty of Britain, with its Crown Jewels and guardian ravens. Bran was not the only god or hero said to be buried here, for legend tells how two other mythological personages, Brutus the founder of London and Molmutius, a roadbuilder and lawgiver, are also buried there.

The name 'bran' is said to mean 'raven' or 'crow', which clearly connects the talisman head with the custom of keeping ravens at the Tower as a protection against invasion from abroad. The Tower itself dates from the eleventh century, but the name 'white mount' is clearly older, and from the Welsh *bryn gwyn* or holy hill, white meaning holy. This connection is shown by a thirteenth-century account which describes the exterior as being whitewashed.

The archaic story of Bran, which although written down in the medieval period clearly contains pagan motifs, survives in the fourth branch of the Mabinogi, called 'Branwen, Daughter of Llyr'. This describes how the god king, who is described as huge in size, wades across the sea to lead an invasion of Ireland. However, the Irish have a magic cauldron given to them earlier by Bran, which can raise the dead back to life, giving them success in battle. Bran is left mortally wounded with a poisoned spear in his foot, and tells his seven surviving companions to cut off his head and carry it with them back to the mainland.

'And take my head,' he said, 'and carry it to the White Mount in London, and bury it with its face towards France. And you will be a long time upon the road . . . and the head will be as pleasant company to you as it ever was at best when it was on me.'[9] Following this request, the seven companions and Bran's sister Branwen (a goddess figure) take the head across the sea on a magical journey to Britain. This 'assembly of the head' stop first at Harlech where they spend seven years listening to the singing of the magic birds of Rhiannon unaware of the passage of time, and then a further eighty years on an island off the Pembrokeshire coast until one of them opens a hidden door and breaks the enchantment. During this time Bran's head remains undecayed, talks and is 'good company' until its burial in London.

A later Welsh account says the magical talisman head was lost in the time of King Arthur who 'disclosed the head of Bran the Blessed from the White Hill, since he did not desire that this Island should be guarded by anyone's strength but his own'. The head of Bran, buried in London to protect England from attack, is a strong folk motif connected with ancient cities in Greek mythology. Some, like Lerna and Rome, had magical talismen, usually the heads of kings, buried in their foundations or boundaries to act as magical guardians. In the eighth century Bede, in his story about the death of King Edwin in battle against the pagan king of Mercia, said the body was dismembered and the head was brought to York to be 'placed in the church of the blessed Apostle Peter' and perhaps fulfil another guardian role.

Deal, Kent

One of the most amazing pagan Celtic ritual landscapes was discovered on the chalkland coast of Kent in the 1980s by a group of archaeologists from the Dover Archaeological Group, led by Keith Parfitt.[10] The site itself is located only one mile from the sea on the top of a prominent ridge known as Mill Hill in the suburbs of Deal. Chalk quarrying in the area during Victorian times had already destroyed some evidence of early occupation, but in 1983 when a new housing estate was planned in St Richard's Road, the team of archaeologists began a rescue dig. This resulted in the discovery of a superb burial of an Iron Age warrior or priest and evidence of ritual stretching from the Neolithic to Late Roman and Anglo-Saxon times.

The earliest feature on the highest part of the hilltop are the ploughed-out remains of a large Bronze Age barrow. Although no burials were found, the mound probably covered the remains of a chieftain and its importance can be seen from the field name 'The White Barrow' (white meaning 'holy') and nearby Barrow Hill Road. The mound appears to have been re-used in the sixth century AD when it became a cemetery for seventy-four pagan Anglo-Saxon settlers.

Exciting as these finds were, the team were not prepared for their next discovery, which came near the end of their excavation in 1988, and is now regarded as one of the richest Iron Age burials ever found in England. It began as an unimposing grave-pit on the very edge of the barrow ditch, located on a narrow spit of land, which had very narrowly escaped destruction in the nineteenth century. Inside a cramped and shallow grave was found the slightly built skeleton of the warrior, chieftain or priest. Still in place, wrapped around the man's skull, was a bronze band or 'crown' which encircled the head, with evidence of a vanished cross-band. This 'crown' or head-dress was decorated with fine La Tene I art designs, and may have also featured feathers or horns at one time. The only similar comparable crowns, which resemble Roman priestly regalia, come from a ritual pit at Hockwold-cum-Wilton in Norfolk, which also feature a cross-band and are decorated with a human face.[11]

An impressive cache of prestige iron and bronze goods were buried with the man. Resting over his right arm was a beautiful iron sword, set within a decorated bronze scabbard. The sword's pommel was found level with the man's right shoulder and close to the top of the scabbard was a circular cast-bronze suspension loop decorated with pink coral beads. Adjoining this was a decorated bronze belt-fitting, another resting on the left forearm, both decorated with coral.

Also decorated with coral was a fine bronze brooch which was found in an unusual position over the lower left leg, suggesting it was once pinned to a cloak covering the man's legs. The brooch and one of the belt fittings were elaborately decorated with designs which seemed to have been worked from a wax model. The mouthpiece of the sword scabbard showed evidence of another technique known as 'repousee' whereby the decoration is raised from the underside of sheet bronze by hammering. The fine metalwork was dated to around 200 BC by the British Museum, who have confirmed that the Deal grave has produced more examples of Celtic art than any other previously discovered, and in addition, it appears to be purely of fine British Celtic manufacture.

Probably the most puzzling find in the grave were the remains of what appear to be a 'ritual shield', which suggests this man was a priest rather than a warrior. A scatter of sheet bronze edge bindings show the shield had long convex sides, a concave top and bottom and therefore had pointed corners. The body of the shield appears to have been made of leather or some other material which has disintegrated, leaving behind only thin cut-out designs in sheet bronze.

Experts including Dr Ian Stead of the British Museum and Celtic scholar Dr Anne Ross identified the shape of this strange object as being of a distinctive British type, only recently recognized as being of ritual origin. The only similar known finds are a group of small ritual shields, some of them decorated, which were recently found in a votive deposit near Stonehenge. This coincidence, and the presence of the unique 'crown' have led Dr Ross to classify the man in the grave as a Druid priest.[12]

Archaeologists are still evaluating the significance of this very unusual find, a burial which was only part of a large ritual landscape on the very edge of England. More evidence for continuity, this time from the early Roman period was found in 1984, when the team found a chalk-cut shaft leading to a strange underground chamber, about eight foot in depth, on the south-eastern part of the site, now an estate road. This formed part of a native farmstead, and the fill of the chamber included Roman pottery dating to the late first to second century AD.

Inside the chamber, large enough to hold five or six seated adults, was found a remarkable chalk figurine or idol, 7.5 inches high, which has become known as 'the Deal Man', but which might equally be a representation of a female deity. The idol has a simply carved face with deep set eyes, a slit mouth, a long slender neck and block-shaped body. Its base had been cut so it sloped backwards, and the excavators found that it neatly fitted into a niche in the roof of the underground chamber or shrine.

The excavator, Keith Parfitt, suggests the effigy was a local deity or god of the Underworld whose function was to bless and guard the contents of the underground 'shrine'. He added: 'The Celtic belief in natural places, such as hills having their own minor deity (the genius loci), who lived in and presided over that place is fairly well documented'. He goes on to state that the subterranean nature of the existing structure could suggest a link with a type of 'earth cult' in the vicinity.' [13]

The underground shrine to a Celtic deity at Deal completes the picture of this remarkable ritual hilltop landscape on the coastline of southern England. Clear evidence has been found here that the original Bronze Age barrow retained its sanctity and acted as focus for over 2,000 years of ritual activity. What other finds lie beneath this extensive hill ridge awaiting discovery?

The Deal Man is currently on display in Dover Museum, Market Square, along with other finds. The remains of the priest and his grave goods have been donated to the British Museum in London.

Guernsey, Channel Islands

The Channel Islands are rich in prehistoric monuments, many of which are surrounded by folktales and legends concerned with the fairies, or Les Petits Faitaux. The most important survival of Guernsey's pagan past is an impressive statue menhir known as La Gran'mere du Chimquiere, a name which means 'the grandmother of the cemetery'. It stands on the southern side of the churchyard at St Martin-de-la-Beilleuse on Guernsey, and is a granite pillar of local stone, five foot six inches in height and one foot seven inches broad, with a rectangular body carved into a rough female shape terminating in a head. The face is finely carved with arched eyebrows, large oval eyes and a long broad nose and slit mouth. The figure appears to be wearing some kind of tight-fitting head-dress and there are carved 'curls' which may represent hair. Immediately beneath the bust are two exposed breasts, very close together surrounded by faint traces of encircling arms.

No one knows when this fertility figure or goddess was originally found, but it may come from beneath the church itself, as a similar phallic statue was found deliberately hidden beneath the floor of the church at Catel in 1878. These stones actually belong to a style of pagan sculpture known as the 'statue menhir', which appears to have originated in the Western Mediterranean during the Bronze Age, though some authorities have classified the style of carving on the head and face of the Gran'mere as being a later Gallo-Roman addition.

Local people have always regarded the stone as a sacred object or idol, and it is said that during the nineteenth century it was 'lucky' to place a little offering of fruit or flowers, or to spill a few drops of wine at the foot of the statue. These offerings seem to have attracted the attention of a hostile churchwarden, who in the same century broke the statue in two and removed it. The parishioners protested vigorously at this outrage, and as a result it was placed where it now stands (the break in the stone can be clearly seen today).

Offerings are still made to the Gran'mere, and one account says that as late as the 1920s the rector found bunches of flowers and other small offerings left at her feet and this respect continues today with the figure occasionally decorated with an ivy chaplet on May Day morning. Some even believe she is capable of making movements and responses to questions in certain circumstances.[14]

Hornchurch, Essex

The name of this town is taken from the extraordinary and unique parish church of St Andrew 'the horned church'. Its most striking feature is a carved stone head of a Highland bull with large hollow copper horns which protrudes from the east end of the chancel. As the church guide admits this carving 'is a most unusual feature to find on a church, as horns are more generally associated with the devil.'[15]

The first record of a religious building here comes from the twelfth century, when Henry II granted land in the parish of Havering to the monastery of St Nicholas and St Bernard at Montjoux. The name first appears in a record of 1222 which mentions the 'Monasterium Cornutum' or the Horned Monastery at Havering, and it appears the name was later transferred to the church in the same parish. The bull's horns are mentioned 400 years later in 1610 when it seems they were made of lead. Repaired in 1824, they were found to be made of copper, so it seems probable they were replaced several times in the intervening period. The horned head of an ox also appears on an ancient seal used by the Masters of Hornchurch Priory, and historians believe the church took its name from the horns, and the building may stand upon the site of an older pagan temple.

One legend says a former pagan priestess from the temple, dedicated to the Roman Diana goddess of the hunt and the moon, converted to Christianity and built the church to atone for her sins. At the late Romano-Celtic temple at Maiden Castle in Dorset, Diana is invoked alongside a statue of a triple-horned bull, and a similar clay figurine of a bull was found in the grave of a child at Colchester in Essex. The bull was a sacred animal to the Celts, and it probably represented power, fertility and good fortune.

There are other local theories for the origin of the bull and the horns, one of which tells of the shooting of a deer by the prior who placed its horns upon the monastery. Whatever the case, there can be little doubt about the pagan origins of the symbolic horns. They may be linked with a strange custom in the parish whereby every Christmas Day the lessee of the tithes provided a boar's head which was carried to Millfield, near the church, on a pitchfork. This was planted in the earth and the head was fought for by the people, with the winner and his friends afterwards feasting upon the trophy. It is therefore possible the head on the church is a symbol of this kind of ritual contest, of which there are examples all over the country.

Heads and skulls of animals were often used as protective or evil-averting talismen when placed upon the gables and roofs of buildings and temples. This custom was widespread throughout northern Europe, and a carved wooden horse's head was used by Finns in Northern Russia as a charm against evil.

The horned church can be reached via the A124 road between Goodmayes and Upminster in the London borough of Havering.

Vale of the White Horse, Berkshire

On recent estimates there were at least fifty landscape figures cut upon the chalklands of southern England. The best known are the white horses, of which there are fourteen examples in Wessex alone. The vast majority of these figures were cut in recent times although several appear to have been developed from earlier designs, including the Westbury White Horse in Wiltshire whose present form dates from 1742, when it was recut over an earlier more primitive figure.

The only truly ancient white horse in England is the famous Uffington horse, whose abstract image was cut high up on a chalk escarpment below Uffington Castle, a hillfort occupied by a Celtic tribe during the Iron Age. Like the other archaic hill figures, the horse is associated with a tribal stronghold or hill-fort, and archaeologists now believe it was carved between 1400-600 BC, before the Roman invasion, as a tribal emblem.

The horse was a sacred animal to the Celtic tribes, and appears in a number of contexts both as a religious and martial symbol, both in the pagan period and later. Horses appear to have been sacrificed at Danebury hillfort in Hampshire, and images very similar to the Uffington figure appear on a number of coins and other metalwork from the territory of the Atrebates, whose capital was at Silchester. The most famous horse deity was the Gaulish Epona (divine horse) whose cult was spread widely in Roman times and appears to have merged with that of insular deities like the Welsh Rhiannon and Irish Macha. In one

113

well-known carving from Wiltshire, Epona appears accompanied by two dogs, while in others she has foals.

Unlike the giants at Cerne and Wilmington, there are indeed very early documentary references to the Uffington Horse. The earliest seems to be a mention of the name White Horse Hill in 1084. The horse also appears in a twelfth century Book of Wonders which describes the figure as 'a horse with a foal', while one century later a cartulary of the Abbey of Abingdon refers to a monk owning certain land 'near to the place which is popularly known as the Hill of the White Horse'. Indeed, the 374 foot-long horse cut in the gleaming white chalk became such a landmark that it was classed by one medieval writer as a marvel second only to Stonehenge. Theories about it have abounded – at one time it was regarded as an Anglo-Saxon work, cut to commemorate King Alfred of Wessex's victory over the Danish invaders in 871. In the eighteenth century, topographers suggested the horse was a symbol of the Anglo-Saxon king Hengist (whose name means 'stallion').

Others have said the horse is really a dragon because of its strange stylized body and beaked head. In the valley below the hill figure is the famous flat-topped Dragon Hill where St George is said to have killed the dragon. A patch of bare earth on the hilltop has been pointed out as the spot where the creature's blood fell. One tradition, recorded by Francis Wise in the eighteenth century was that the horse was St George's mount, and another says it is a portrait of the dragon he slew. Whatever is the truth, recently experts have suggested a chapel may have been built upon Dragon Hill in the Middle Ages to Christianize the hilltop.

In order for the horse to have physically survived from Celtic times it had to be regularly scoured so that it did not disappear beneath the turf. The earliest record of this pastime is from 1650, and the work seems to have always been followed by great feasting and ceremony, which may point back to a time when the horse was regarded as sacred.

By tradition, scourings took place once every seven years and the event was immortalised in Thomas Hughes' treatise *The Scouring of the White Horse* which details the last great scouring in 1857, when a colourful country fair was held alongside a number of curious ceremonies including the rolling of cheeses into a field below the hill. Hughes' novel *Tom Brown's*

Schooldays is also set in the village and contains much folklore about the horse.

Attempts to date hill figures and other inconography from pagan times is notoriously difficult on stylistic grounds alone, but recent work by David Miles, and a team from the Oxford Archaeological Unit has added new evidence to what we already know about the history of the horse.[16] The team from Oxford began work in the 1980s in an attempt to answer the question of whether the present abstract design of the horse was 'original', or if it overlaid a more naturalistic design. In order to establish the true chronological sequence they tried to date the horse and its surroundings by means of limited excavation and by using a new technique to date silt-deposits. This first established how the land surrounding the image appeared to have been deliberately kept clear of arable use and left under pasture, perhaps an indication this was a 'sacred place'. The horse is cut into a specially prepared artificial trench which had been filled with chalk, so that the whole animal was made of chalk rather than just being cut into the hillside.

The Oxford team's trial dig at the beak of the figure found there had been four successive chalk-filled trenches separated by hillwash; this showed that earlier 'beaks' were larger and the belly of the beast was once much thicker. This provided some evidence to suggest the horse has always possessed its curious elongated shape, and it is therefore more likely to have a genuine Celtic origin. The project is still ongoing, but the most recent findings indicate that the Uffington White Horse was only one part of a major funerary complex or ritual landscape which originated in the Neolithic. A Bronze Age burial mound has recently been excavated just above the head of the horse, and evidence of later Roman and Anglo-Saxon burials have been discovered.[17]

Uffington Castle and the White Horse command a strategic strongpoint above the prehistoric Ridgeway path, which cuts across southern England from Dover to Ilchester in Somerset, and it is clear that whoever held this hillfort could control movement across a large part of south-west England. Moving west along the Ridgeway, the visitor should call at the impressive Neolithic burial chamber known as Wayland's Smithy, or Wayland Smith's Cave, situated in an eerie grove of trees just over one mile from the horse. The name was recorded as

Welandes smidde in a charter of AD 855, and folklore says this is where the Uffington horse's shoes were made by Wayland, the lame smith of the gods in Anglo-Saxon mythology. Wayland ('the craftsman in the mound') was a giant or elf whose trade was associated with magic in tribal societies.

The horse, on Department of the Environment land, can be seen best from the B4507 between Ashbury and Wantage. Five miles west of Wantage, opposite a turn for Uffington village, a minor road leads to the car park, and a short walk to the figure itself.

Wilmington, Sussex

The Anglo-Saxon kingdom of Sussex (land of the 'South Saxons') remained with old gods for the longest, for it was not until the late seventh century that a mission by St Wilfrid of Northumbria brought Christianity to their shore. His *Life* tells us while some of the South Saxons were converted willingly others 'were compelled by the king's command' and it is clear that here at least the pagan priests made a stand against the new religion.

A story is told of how St Wilfrid and a band of followers landed in Sussex after their ship was blown off course when returning to Britain from Gaul. A huge army of pagans arrived intending to seize the ship and make off with money and captives. St Wilfrid spoke to them soothingly and sought to save the lives of his companions by promising a large sum of money. The pagans, however, were unwilling to let the churchmen go and the 'chief priest of their idolatrous worship' took stand on top of a high mound, and attempted to curse them and 'bind their hands by the magical arts'. At this point one of Wilfrid's followers took a stone and hurled it from his sling towards the Druid. 'It pierced the wizard's forehead and penetrated to his brain as he stood cursing ... and his lifeless body fell backwards on to the sand,' according to the story.[18]

A number of place-names suggestive of Anglo-Saxon or earlier pagan worship have survived in the Sussex region, including the Domesday hundred-names associated with nature shrines like Ghidenetroi ('tree of the goddess').[19] Probably the most interesting signpost to the past is the huge 230 foot high figure of a man cut into the turf on the north face of Windover Hill, overlooking the village of Wilmington. The famous 'Long Man' or the Green Man (as he is known locally), is clearly the image of a deity or tribal god of some kind whose real identity has been long forgotten.

The featureless, but muscular outline of the Long Man is said to be one of the largest drawings of a human figure anywhere in the world, and stands in prominent natural hollow grasping a long 'staff' or spear in each outstretched hand. His present appearance dates from 1874, when he was cleaned up and restored by the Duke of Devonshire, but early illustrations seem to show the remains of a cap, or the neckguard of a horned helmet, similar to those depicted on that from Sutton Hoo.

Today, the Long Man remains annoyingly anonymous despite the efforts of many to explain his identity. Some experts believe the figure may have been cut in the chalk as far back as the Celtic Iron Age, when Sussex was the territory of a tribe known as the Atrebates and in that case he may represent a divine guardian of the region, perhaps Succellos, the hammer wielding god, or the Roman Hercules.

The evidence suggests it is more likely the Long Man is the image of an Anglo-Saxon god or hero. Folklorist Jacqueline Simpson has found that the figure lay within an area recorded in the Domesday Book as 'Wandelmestrei' after the Germanic Waendal, a god of war also found in Cambridgeshire. He may be the same deity depicted as a naked warrior, wearing a horned helmet and carrying two spears, engraved upon a belt-buckle found in a seventh century AD grave at Finglesham in Kent.[20]

As with the other famous hill figures at Cerne Abbas and Uffington, the periodic 'scouring' of the giant, in order to keep his outline clear and free from weeds, was a communal festivity involving much dancing and merrymaking, perhaps at harvest time on the hilltop, which is crowned by a Neolithic long barrow. The earliest recorded description of the Long Man was made in the eighteenth century, when he was described as holding a scythe and a rake in his hands, and there are other stories about a 'cock' visible on a hillside to his right. It appears possible that at some point he was emasculated, perhaps by the monks from nearby Wilmington Priory, which some historians have suggested was built nearby in an attempt to stamp out or exorcise the pagan power which the giant symbolised.

In folk-tales the giant appears as a living person, one of a pair (the other giant lived on Firle Beacon in the Cuckmere Valley, three miles away) who battled by hurling huge boulders at each other. Where the boulders fell craters were left, actually the remains of Neolithic flint mines. Eventually, the giant was killed and laid out on Windover Hill, his outlines marked so that future generations may remember him. This legend is similar to another connected to a more nebulous hill figure at Penhill in North Yorkshire, and there are several alternative versions of how the giant or deity became part of the Sussex Downs landscape. One says he slipped on the steep hillside, breaking his neck and another story tells how he was attacked and killed by pilgrims on the way to the abbey at Wilmington.

Perhaps the most intriguing idea about the Long Man is that he is positioned in such a way on the hillside that he would have been visible only when the sun's rays hit him at a certain angle, and indeed some have suggested the positions of the staves the giant holds altered with the movement of the sun. There are many other examples of subtle interplay between ritual and landscape in the Celtic world, and it is clear that great skill was employed by the tribesmen who originally designed this religious and perhaps martial image.

Twenty miles north-east of Wilmington is the village of Rushlake Green, the home of two peculiar human skulls which were carefully preserved for hundreds of years in the walls of the old Warbleton Priory.[21] A farmer kept one skull on his bible in Warbleton Priory Farm for a number of years, and the tradition describes how on two occasions when it was taken away strange happenings occurred – once when taken to an inn at Rushlake Green its eerie power turned the beer mouldy!

The Long Man is maintained by the Sussex Archaeological Trust and can be reached by a footpath from the minor road linking Wilmington to Litlington, and is signposted towards Westdean between the A27 and the A259.

Windsor, Berkshire

What may be a folk memory of the pagan cult of the horned or antlered god Cernunnos ('the Horned One') has lingered in the grounds of royal Windsor Park for many generations. Here the horned god became known as Herne the Hunter, and was referred to in Shakespeare's play *The Merry Wives of Windsor* (1623), in the following lines:

> There is an old tale goes that Herne the hunter,
> Sometime a keeper here in Windsor Forest,
> Doth all the winter-time, at still midnight,
> Walk round about an oak, with great ragg'd horns,
> And there he blasts the tree, and takes the cattle,
> And makes milch-kine yield blood, and shakes a chain
> In a most hideous and dreadful manner.[22]

The legend of Herne is just one example of a range of beliefs about the supernatural world utilized by Shakespeare, all of which appear to have been rooted in the popular tales and traditions of his time. More than a century later Samuel Ireland tried to identify the figure of Herne with a real man, one Richard Horn, who was 'a keeper in the forest in the time of Elizabeth'. The legend tells how Horn fell from royal grace when he was framed by two jealous huntsmen and is said to have hung himself in shame upon a great oak tree which in later years became known as Herne's Oak. This curious historical legend connects Horn/Herne with the god Woden/Odin, who is said to have hung himself upon the world tree Yggdrasil, here represented by the sacred oak. The oak is the most important tree in Celtic mythology and to the druids in particular, and here the centre of the cult was located in the grounds of an ancestral home of the English Royal Family, whose Anglo-Saxon ancestors traced their lineage back to Woden himself (one of Woden's sacred animals, the raven, is associated with another well-known royal building, the Tower of London).

Both the late Dr Margaret Murray (author of the controversial *Witch Cult in Western Europe*) and writer Colin Wilson have suggested Windsor Park was a former stronghold of the old religion, connecting it with the worship of both the horned god and the goddess Diana. Nearby are two important early churches at

Taplow and Hedsor, both dedicated to St Nicholas or Old Nick, the devil with whom Woden was equated by Christianity. Bearing in mind Windsor Castle and Great Park's connections with the Kings of England, there is anecdotal evidence that it may well have been the centre of the Anglo-Saxon pagan religion in this region before the arrival of Christianity.

The fate of the 'great oak' of Herne in Windsor Home Park, which stood upon the edge of a hollow known as Fairy Dell, is a mystery because one story says it remained alive until 1863 when it was uprooted during a great gale. Another more accurate account says the remains of the oak were cut down late in the eighteenth century by mistake on the orders of the mad king George III. A new oak was planted on the site of the original by Edward VII in 1906.

Whatever the truth, in local legend the figure of Herne appears in the shadow of the tree, riding at the front of a pack of baying hounds and blowing a hunting horn as the group pursues a white deer. Herne is said to dress in the garb of a woodsman, carries huge antlers on his head and trails rattling chains behind him. According to Peter Underwood, the 'Foul Fiend of the Forest' (as Herne is described in Harrison Ainsworth's romance *Windsor Castle*) is only seen at night as a horned figure, often identified as Woden himself, on a horse followed by spectral hounds.[23] This description clearly draws upon the well-known folk-tale of the Wild Hunt, a phantom aerial host hunting lost souls, which appears in writing as early as the twelfth century in the pages of the Anglo-Saxon Chronicle.

In Windsor Forest, the appearance of Herne and his Wild Hunt is said to herald crises or major disasters facing the country. He is said to have been seen in 1931 before the economic crisis, in 1936 before the abdication of Edward VIII, and again in 1939 before the outbreak of the Second World War.

One eye-witness account was given in 1926 by a Mrs Walter Legge, a JP and member of the Windsor Board of Guardians and the Rural District Council who lived in a farmhouse within the Great Park. She described how one night that year she heard the sound of baying hounds coming from the direction of Smith's Lawn and appearing to move, dying away as they moved along the Long Walk towards Windsor Castle. Two weeks later, she heard the same sounds again at midnight along with her daughter who came running into the room to describe them 'as almost like Herne the Hunter's hounds.' [24] Although the family lived there for many years afterwards, the strange baying was never heard again.

Herne's 'last appearance' is supposed to have been as recently as 1962, when a group of youths found a hunting horn in the forest and blew upon it at the edge of a clearing. Immediately, they were answered by the blast of another horn and heard the baying of hounds. They fled terrified when a black horse appeared, the rider's ragged antlers silhouetted against the sky. Eerie happenings continue, for in October 1976 a young guardsman on duty at the State Apartments on the East Terrace at Windsor Castle was discovered unconscious when his relief arrived. Afterwards he described how he saw a statue 'come to life'. His adjutant, asked whether the soldier had seen Herne, replied: 'Whether he saw something or whether it was all in the mind is anyone's guess'. However, Buckingham Palace's press office was in no doubt: 'We have never heard of a ghost at Windsor Castle.' [25]

Windsor Great Park is south of the town and castle; public access is allowed but visitors should check with Tourist Information for details.

South-west England

Bath, Somerset
Bettiscombe, Dorset
Cerne Abbas, Dorset
Madron Well, Cornwall
Padstow, Cornwall
Wistman's Wood, Devon
Wookey Hole, Somerset

Bath, Somerset

Wondrous is this stone-wall, wrecked by fate;
the city buildings crumble, the work of the giants decay.
Roofs have caved in, towers collapsed,
barred gates are broken. hoar frost clings to mortar,
houses are gaping, tottering and fallen.
undermined by age ...

The Ruin (eighth century AD)

The art of building in stone was unknown to the Anglo-Saxon tribes, and poems and accounts written during this period often refer to the crumbling remains of Roman villas and towns as 'the work of giants'. *The Ruin*, which marvels at the great stone buildings, bath houses and gateways of a deserted Roman town may refer to Bath, which the Anglo-Saxon Chronicle says was captured by the West Saxon warriors Cuthwine and Ceawlin following the defeat of the Britons at the Battle of Dyrham in AD 577.

It appears the vault of the great bath adjoining the Classical temple, dedicated to the Romano-British cult of Sulis-Minerva, was standing at this time perhaps with the famous sculpture of the Gorgon's head still displayed upon the richly carved tympanum. In the ninth century Nennius, a Welsh monk, refers to Bath as being in the territory of the Hwicce: 'it is surrounded by a wall, made of brick and stone, and men may go there to bathe at any time, and every man can have the kind of bath he likes.[1] This appears to suggest the springs continued to be used for healing despite the ruin of the city which surrounded them.

The powers of the hot mineral springs beside the River Avon, which gush from the ground at the rate of a quarter of a million gallons every day, have been in use for more than 7,000 years and were probably regarded as miraculous by the Celtic tribes who ruled the Severn estuary during the Iron Age. Shrines associated with therapeutic springs are well-known in the Celtic world, and were usually presided over by female deities or the Mother Goddess herself.

At Bath, the goddess Sulis (a name with solar connotations) was equated with the classical Minerva by the Romans, but the Celtic goddess remained the dominant partner. The Romans gave Bath the epithet Aquae, one of only two water shrines in Britannia with that classification, and the springs became the centre of an important pagan complex.

Archaeologists believe that sometime in the late first century AD Roman engineers converted the Celtic shrine at the springs into a great ornamental pool, enclosed within a building which was associated with a Graeco-Roman style temple, theatre and bath-suite. The central focus of the cult at the temple was the springs and the reservoir they emptied into. Here, more than 16,000 coins, some dating from the Iron Age, were cast into the waters along with votive objects, some of them being ritually 'killed' so they could not be stolen. Curses written in Latin on strips of lead had also been cast into the waters, invoking Sulis who remained the tutelary goddess of the springs long after the arrival of the Romans.

Sulis herself appears to have been represented by a huge bronze statue of which only the head survives. Other goddesses called the Suleviae appear to have been depicted, along with the classical Mercury and his consort Rosmerta. A relief on view in the baths shows a divine couple, the horned Leucetius ('lightning'), and seated next to him, Nemetona ('goddess of the sacred grove'), an aspect of the patron goddess. They are associated with a ram and the mysterious genii cucullati, a trio of hooded deities.

It is unclear what kind of structure existed here before the Romans, but it seems they replaced the native shrine with a wooden structure enclosed by a ring of timber pile. A huge wall was built to enclose the temple, lined with lead which remained in place until the end of the nineteenth century when the complex was renovated. It was during the renovation of the baths that an extraordinary 'ritual mask' made of tin was discovered in an aqueduct used to drain the waters. The mask is a stylized representation of a human face with a head-dress, and experts believe it may have been used by a priest in ceremonies at the temple or attached to a wooden idol.

The most striking pagan symbol to survive at Bath is the Gorgoneion or Gorgon's Head, mounted on an impressive triangular pediment of the temple which was built to the north of the spring. This head has been described as 'the most remarkable manifestation of Romano-British art' and archaeologist Barry Cunliffe has suggested the head may have been buried by Christians or by natives in fear of the old gods.[2] The deity represented by the Gorgon head is undoubtedly male, and its two-dimensional form with deeply furrowed brow and moustache has been compared with the archaic Celtic carved heads of the same era. Behind the face the Gorgon's hair can be seen writhing serpent-like from its face and beard.

Experts see the carving as a fusion of the classical Gorgon and the Celtic cult of the head, both of whom were associated with cults of thermal healing waters. The presence of the head in the ruins of the Roman bath complex during the Middle Ages may have given rise to the strange legend of King Bladud, 'the flying king of Bath', referred to by Geoffrey of Monmouth in his *History of the Kings of Britain*. He says Bladud lived in the ninth century BC and was the founder of the the town of Caerbadum (Bath), and 'made hot baths in it for the benefit of the public' which he dedicated to the goddess Minerva.[3]

Another version of this legend says Bladud was a leper and swineherd who was cured of a skin disease when he followed his herd of pigs into medicinal mud in the valley bottom. However, Geoffrey refers to Bladud (whose name appears to mean 'Wolf Lord') as a necromancer or druid whose greatest achievement and ultimate downfall was his power of magical flight 'till he attempted to fly to the upper region of the air with wings he had prepared, and fell down upon the temple of Apollo in the city of Trinovantum (London) where he was dashed to pieces.' Magical flight was one of the powers possessed by a powerful Irish druid, Mog Ruith, who wore the hide of a bull and 'speckled bird dress' before rising into the air, seemingly during a shamanic ritual.

Bath can be reached by the A4 from Bristol, or from junction 18 on the M4. The Roman Baths Museum in the Abbey Churchyard containing the Pump Room and stones from the temple is open daily, and opening hours can be obtained from the Tourist Information office.

Bettiscombe, Dorset

At the time of the Domesday Survey, the village of Bettiscombe was a small settlement within the great forests which surrounded Marshwood Vale, land which then belonged to the Benedictine monks of St Stephen's from Caen in Normandy. Long before then, the Romans had built a camp on Waddon Hill near Broadwindsor in an attempt to control those who dwelled in 'Haucombe' the great oak wood which contained Bettiscombe.

Bettiscombe Manor, six miles north-west of Bridport in Dorset, lies at the foot of Sliding Hill, topped by an important Iron Age temple known as Pilsdon Pen, a former beacon site which acted as a guide for mariners. In the house, which dates from the seventeenth century but lies on a site which has been inhabited since the beginning of recorded history, lives a famous petrified human skull which according to local legend, refuses to be moved from its adopted place of residence. Anyone who removes this 'Screaming Skull' will die before the year is out, and like the head of Bran the Blessed in the Welsh Mabinogion, it is prophetic – weeping blood before the outbreak of the last two world wars.

In 1874, a collector of curious stories, John S. Udal, described the skull in the following terms:

At a farmhouse in Dorsetshire at the present time is carefully preserved a human skull, which has been there for a time long antecedent to the present tenancy. The peculiar superstition attaching to it is, that if it be brought out of the house, the house itself would rock to its foundation, while the person by whom such an act of desecration was committed, would certainly die within the year. It is strangely suggestive of the power of this superstition, that through many changes of tenancy and furniture, this skull still holds its 'accustomed place' unmoved and unremoved.[4]

Although Udal dismissed the yarns about the jawless skull 'screaming', he recorded stories about violent disturbances if it was moved, with cattle and crops apparently suffering and bad luck striking all those employed upon the farm. One tale describes how the skull was once cast into a duckpond opposite the house by a tenant. He was seen later raking out the pond after he was plagued by strange and unearthly noises, and the last time the skull was removed from the house by a tenant (before he emigrated to Australia), it is said to have resulted in the premature death of the desecrator just as the legend predicted.

The skull has defied all attempts to bury it and several visitors are said to have heard the skull 'screaming like a trapped rat' under the rafters in the attic where it was kept by tradition until recently. This is not the only guardian skull of its kind in the West Country, for there is another kept in a house at Chilton Cantelo, Somerset, and others on Bodmin Moor and Exmoor.

Records show the home of the Bettiscombe skull was built by the Pinney family, one of whom, Azariah Pinney, was exiled to the West Indies after taking part in the rebellion of the Duke of Monmouth in 1685. There the family prospered, and eventually his grandson John was able to return to Dorset bringing with him a negro slave. Judge Udal, who was familiar with this story, concluded the skull belonged to the slave, and a tale arose that, on his deathbed, the negro made Pinney promise to return him for burial in the Caribbean. The promise was broken, as would be expected, and he was buried in the churchyard. However, such horrible screaming and moaning noises ensued that his skull had to be disinterred and placed in the manor house to placate it.

In 1963, archaeologist Michael Pinney, then owner of the

hall, tested the legend by having the skull examined by Dr Gilbert Causey of the Royal College of Surgeons. His report said: 'It is probably a female skull aged between 25 and 30 years . . . I think all these quantitative data lead to just one conclusion; that this is a normal European skull, a bit small in its overall dimensions, but certainly not negroid.'[5]

It is now believed the Bettiscombe skull is actually that of an prehistoric woman with delicate features who died from a head wound around 2,000 years ago. Some writers have suggested the woman was buried in a building or temple on the site of the house as a grisly 'foundation sacrifice', but Michael Pinney thinks it is more likely the skull was brought down by a natural spring on the hillside below Pilsdon Pen, as the skull has a brown, glassy texture which is consistent with minerals absorbed through immersion in mineral water. Mr Pinney believes that the skull was discovered at the rear of the manor in a Celtic shrine and was introduced into the house, when it was rebuilt around 1690, in order to bring good luck. The skull is the luck, not the curse, of Bettiscombe, going back to a very ancient sacrifice.'[6]

The Celtic shrine referred to by Mr Pinney is the complex earthwork on Pilsdon Pen, above the house, which was excavated between 1964 and 1971. The 'fort' here is situated on the end of a long hill and has three entrances, one of which has a trackway leading to a square enclosure, built from wood, which was situated in the centre of the earthworks. Also in evidence was a hole for a giant wooden post or totem pole, similar to those found at the ritual sites at Navan Fort, Ireland and Crickley Hill in Gloucestershire. Celtic scholar Dr Anne Ross has suggested the 'temple' at Pilsdon Pen was a school for druids, and she points to the discovery of a gold coin on the site belonging to a tribe from Belgium, one of whose kings was said by Caesar to have once exerted influence over parts of Britain. This may add credence to the opinion of the excavator that foreign architects may have been at work in the creation of the 'sanctuary square' on the Pen, because similar examples have been discovered on the Continent.

Bettiscombe village is reached via the B3164 three miles southwest of Broadwindsor. The skull is in private ownership, but Pilsdon Pen can be visited to the south, overlooking Marshwood Vale.

Cerne Abbas, Dorset

One of the most striking landmarks of southwest England is the Giant of Cerne, a huge, primitive figure cut into white chalk upon a hillslope, hidden in a landscape made famous by Thomas Hardy. Naked and blatantly sexual, the 200-foot-high giant brandishes a knobbly 100-foot-long club in his right hand, and sports a huge erect phallus, his feet resting almost against the walls of a ruined medieval abbey.

The Cerne Giant has baffled and intrigued antiquarians, travellers and historians for centuries, and continues to baffle visitors to this beautiful region today. Of the oral traditions, the most popular is one which suggests he was a sheep thief who fell asleep on the hillside and was there killed by villagers, who cut his outline in the turf. Conclusions about the age of the giant are hampered because there is no mention of the figure in any document until the middle of the eighteenth century; even a detailed survey of the land in 1617 fails to make any mention of it. This has led some to suggest the giant was a piece of medieval graffiti poking fun at the last abbot of Cerne Abbey, Thomas Corton, who was charged with gross immorality when his house was dissolved in 1539.[7]

The first reference to the giant appears in 1742, and shortly afterwards in an exchange of correspondence between a local man and the Dean of Exeter, it is said: 'It has been handed down by ye Tradition of many ancient people of that place in several Generations that it has been here in a remote Age. It was no doubt intended for a memorial of ye Saxon idol heil.' Although there was some suggestion it had been cut in recent times it is more likely an earlier giant had been repaired. Writing to the Dean in 1774, Hutchins said: 'some people who died long before 1772, 80 or 90 years old, when young, knew some of the same age that averred it was there beyond the memory of man.'[8]

On the ridge above the figure's left arm is a small rectangular earthwork known locally as The Trendle or Frying Pan. At the turn of the century, a village sexton was recorded as saying that people from Cerne would drag a newly cut maypole to the Trendle, raise it at night and dance around it on 1 May. There was also a sacred well at the foot of Giant Hill dedicated to St Augustine, which may have played a part in the fertility rituals in this landscape.

What can be said for certain is the giant is a fertility figure, and even today barren women continue to make pilgrimages to him, sitting upon the base of the phallus. This tradition was first recorded in 1888, and in 1968 it was said:

> Women about to get married ... used to look upon it not only as a normal and respectable act but the duty of commonsense to visit the Giant to express their hopes during the week prior to marriage . . . some confess to having sat on the appropriate portions of the erstwhile god to assure themselves of the future.[9]

If the giant does represent a pagan god of fertility, which god was it? In the Celtic Iron Age Dorset was the territory of a tribe known as the Durotriges. Dr Anne Ross has suggested the club-bearing god could be the Celtic Succellos 'The Good Striker', or his Irish equivalent In Dagdae. Archaeologists Stuart Piggott and Leslie Grinsell believe the giant was first cut in the turf in the Romano-British period and is an image of the Roman god Hercules, who was often depicted by Celts with attributes of native guardian deities. Hercules was an important god during the Roman occupation of Britain, especially after the Emperor Commodius set up a cult in AD 191 to worship himself as the incarnation of Hercules.

The Hercules theory appeared to be supported by a clue given by the antiquarian William Stukeley in 1764, who wrote: 'the people there give the name of Helis to the figure'. Although this name does not seem to have survived to the twentieth century, Piggott pointed out the similarity of the name with a thirteenth century legend recorded by William of Coventry, concerning a mission by St Augustine to Cerne at the end of the sixth century to stamp out paganism. Although its authenticity has been doubted, the account clearly states the local pagans worshipped a god known as 'Helith'. St Augustine founded the abbey at Cerne 'when hee had broken there in pieces Heil the Idol of the heathen English-Saxons, and chased away the fog of paganish superstition.'[10]

It has been suggested that Cerne Abbey was founded below the giant in the tenth century, in an attempt to Christianize the giant, but it is strange that the monks tolerated the figure for so long. Evidence of continuing pagan belief is found at the medieval abbey church of St Mary, where a large Celtic-style head is built into one of the outer walls. But of more immediate interest are grotesque carvings of four grimacing giants on the façade of the building; they are 'giants' in context with smaller flanking figures who help the larger figure pull open his gaping mouth.

The evidence appears to suggest the Cerne Giant is a depiction of a native, tribal or ancestral god whose image may have acted as a guardian or protector of the land. Even today, the giant continues to generate new folklore and tradition. In 1978 the Wessex Morris Men, following the tradition of maypole dancing which is supposed to have taken place in the Trendle, revived the tradition by dancing at dawn on 1 May, on the first few occasions bringing with them a replica of the horned mask known as the Ooser, once a feature of village festivals in the West Country. The frightening Ooser mask, with its bulls horns, staring eyes and whiskers could well be a folk version of the Cerne giant himself.

The fertility associations of the Cerne Giant remain, for in 1982 a local newspaper reported how the Marquis of Bath with his wife and daughter were to make an annual pilgrimage to the giant. 'Some 22 years ago the Marquis is said to have called upon its power after five years of childless marriage. His daughter arrived nine months later, and every year since, the trio visit the Giant where, it is claimed, they talk to it at length about their problems.'[11]

The Giant, owned by the National Trust, can be reached on foot from the centre of the village, and via the abbey ruins A good view can be obtained from the A352 road, which runs north towards Sherborne.

Madron Well, Cornwall

West Penwith, is a 90-square-mile gritstone peninsula at the western extremity of the country, surrounded by rugged coasts and with rising hills and moors at its centre. This ancient land is rich in all kinds of archaeological remains including standing stones, dolmens and mysterious underground chambers known as fougous.

The whole peninsula is rich with legend and folklore containing elements of early pagan beliefs intermingled with Christianity, most notably in connection with Celtic missionary saints and their holy wells and springs. These natural shrines are often found close to ancient chapels associated with the saints during the Dark Ages. Some appear to be of considerable age, and at two places, Madron and Sancreed, the remains of early temples are found close by healing wells frequented from time immemorial.

Madron holy well near Penzance is particularly beautiful, isolated as it is from the outside world. It retains its reputation for healing, as is clear from the hundreds of pieces of rag and bits of clothing which the visitor will see covering the trees surrounding the marshy well and nearby ruined chapel. A writer who visited the well in 1845 observed the custom of hanging offerings from trees and bushes which he said was unique in Cornwall, although it is known of in Ireland and Scotland where the rags are called 'clouties'.

A noticeboard at the site notes that 'the well has been venerated since pagan times for its curative and prophetic powers', but the structure itself is for most of the year hidden by a swamp. This well has clear pagan associations, for people would visit it on the first three Thursdays of May, with village maidens dropping crossed straws fixed with pins into the water as a method of foretelling their marital prospects. As late as the nineteenth century the well had a woman attendant who was familiar with correct rituals, like the priestesses of former times.

In their book on the holy wells of Cornwall published in 1894, M. and L. Quiller-Couch described how children used to be taken to the well on the first three Sunday mornings in May to be dipped in the water so 'that they might be cured of the rickets, or any other disorder with which they were troubled'. Three times they were plunged into the water, after having been stripped naked, with the adult standing facing the sun. And after dipping they were passed nine times round the well from east to west then they were dressed and laid on St Madern's bed; should they sleep, and the water in the well bubble, it was considered a good omen. Strict silence had to be kept during the entire performance, or the spell was broken.'12

The water from the spring feeds another well of water in the wall of a ruined chapel a short distance away to the north-east.

This place is supposedly the hermitage of 'St Madron', of whom nothing is known, not even the saint's gender! It lacks a roof, but contains benches for pilgrims, an altar slab and in the corner a baptistry with a constant flow of holy water. The structure of the building has been dated to the fourteenth century, but it is likely to be of earlier origin.

It was here that a celebrated miracle cure was recorded in 1640. John Trelille, who had been a cripple for sixteen years following a football accident which shattered his spine, 'dreamed that if he did bathe in St Maderne's Well, or in the stream running from, he should recover his former strength and health'. Following local custom, he visited the well on the first Thursday in May and with the help of a neighbour, crept into the chapel, lay on the altar and then washed himself in the water. He then slept on a grassy hill known as St Madron's Bed, after which he felt relief from his handicap. He returned the following Thursday on crutches, and again for a third Thursday, following the ritual on each occasion, becoming ever stronger until he was cured. History says he made such a complete recovery that he was able to enlist in the Royalist army where he was killed in a battle in 1644.[13]

Analysis of the waters has failed to find any mineral content with which to associate the healing cures, but Earth Mysteries writer Paul Devereux has investigated the possibility of natural radiation playing a part. The chapel is made of granite which increases the radiation count of the area above background levels, but when he floated counters on the water surface he found readings 'over double that of the environment, and 49 percent higher than the interior of the chapel.'[14]

Magical cures were not the sole province of holy wells and springs in pagan times, and were also associated with trees and standing stones. Also in West Penwith, on the moor near Morvah, is the famous ringed healing stone known as Men-a-Tol (meaning 'stone of the hole'). It is actually in the middle of a line of three standing stones, which are believed to be the remains of a neolithic burial chamber or stone circle. Writing in the eighteenth century, the antiquary William Borlase noted how people visited the stone, again in May it seems, to cure pains in their back and limbs (it was also known as 'the Crick Stone').To cure rickets, children were passed through the holed stone three times, and then drawn through the grass, with adults performing this ritual nine times for a cure.

An early reference to pagan rituals at a standing stone in Cornwall is found in the seventh century *Life* of Saint Samson of Dol. St Samson was a Welshman who was moved by a vision in 521 to set sail to Cornwall and finally to Brittany. After landing at the mouth of the River Camel, he travelled southwards through Cornwall and arrived in a place called Tricurius (the modern Trigg) where he came upon a hilltop where a crowd of people were worshipping 'an abominable image' and taking part in some kind of strange ritual drama. The Life tells how St Samson persuaded these heretics to be baptised after a miracle, marking his triumph over paganism by cutting a cross on the standing stone near 'the idol'.

Madron Well is reached from a lane signposted 'Wishing Well' off the road to Morvah north-west of the village. Walk along the lane and turn right along a footpath through woods for one quarter of a mile.

Padstow, Cornwall

This seaport on the north coast of Cornwall is famous for its Obby Oss, a magical event which takes place on 1 May every year. The sinister-looking Oss is probably one of the most archaic and pagan customs which survive in Britain today, and even the most sceptical of visitors cannot fail to be impressed by the intense, almost primitive, atmosphere of the joyous festivities which transform the little town at Beltane.

Hobby Horses play a well known part in Mumming Plays, but although reference is made to them in Shakespeare's *Hamlet*, it is not known how old the tradition actually is. What is certain is the connection with springtime or May Day in the West Country. The earliest reference to the Padstow horse appears in the early nineteenth century, and it is curious that earlier accounts by local writers fail to make any mention of the event.

One theory is the Oss was created by a local woman, Aunt Ursula Birdhood, as an image of the devil in order to frighten away a French warship which appeared on the coast in 1347. True or not, we know Padstow was named after a missionary, St

Petroc, who according to one legend crossed the sea from Wales in the sixth century. Another account says Petroc was a Cornish saint who battled with a fearsome dragon which terrorized the seaport during the May Day celebrations, binding the creature in a girdle and casting it out to sea. This has led some to speculate that the Oss represents this dragon or monster, and the 'teaser' who dances with it, St Petroc.[15]

May Day in Padstow actually begins on the night before, when the townspeople bring flags and greenery in from the surrounding countryside to decorate the streets of the town. As the excitement grows towards the break of dawn, a large maypole is planted in the square and groups of mayers spend the night going round the town singing and drumming a traditional tune which can be heard for miles around. At midnight, the mayers go to the Golden Lion Inn, where the Old Oss is kept or stabled, and sing the first verse of the 'Morning Song' before serenading the landlord and his wife:

> Rise up, Mr Hawken and joy to you betide,
> For summer is acome unto day
> And bright is your bride that lies down by your side,
> In the merry morning of May.

Early that morning a number of colt Osses appear on the streets. These are smaller versions of the Old Oss, made by the children of the town, and they appear and disappear at various points during the day. A great cheer is reserved for the Original Old Oss which emerges from the Red Lion at eleven o'clock to begin the perambulation of the narrow streets and lanes of the town. By the time the ceremony is in full swing, Padstow is crowded with thousands of people.

Emerging from the inn to the sound of drumming and accordion music, the Oss bounces up and down, dances and rushes around to frighten onlookers while the white-clothed 'teaser' prances around in front of the beast. Accompanied by the throbbing drums and chanting of the Day Song, the plunging movements of the Obby Oss produce an effect which some have compared with tribal rituals in the tropics, quite out of character for a small seaport in western England.

The construction of the Oss is unique. It is made up of a circular frame, around six feet in diameter, over which is stretched a shiny black oilskin covering, at the front of which is a small carving of a horse's head. The operator of the Oss stands in the middle of the horse, his legs obscured by the oilskin which hangs down from around the edges of the frame. His head sticks out from a hole in the centre of this construction, but his face is covered by a pointed hat and a grotesque painted mask, of frightening and archaic appearance.

The Oss and its attendants travel some distance during the day around the boundaries of the parish, visiting elderly people and those who are confined to house because of illness or infirmity. As with other customs of this kind, the purpose of these visits was to bring 'good luck' to the household. As a curious break to the furious energy of this dance, at certain points the mood of the music will change, becoming slow and sad, at which point the Oss sinks to the ground, and the mayers begin to sing a song invoking St George. The teaser then slowly strokes the the Oss with his club, and after a loud crescendo of drumming the creature leaps up and the dance begins again. It is this part of the custom which has led to speculation that the 'dying' Oss symbolizes the passing of the old year, which may have been represented by the ritual death of the old deity and his replacement by a more youthful god.

There are two other important features of the Obby Oss which point to its pagan origins. The most important is the connection with fertility, for the Oss would traditionally jump towards young women and try to drag them beneath its oilskin skirt. At one time the skin would be smeared with soot or blacking, and if a young woman was singled out for treatment it was said she would have 'good luck' and would undoubtedly be pregnant within a year. The other important element is the connection with the sea, for at one point during the day, the Obby Oss goes down to the harbour and is 'dipped' in the water at the quay, which is known as 'the Obby Oss slip'.

Since the First World War, the Padstow ceremony has been changed somewhat by the addition of a second Hobby Horse, which is known as the Blue Ribbon Oss. This was a 'temperance oss' developed by townspeople as an alternative to the drunkenness associated with the original. All the attendants who follow the Osses are dressed in white clothes, but are identified by the red or blue ribbons, red being the symbol of the Old Oss. The younger Blue Ribbon Oss, which is constructed in the same way, emerges from the Padstow Institute at 10 a.m. and follows a different route through the town, meeting up with the Old Oss at the maypole in the square towards the end of the day. Both Osses then dance together, a farewell song is sung and collections are made.

A very similar custom is found further northeast along the coast of Somerset, at the town of Minehead, where two other ritual horses appear on May Eve and dances around the parish for the following three days. The Minehead horse is constructed differently, with an elongated framework seven to eight feet in length covering the operator. The frame is draped with coloured sacking and hung with brightly-coloured strips of cloth and ribbons. At the centre of the frame the man's head is covered once again by a pointed mask painted with a frightening demonic face, while at the end of the horse hangs a heavy knotted cow's tail, which is swung to and fro during the dance.[16]

The two Minehead horses are paraded through the town accompanied by musicians, visiting various places, and rushing to and fro, chasing children. The horses' attendants stop people and cars to collect money, and during the three days girls and women will dance with the horse and are 'booted', or struck ten times by the bow of the horse. Although there is some ancient dispute between Padstow and Minehead as to the origin of these strange customs, it is clear there are many points of similarity which point towards an archaic origin for these patently un-Christian customs.

Padstow is located on the A389, which branches from the A39 between St Columb Major and Wadebridge.

Wistman's Wood, Devon

Many books have described this ancient oakwood (the oldest natural copse in England) as Dartmoor's most evocative mystical site. The wood, owned by English Nature and the Duchy of Cornwall, covers four acres and stands on a steep western valley slope, filled with stunted, gnarled and weird-shaped oak trees, most of which are around 200 years old.

The eerie appearance of Wistman's Wood, enhanced by its loneliness and impenetrable nature, has undoubtedly contributed to its reputation and its strange aura of otherworldliness which led antiquarians to connect it with the druids and the Wish Hounds. The Revd Samuel Rowe in his book *A Perambulation of Dartmoor* wrote of it in 1848: 'The whole world cannot boast . . . a greater curiosity in sylvan archaeology than this solitary grove in the Devonshire wilderness ... the ancient storm-stricken oaks of Wistman are without recorded parallel, there is something almost unearthly in their aspect.'[17]

The name was first mentioned in 1605, and the word Wist or Wisht appears to be an old Devon term meaning 'eerie' or 'uncanny', but it has also been used to refer to the devil.

Although the connection with the Wild Hunt appears to be a genuine local tradition, stories concerning druids, sacred groves and mistletoe are on less firm ground.

It is probable that the wood was one of the last remnants of a primeval forest which once covered a large part of Dartmoor before deforestation in the Bronze Age. Its size was again reduced in the summer of 1882 when a group of visitors destroyed part of it during an abortive attempt to boil a kettle! Separated from Wistman by nine miles across the moor are two similar woods, known as Black Top Beare or Copse and Piles Wood Copse, making up a unique group of ancient groves.

The best known supernatural tale connected with Wistman's Wood is the legend of the Wish Hounds, packs of infernal creatures breathing flame led by a hunter, usually the one-eyed Odin of Germanic mythology. In tradition the sound of their terrifying baying can be heard in the wood before the pack set out across the moor on Sabbath nights. They are said to leave at midnight, Odin or the devil riding a headless black horse, chasing victims towards the Dewerstone and then over a precipice and into the River Plym.

The Wish Hounds are clearly connected with the phantom black dogs which are very well known in British folklore, and are believed to have been the inspiration behind Arthur Conan Doyle's famous story *The Hound of the Baskervilles*, which was set on Dartmoor. Ghostly black dogs, sometimes ominous, sometimes friendly to man, are found throughout Devon and Dorset, often patrolling liminal locations like crossroads, bridges and ancient pathways.[18] There is a Black Dog Path running from Wistman's Wood to the Dewerstone, and the creature is also said to haunt the Lych Way, now a popular path for walkers which runs parallel to the wood.

Belief in the Wish Hounds remained strong until the end of the nineteenth century. Ruth St Leger-Gordon[19] writes of an inquest held in 1870 on the body of a man found by the banks of the River Yealm, on Dartmoor. Unable to find any obvious cause of death, the jurors decided the man must have been 'struck down by the phantom hunt', and so certain were they of this explanation that the coroner had great difficulty in persuading them to return a verdict of accidental death rather than the one they preferred, 'death by supernatural agency'!

A phantom hunt is also featured in a scary story heard by the Revd Baring-Gould in the neighbourhood of Widecombe-in-the-Moor.[20] This told how in the seventeenth century a farmer returning home from the fair one night worse for drink, was crossing the moor when, as he passed a circle of standing stones, he was amazed to see a pack of supernatural dogs fly silently past him led by a figure on a horse. Encouraged by the drink, the man called out to the figure, asking for some of his game. Laughing, the figure on horseback tossed him a bundle which the farmer thought contained a dead animal. It was not until he returned home and unwrapped the bundle in the light of a candle that he was horrified to find the bag contained the corpse of his own unbaptised child.

Desolate Dartmoor is truly one of the wildest and beautiful parts of the British Isles, and has hundreds of prehistoric sites, including the remains of prehistoric hut circles and stone circles, a number of which are said to have an uncanny atmosphere. Strange voices are heard calling from Clakeywell Pool, adjacent to one of the hut circles on Coombshead Tor, and the River Dart itself is said to cry out for a tribute of human life. This is heard only when the wind is blowing down its deep valley, and it says:

The Dart, the Dart – the cruel Dart
Every year demands a heart.[21]

Supernatural forces had to be placated by offerings and sacrifice, and there are many records of animal offerings to standing stones around the southern borders of Dartmoor, some of them in recent years. At Holne there was long ago a Ram Feast held on May morning when the young men of the village would gather before daybreak beside a seven-foot-high monolith, then set out for the moor where they would select a ram. The animal was brought back to the stone to which it was tethered, its throat was cut and then the carcass roasted whole. At midday everyone would take part in a struggle for the slice of the meat, which was believed to bring good luck and had fertility associations. The day ended with dancing, wrestling and drinking.[22]

At Buckland-in-the-Moor a ram was sacrificed in a similar manner on Midsummer Day, and the custom survived until recent years at Kingsteinton where on Whitsun Monday a lamb was drawn around the parish 'in a cart covered with garlands of lilac, laburnum and other flowers'. The following morning it was killed and roasted whole in a huge fire in the centre of the village, slices of meat being distributed to the poor. A story to account for the custom describes how once the stream which flows through the village ran dry and a ram was sacrificed in the stream bed to start the waters flowing again. Every year since that time, the ram has been roasted every Whitsuntide 'as a return offering'.

The Revd Baring-Gould writes of a farmer he knew 'on the edge of Dartmoor' whose cattle were afflicted by sickness in the year 1879. He took a sheep to the ridge above his house, where it was sacrificed 'as an offering to the Pysgies'. Almost immediately the cattle began to recover, 'nor were there any fresh cases of sickness amongst them, and since then I have been told of other and very similar cases.'[23]

The wood is owned by the National Trust and can be reached by footpath only. It runs north for a mile from Two Bridges, a village reached on the B3357 road.

Wookey Hole, Somerset.

For hundreds of years people have visited the spectacular limestone caves at Wookey Hole to peer inside the dark and mysterious caverns at the colourful stalagmites and stalactites, and wander along the underground river which flows alongside them. In the distant past, visitors here would surely have regarded these vast caverns as a holy place, an entrance to the Otherworld or the very body of the earth. The official guide-book to the site[24] quotes two lines from Coleridge, who they suggest may have been inspired by the underground river:

> Where Alph, the sacred river, ran,
> Through caverns measureless to man

Today we know the caverns have been formed over millions of years by the slow erosive action of water from the River Axe, flowing through the soft limestone fissures. We also know that Wookey Hole was inhabited from the earliest times, during the old Stone Age some 50,000 years ago when hunter-gathering peoples hunted wild animals from here with their basic weapons.

In the fourth chamber of the caverns, now closed because of the raised water level, the remains of dozens of human bodies dating to the second or third centuries of the Roman period have been discovered, along with their jewellery, a purse of coins, and grave goods which included pottery, perhaps containers for the food required for the journey to the Otherworld.

The reason for burial here is a mystery, but the lack of cuts on the bones suggested to excavators in the 1970s that sacrifice was an unlikely explanation, and it is probable the bodies were buried here because it is the furthest point into that cave which man could reach[25]. Here the underground water wells up out of the rock, which could have been of great religious significance.

This awe for the underground world and dark watery places on the part of the Celtic tribes seems to have continued into the Roman period, as evidence of similar burials or offerings have been found for example at Poole's Cavern in the Peak District. At Wookey Hole there is a suspicion that the cave system was used for pagan rituals, perhaps initiation ceremonies or offerings to the gods or goddesses of the underworld, for there is evidence of steps cut down into the river whose level has risen in recent times.

Much evidence of Iron Age and Roman occupation and burial has been found in different parts of the entrance caverns by archaeologists. Finds have included pottery, bronze jewellery and human remains, in particular skulls, some of them with discs of bone removed from the forehead. In 1946, cave divers found three human skulls, other bones and pottery dating to the Romano-British period in an underground pool of the river, between the first and third chambers upstream from the famous

Witch stalagmite. Further work by divers in the stream between the Third chamber and the resurgence of the river uncovered more pottery dating to the first and second centuries AD bringing the number of human skulls to eighteen, all but one of which appear to have belonged to young people, two of whom were female[25]. Also found was more Romano-British pottery, wine bottles and a Roman coin of the Emperor Gratian (AD 378-83).

The dedication of human heads to sacred pools and rivers is a well-known feature of Celtic ritual, and some have suggested these heads were battle trophies or sacrifices made to the Witch stalagmite which grows from the floor of the cave in the First Chamber. Archaeologists have tried to play down these ideas, pointing out that most of the skeletal remains had come to rest upstream of the Witch, most of them behind natural barriers of rock in the streambed.

This chamber is known as the Great Cave of Wookey Hole and it is quite possible this grotesque stalagmite, the product of natural forces over thousands of years, was regarded with religious awe by those who visited the cavern for ritual purposes in the past. Although there is no direct evidence that offerings were made to the Witch, it is probable there was a ritual origin behind the presence of the skulls in the underground pool further downstream.

The stalagmite is known in folklore as the Witch of Wookey, and in the eighteenth century local people believed she was an evil old woman who lived in the cavern with her dog. The dog is represented by another small stone at the foot of the large stalagmite. Although completely natural, the Witch is said to be the petrified remains of the old crone who was turned to stone at some point in the Middle Ages. The story runs that the people of Wookey had appealed to Glastonbury for help, and its abbot sent a monk to the cave. He confronted the witch and sprinkled her with holy water, turning her into the stalagmite which still stands today beside the River Axe.

No one knows how old this story really is, but an even earlier Welsh legend tells how King Arthur killed an evil black witch 'who lived in the cave at the head of the Stream of Sorrow on the confines of Hell.' The underlying grain of truth, or folk memory, at the source of this legend was revealed in 1912, when the archaeologist Herbert Balch, excavated the cave and discovered a complete skeleton of Iron Age or Romano-British date. Although never subjected to an in-depth scientific study, these are thought to be the remains of a woman, buried together with a comb, a bronze dagger and a white alabaster ball (a witch ball) which may have come from the Mendip hills. Alongside her were the remains of a goat and kid, the remains of which are preserved in the Wells museum nearby. Are these remains those of the original witch of Wookey, or are they those of a priestess or guardian of the cave, who lived here in the Celtic period?

The caves and mill are reached from the A371 road northwest of Wells town centre. The visitor's centre is open all year except between 17 and 25 December, with guided tours and free parking. For opening hours phone (01749) 672243.

Scotland
including the Isle of Man

Glen Lyon, Tayside
Island of Iona, Strathclyde
Isle of Lewis, Western Isles
Isle of Man
Lochmaben, Dumfries & Galloway
Loch Maree, Wester Ross, Highland
Well of the Heads, Invergarry, Strathclyde

Glen Lyon, Tayside

In Gaelic Glen Lyon is *cromghlearn nan clach* meaning 'the crooked glen of the stones'. It is Scotland's longest and most magical glen, a place where Celtic belief and tradition is written upon the landscape in a way long since lost in other areas. Hidden deep in the Grampian mountains on the borders of central Perthshire, it begins at the wooded Pass of Lyon and runs for 35 miles with mountains towering skywards on either side.

Every pass into the valley is guarded by ruins of stone-built Iron Age ring forts known as duns, on whose origin archaeology says nothing. Maps identify them as 'homesteads' but the thickness of their walls suggest they were defensive in nature, and a strong folk tradition in the valley associates them with Fionn MacCummail. Fionn was a supernatural god king and legendary Celtic hero and his elite war band the Fianna, were chosen through ordeals of strength and valour.

Near one of the old forts at the hamlet of Cashlie is a large standing stone which resembles the head of a dog. It is known as the Bhacain ('dog stake'), and locals will tell you this was the stake upon which the Fianna would tether their hounds when they returned from the chase. Even in recent times, the stone was regarded with 'superstitious awe' and was said to have the power both to promote and prohibit fertility in young girls who visited it in secrecy. The Bhacain is just one of the many magical stones in this hidden valley around which a living tradition survives.[1]

Celtic scholar Anne Ross visited Glen Lyon in the 1950s to gather some of the folk-tales and managed to learn much first-hand lore of the locality. She was shown stones along the glen, which locals believe were creatures from Gaelic mythology, and other weird water-worn stones on gateposts, drawn from the bed of the River Lyon, which were thought to have healing and evil-averting power. In the parish churchyard is the Fortingall Yew, said to be the oldest tree of its kind in Europe, at whose roots the boys of the village once lit their Beltane fires. The plaque which accompanies the tree claims it may be as much as 3,000 years old.

Travelling west from Fortingall, past the Bridge of Balgie the visitor will reach the most mysterious part of Glen Lyon hidden away at the source of the river, on a lonely moor beyond Loch Lyon. The loch is a modern creation, for here the valley and natural loch were flooded earlier this century to make way for a huge hydroelectric dam after the glen was depopulated. In the late twentieth century the Celtic past sits uncomfortably side by side with the new concrete dam and its electric pylons.

Beyond the six-mile loch, at the head of the glen lies the remote and mysterious Tigh nam Cailliche, 'the Hag's (or Old Woman's) House', a crude rocky shrine above a rushing burn which in all probability is connected with the cult of the Mother Goddess. At the door of the little stone house, from May to November, stand three extraordinary anthropomorphic stones known as the Cailliche or Hag, the Bodach (Old Man) and the smaller Nighean, or daughter. Today, there are six stones in the family, gazing down the glen as they have done for centuries. Although some of the stones appear carved, the Cailliche and her children are in fact natural water-worn stones, like dumb bells, a shape that is found only in one small part of the Cailliche Burn.

Dr Ross has recorded a unique oral tradition which has been

passed down in the oral tradition of the valley which seeks to explain the ritual connected with Tigh nam Cailliche. It tells how centuries and centuries ago during heavy snow at Beltane, a man and his heavily pregnant wife came over the mountains and sought shelter in a bothy by the rushing burn. The couple, described as giants, were homeless in this wild and rugged country but the clans who lived in the glen built them a large stone house for them to live, and thatched it. The story tells how the woman or goddess gave birth to a daughter 'and they lived there forever and ever and blessed the glen and all its flock and stock and progeny provided the correct ritual was carried out'.[2]

In legend, the three weird anthropomorphic stones which represent the deities guarantee good pasturage and fine weather, but strange and unpleasant things will happen if the stones are disturbed from their winter's sleep. Before the First World War, this miniature black house was annually thatched on May Eve and the stones brought out to watch over the flocks, but since the depopulation of the glen the little house has been roofed with stones, which until recently included a lump of white quartz, acting as a marker in the wild hill country. Now the shrine has a rough roof of rock, and it is the duty of the shepherd who patrols Glen Cailliche to perform the vital ritual twice every year.

More of these strange water-worn stones invested with magical properties can be found at the small town of Killin, at the head of Loch Tay, south of Glen Lyon. They were kept beside the Falls of Dochart, hidden behind bars in the gable wall of St Fillan's Mill. Inside a niche in the wall were eight water-worn stones said blessed by a Dark Age saint, St Fillan. They sat on a bed of rushes and all were once used to heal various afflictions of the head and body. Early in the nineteenth century the keeper of these stones was an old woman whose office was hereditary, and it was her job to rub the stone three times upon the diseased limbs of those who came to be healed, and recite a benediction in Gaelic. When last the stones' healing power was invoked by local people is not clear, but the tradition continues whereby every Christmas Eve the keeper of the mill goes down to the river to collect new rushes with which to change the bed upon which they sit. Belief in the power of the stones may have lapsed, but it still would not do to neglect them![3]

While visiting Killin, a visit should be made to a Victorian standing stone in a field behind the village school. This is said to mark the grave of the legendary Fionn MacCummail, whom we met earlier in this excursion!

The head of Glen Lyon lies in the mountains 5 miles east of Bridge of Orchy and extends for 35 miles to the confluence of the Rivers Lyon and Tay near Kenmore. An ideal starting point is Fortingall, 5 miles west of Aberfeldy on the B846.

Island of Iona, Strathclyde

This tiny three-mile-wide rocky island with its white sands, lies off the western shore of the larger Isle of Mull in the Inner Hebrides. This peaceful and mystical place was described by Marc Alexander as 'an amalgam of everything that is magical about Britain . . . pagan and Christian influences blend to create an essence of spirituality which once was common in many parts of the land and which still lives on here.'[4]

The name Iona or Hii is a puzzle, for the seventh century abbot Adamnan referred to it as Ioua Insula, meaning an island of yew trees. Coincidentally, Iona is also a Hebrew word meaning 'dove' an animal connected with the Irish St Columba or Columcille ('Dove of the Church'), who landed here in AD 563, more than thirty years before the Roman mission to convert the Anglo-Saxons in southern England.

However, there is evidence to suggest Iona had a special pagan sanctity before the arrival of Christianity. Tradition suggests pilgrims had been making journeys to the island before Columba's time when it was known as Innis-nam Druidbneach – the Isle of Druids. Offshore islands have a particular reputation as magical places in the Celtic tradition, for Tir nan'Og or the Land of Youth was believed to be a glistening Otherworld island situated in the Western Ocean. Islands were also used as burial places, and guidebooks say 48 Scottish, 8 Norwegian and 4 Irish kings are buried in the cemetery close to the Benedictine abbey, built around 1200 upon the site of the Celtic monastery founded by St Columba.

Columba was one of the great Celtic Christian holy men whose influence shaped the establishment of Christianity in Britain during the Dark Ages, but mystery surrounds his early life and mission to Britain. He was born an Irish prince in Donegal in 521 and his early education was in the native tradition of his homeland during the period of transition from paganism to Christianity. Some sources describe him as a druid, and his understanding of the old ways is clear from some of the verses attributed to him, including the following which express his inner struggle to come to terms with the past:

> I adore not the voice of birds.
> Nor a destiny on the earthly world,
> Nor a son, nor chance, nor woman:
> My drui is Christ the son of God.[5]

Columba's identification with the animal world is just one of the many connections with the animistic beliefs of his people, and it was against this background when still a young man that he began his career as a Christian missionary. Writing more than a century after his death, Bede said 'whatever type of man he may have been' it was clear he left successors at Iona who were distinguished for their 'purity of life, their love of God, and their loyalty to the monastic rule'.[6] The facts show how Columba was banished from his homeland in the early sixth century because of a bitter feud which ended in the slaying of 3,000 tribesmen in a battle. Following this very obscure episode Columba was excommunicated by the Irish Church, a sanction which was removed later on the understanding that he would win the same number of souls for Christianity as had been lost on the battleground.

Legend tells how he took eleven devoted monks with him on his exile and travelled across the sea by coracle to the Inner Hebrides, landing upon the north eastern shore of Iona, an island sacred to paganism. Here he banished 'false bishops' and set out to preach the faith to the pagan Picts and found the Celtic Church in Britain, with his missionaries like St Aidan founding new monasteries at Holy Island (Lindisfarne) in Northumbria and Bardsey Island in Wales.

St Columba's famous monastery church and cell on Iona survives as a centre of pilgrimage to this day, but despite his Christian mission, it seems the method he used to consecrate it had clear connections with the pagan tradition of his homeland.

His successor, Abbot Adamnan, penned a biography of the

saint around less than one hundred years after his death in 598, which has survived in several versions. One of the early Irish lives of the saint describe an episode whereby Columba tells his people 'it would be well for us that our roots should pass into the earth here' and adds 'it is permitted to you that some one of you go under the earth of this island to consecrate it.' One of his retinue, Odhran, quickly volunteered and the account ends: 'Odhran then went to heaven. He [Columcille] founded the church of Hy then.'[7]

Although the meaning of this passage has been questioned, it is a fact that the cemetery existing on Iona today is called the Reilig Orain, named after Odhran and not St Columba. One authority writes that the evidence makes it clear that Columba 'called for and received a volunteer human sacrifice to consecrate his new house,' and suggests that he used the same 'technique' when building other early churches, of which he founded some 300![8] If this is accurate, then it seems St Columba consecrated the island of Iona by burying one of his own followers – a case of what we would today call human sacrifice. The practice of using a human sacrifice in the foundations of a new structure is supported by much archaeological evidence, and was practised by the druids in Gaul. Many examples are known from the Iron Age and Romano-British period in Britain, particularly relating to the construction and reconstruction of hillforts and temples.

Of the 360 Celtic crosses once present on Iona, only 3 have survived the reformation when in the sixteenth century the Synod of Argyll ordered their destruction and removal. Three magical white marble balls or 'fairy stones', kept in a stone slab alongside the chapel of St Oran, seem to have been lost. Other relics of the past were looted from the island during repeated Viking raids during the eighth and ninth centuries, when the famous Book of Kells, begun on Iona, was moved to safety in Ireland. Elsewhere there are springs named the Well of the North Wind and the Well of Eternal Youth, and a mound known as Sithean Mor, where St Columba is said to have communicated with angels (this too is also the home of the island's fairies).

Iona can be reached from Oban on the mainland via car ferry on a journey which takes under one hour to reach Craignure on the Island of Mull. From here a car or bus journey is required on the A849 to Fionnphort, where a second ferry takes foot passengers on a five-minute journey across to the white sands of Iona. Information and timetables can be obtained from the Tourist Information office in Oban.

Isle of Lewis, Western Isles

This group of islands off the north-west coast of Scotland was known to the Romans as Dumna Insula and were settled very early in the history of Britain. They contain many megalithic remains, most mysterious and remote of which is the stone circle of Callanish on the Island of Lewis. There are 13 tall thin pillars of stone in the inner circle which enclose a chambered cairn, approached by a 270-foot-long avenue, with shorter arms, which make the site appear like a cross from the air. The avenue appears to have been used, even in historical times, for communal processions on May Day and Midsummer's Day, when the powers of the stones were believed to be at their greatest.

Martin Martin in his *Description of the Western Islands of Scotland*, published in 1703, refers to Callanish as 'a heathen temple' and folklore tells how the stones are the remains of giants who formerly inhabited Lewis. They were turned to stone by St Kieran upon the arrival of Christianity because they refused to be converted or build a church in his honour. Another story tells of the arrival on the islands of a priest-king adorned in mallard feathers, who brought slaves to erect the stones, which were dragged from a stoney ridge one mile from the site.

One antiquarian described how he was told by an old man that in his childhood people visited the circle in secrecy on the two festival dates: 'His parents had said that when they were children people went openly to the circle but the Ministers had forbidden all that, so now they went in secret for it would not do to neglect the stones.' and he added: 'And when the sun rose on Midsummer morning "something" came to the stone walking down the great avenue heralded by the cuckoo's call.'[9]

The archaeologist Dr Aubrey Burl has drawn attention to the proximity of the Callanish stones to the waters of the Tob na Faodhail or Bay of the Ford nearby. If this is relevant then Callanish is only one of a group of prehistoric stone circles and isolated standing stones which are associated with processions to sacred water sources.

In other parts of the Island of Lewis, it seems a sea god named Shoni was worshipped with propitiary offerings of animals by the fishermen who depended upon the ocean for food to supplement the few crops which could be grown on the rocky soil.

On the west side of Lewis it was recorded in the nineteenth century how after a successful fishing expedition, or at the beginning of a season when one was expected, a goat or sheep was bought by the fishermen and then brought to the seashore where they were in the habit of landing their catches. Then the oldest fisherman in the district 'revered alike for his age and seamanship' was appointed to conduct and preside at the public sacrifice, leading the animal victim to the edge of the sea so that any of the blood spilt would fall into the water.

The seaman or temporary priest, 'conscious of the solemnity and dignity of his position reverently uncovered his hoary head, and on bended knees slew the victim by cutting off its head. With scrupulous care the blood was caught in a boat's bailer. When the blood had ceased to flow he waded into the sea and there poured it out to him whom he considered the ruler of the deep and its numerous inhabitants.' He then turned to the carcass of the victim and divided it into as many portions as there were paupers in the district, sending a piece to each 'for it was touched by no one else.'[10]

It seems this religious ceremony, known as Tamnadh or Tamradh (from the Irish tamhnadh or 'beheading') was last performed during the nineteenth century, when the islands were relatively isolated and seldom visited by Englishmen. At another location on the island, a group of wisewomen would in the spring collect a quantity of grain which they made into malt. When this had been dried and ground they went, according to custom, to a ruined chapel where it was brewed into ale, which was then taken when ready to the seashore. The women waded in knee deep, pouring the ale into the water, shouting 'Shoni, Shoni! Send us plenty of seaware this year and we will give thee more ale next year.'[11]

The temple of this god was near the Butt of Lewis, where there are the ruins of St Mulvay's Chapel, known locally as 'The Great Temple'. Here there was a similar custom whereby inhabitants of the island came to the crude rocky shrine late at night at Hallow-tide, each bringing an offering to the deity, with every family providing a peck of malt which was used to brew the ale which was poured into the sea as a libation.

In 1703 Martin described how after this ceremony the people all went to church, where there was a candle burning upon the altar; 'and then standing silent for a little time one of them gave a signal, at which the candle was put out and immediately all of them went into the fields where they drank ale and spent the remainder of the night in dancing and singing'.

Stornoway on the Isle of Lewis can be reached by ferry from Ullapool, or by air from Glasgow. Callanish stone circle is a 15-mile drive west from here on the A858.

Isle of Man

This island, 30 miles long by 11 miles wide, takes its name from Manannan Mac Lir, who was a Celtic sea god remembered in folk tradition as a giant and magician. He has been equated with the Celtic sun god Lugh, who is said to have spent his boyhood on the island as Manannan's foster son, and the great harvest festival at the beginning of August, known as Laa Luanys (Lammas Day) was named after him.

To the Manx, the beliefs of their Celtic and Norse forefathers died hard, and traditions about the god Manannan remained particularly strong. As well as his skill at seafaring, Manannan was said to be equal to a host of druids, and travelled around, like the Norse god Odin, in disguise. In folklore he is said to have lived in a ruined castle on the top of Barrule, and his main lookout was said to be an earthwork known as Manannan's Chair on the uplands of Kirk German, from where he could survey his kingdom. Like other giants who inhabited the island, his last resting place is said to be a grassy mound below the walls of Peel Castle, near the seashore. Medieval hagiographies describe him as a descendant of the Tuatha De Danaan, one of the divine fairy race who founded Ireland, and he is depicted as a god in the early Irish sagas and legends.

In the Irish tales, the Otherworld was located on magical

islands and the Isle of Man's frequent covering by mist must have given it an enchanted reputation among the early settlers. The legends say Manannan used his powers of enchantment to cover the island in a magic cloak whenever danger threatened, raising mists and magical illusions to deflect Viking raiders. Even in recent years, according to folklorist Margaret Killip, on the occasion of a royal visit 'the island was completely concealed in a blanket of mist that stretched from the Calf to the Point of Ayre . . . the significance of this could not be disregarded, and people looked knowingly at each other and murmured slyly and rather gleefully about Manannan's cloak.'[12]

Writing in 1891, A.W. Moore said the ancient Manx were accustomed to make an offering or tribute of green sedge or rushes to this god each midsummer day, and he mentions that a pathway leading up to St John's Chapel, which is connected to Tynwald Hill, was in his day 'still covered with rushes supplied by a small farm close by, which is held on the tenure of doing this service.'[13]

Tynwald Hill appears to have been built upon a Bronze Age burial mound, a very ancient place of assembly, where for centuries the island's parliament, analogous to the Icelandic Althing, gathers to hear new laws proclaimed in Manx and English on Midsummer Day, 5 July in the old calendar. Upon the arrival of Christianity, this pagan sun festival was Christianized as the Feast of St John the Baptist. How far the Tynwald Court dates back is unknown, but its origins are undoubtedly pagan, for a letter written by Bishop Parr to Archbishop Neile in 1636, tells how on St John the Baptist's Day he found people in St John's Chapel 'in the practice of gross superstitions' which he caused to be 'cried down' and in the place of them 'appointed Divine services and sermons.'[14]

Midsummer eve, the night before, was a great festival in former times, with bonfires lit on hilltops, firewheels rolled down their slopes and cattle driven between the embers. One account reads 'on the eve of St John the Baptist, the natives lighted fires to the windward side of every field, so that the smoke might pass over the corn; they folded their cattle and carried blazing furze or gorse round them several times.'[15] This was the beginning of a two-week long festival which involved feasts with fairs and merry-making of all kinds.

Christianity is said to have arrived in Man with St Patrick and his follower St Maughold, after whom many holy wells on the island are named. It is possible that, as in Ireland, St Patrick took over the role of the sun god, and St Brigid took over the role of the female deity, who presided over the many rag and pin wells on the island which are visited for cures and divination.

The Isle of Man is of course best known for its enduring fame as the home of fairies, who in dialect were often spoken of as 'the ones' or 'them', because the Manx believed it was best to refer to the supernatural obliquely, as elsewhere in the Celtic west. Fairies were small beings or spirits who were said to inhabit the sidh mounds and prehistoric forts, and frequented certain thorn trees, stones and holy wells sacred to earlier peoples. Some were said to travel in hosts or armies which could abduct people to magical islands or underground worlds, while others lived a solitary existence as the genius loci of lonely hills and lanes. The fairies often had a distinctive name, best known of which are the lhiannnan shee (the Woman of the Fairies), the fynnoderee and the glashtin (both brownies), and malicious animal spirits like the mhoddy doo (a giant black dog) and the buggane.

The Buggane of St Trinians is described as one of the most notorious of its kind in the island. The ruined chapel here, founded by the early missionary St Ninian, may have been built upon an earlier place of worship and was granted to the Priory of Whithorn in the twelfth century. It was called the Keeil Brisht or Broken Church because of an enduring tradition that work to put a roof on the structure was never completed, because every night a mischievous Buggane or evil spirit with a head of coarse black hair and luminous eyes rose out of the ground and 'amused himself with tossing the roof to the ground accompanying his achievement with a loud fiendish laugh of satisfaction.'

The Buggane's reign of terror was brought to an end by a tailor called Timothy who decided to spend a night in the church making a pair of breeches, waiting for the spirit to appear. As the horrid creature rose from the ground, Timothy stifled his terror and continued stitching, and as the creature roared he fled down the hill with the roof crashing to the ground behind him. As he reached the safety of the churchyard at Marown, the Buggane which was following found it could not enter the sacred space, and in fury it ripped its head off its own shoulders and hurled it at Timothy, dashing it to pieces among the grave-stones. Historians have been unable to find any convincing explanation to account for the ruined state of the church and folklorist Margaret Killip concludes that 'a pagan origin for the buggane is just as likely ... an ancient god of some disestab-lished religion showing his disapproval when a Christian church was built in the place formerly sacred to him.'[16]

The ruins of St Trinian's Church can be found beside the A1 road, four miles north-west of Douglas in the centre of the Island which can be reached by air from London or ferry from Belfast, Dublin, Ardrossan, Heysham, Fleetwood and Liverpool. The Manx Folk Museum in the town should be the first port of call for those wishing to explore the folklore of the island.

Lochmaben, Dumfries & Galloway

In the British section of the Ravenna Cosmography, a Roman document listing the towns, rivers and features of the known world, there is a list of eight meeting places which appear to have been tribal sanctuaries of a religious nature. The first four of these name tribal regions in the Scottish lowlands, and the fifth, Locus Maponi seems to refer to a fanum or shrine in the Annandale region, a name meaning 'the place (or shrine) of the youth god'.

Maponi or Maponus was a Celtic deity equated by the Romans with Apollo the Harper on four inscriptions at the military base of Corbridge (Corstopitum) on Hadrian's Wall, set up by soldiers from the Sixth Legion. One altar portrays Diana the huntress, suggesting he was associated with a goddess, and other altars bearing his name come from Hexham, Castlesteads in Cumbria, and Ribchester in Lancashire.

Some experts have suggested Maponus was purely a north British deity, but the name occurs in the medieval Welsh collec-tion of stories known as the Mabinogion and also in Europe, where in the eleventh century AD a sacred spring dedicated to the god is mentioned in the cartulary of an abbey in Rhone, south-eastern France. He seems to have been associated both with healing springs and with hunting, and in the mabinogi of Culhwch and Olwen, the hero Mabon ap Mapon, stolen from his mother at birth, is depicted as a hunter.

Although his cult seems widespread, Maponus or 'Divine Youth' seems to have had an important shrine or cult centre in Dumfriesshire, which in Roman times was on the frontier between the territories of the Brigantes and the tribes of the Scottish lowlands. In this area a number of archaic stone heads have been discovered, and there are also placenames containing the name of the god. Professor Ian Richmond identified the 'cult centre' with the Clochmabenstane, which lies on the north shore of the Solway, 'the site of a megalithic monument and the great traditional meeting place of early medieval folk on the Western March'[17]. The megalith, a short distance from Gretna Green, is a large boulder, 8 foot high and 18 feet in girth, which lies on its side in a field alongside a smaller stone. It is possible they are all that remains of a prehistoric stone circle, which stood at the north end of a ford commanding a fine view across the Solway estuary. This was the site of a traditional meeting place for the settlement of frontier disputes between the Scots and English in the Middle Ages, and may also have functioned as a shrine of the tribal god.

Another expert, C.A. Ralegh-Radford, argued there was no evidence at the Clochmabenstane of earthworks which are usually associated with Celtic tribal meeting-places, like Tara in Ireland. He suggested as an alternative Lochmaben, near Lockerbie, which is the name of both a village and earthwork a short distance away on the northwest side of a loch. Here there was a Norman church dedicated to St Mary Magdalene and, on the south shore was a fifteenth century castle, built on a promontory above the earlier earthworks, which are badly eroded.

He wrote: 'this enclosure formed the temenos of Maponus . . . Lochmaben lies in the centre of the natural region comprising Nithsdale, Annandale and the encompassing uplands . . . the promontory with its marshy shore and a small island off the point recalls the Celtic predilection for sanctuaries in pools and marshes.'[18]

It was from a marsh at Lochar Moss, near the village of Collin, that in the 1950s peat cutters found a small carved whetstone bearing a human head, which has been tentatively identified as a representation of the god Maponus. Dr Anne Ross has noted how the features of this head, including its long narrow nose with a peculiar twist, closely resemble those of a striking sandstone head from Corbridge, which Dr Ian Richmond identified as portraits of Maponus.[19] Others have thrown doubt upon this theory because the head is sombre and mature rather than youthful in appearance. Like other archaic heads, the Maponus head has a prominent brow, large lentoid eyes, and a circular focus on the top which is thought to have been an altar for offerings to the deity inhabiting the carvings.

Although this identification cannot be proven, there can be little doubt the head represents a god or deity, for a number of other ritual whetstones have been discovered featuring carvings of human faces which seem to represent divine ancestors of the ruler or chieftain who carried the stone. The most famous example is of course the beautiful whetstone, bearing four faces possibly of the god Woden, found in the seventh century Anglo-Saxon ship burial at Sutton Hoo in Suffolk.

The megalith is found at the end of a minor road south of Gretna, signposted to Old Graitney. The town of Lochmaben itself is four miles west of Lockerbie on the A709 road to Dumfries; the castle can be reached by the B7020 south of the town centre.

Loch Maree, Wester Ross, Highland

L akes and lochs (loughs in Ireland) are regarded in Celtic mythology as the abode of powerful spirits, and islands in the middle of these enchanted waters had a special significance. One of the best examples of a venerated loch and associated holy island in Scotland is Loch Maree, in the remote and wild coastal region known as Wester Ross. It is associated with the Irish saint St Maelrubha, a disciple of Columba,who founded a religious house at Applecross on the coast facing the Isle of Skye. His name appears to have become confused at some point with an important Celtic deity known as Mourie, a god or genius loci who haunted the lake and its vicinity. His feast day was 25 August and was probably a 'first fruits' or Lughnasa ceremony, held on this date in the northern part of Scotland because of the later harvest in the Highlands.

The Lughnasa feast here appears to have been connected with

a belief that lunatics brought to an island in the loch could be cured through a special ritual. Innis Maree or Eilean Maree is the name of the small sacred island in the loch. This contained an ancient wishing tree and beneath it an oracular well which had the gift of curing lunacy and also received offerings.

Innis Maree seems to have had a reputation over a wide area as a pagan temple and meeting place as late as the eighteenth century, when the traveller Thomas Pennant recorded how mentally ill people were brought from all parts of Wester Ross to the well for a cure. He described how unfortunate lunatics were rowed to the island and made to kneel inside the ruined church while attendants made offerings to an altar and the tree. Then they drank from the well, and were then dipped into the lake three times, some of them being dragged shrieking through waters at the tail of a boat, in the hope of a cure.[20]

Although these kind of rites have not been seen for more than a century and a half, the island is still regarded as sacred. The holy well is dry and its powers gone, some say because it was defiled when a visitor brought a mad dog to the island for a cure.

Nineteenth-century accounts describe how the wishing tree which grew next to the well on the southern side of the island was studded with coins, nails, screws and hung with scraps of clothing as offerings. The tree was still alive in September 1877 when Queen Victoria visited the island, and following the custom, duly made a wish and hammered pennies into the trunk.

From old accounts it appears there even existed a priesthood on the island who seem to have been lunatics or people suffering from possession, for they are described by the local presbytery as 'Mourie and his derilans' (derilan from the Gaelic *deireoil* or 'afflicted'). That 'Mourie' was no real saint is shown by the fact that the name of the island has been shown to be a corruption of the Gaelic 'Eilean a Mhor Righ', that is 'the island of my king' or 'the great king'. Lewis Spence suggested this may have been a sacred king associated with a pagan divinity who actually symbolized the god and reigned upon earth as his mortal surrogate.[21]

A visitor to the island at this time wrote: 'The people of the place speak of the God Mourie,' and outraged records in old kirk sessions of the Presbytery of Dingwall tell of the regular sacrifice of bulls to this deity on 25 August, a practice it was unable to put down despite repeated attempts. Bull sacrifice continued at Loch Maree until the end of the seventeenth century, and Ronald Hutton notes how oxen were also killed in honour of 'St Benyo' in another remote area, Clynnog Fawr in Gwynedd, Wales until 1589.[22]

In September 1656, the Presbytery met in a town bordering the lake in order to inquire into these 'abominable and heathenische practices' which included the sacrifice of bulls 'at a certaine tyme upon the 25 August, which day is dedicate, as they conceive, to St Mourie as they call him.' Other records tell of the 'adoring of wells' and a sacred oak tree, 'the pouring of milk upon hills as oblations', the circling of a ruined chapel on the island and divination using a hole in the ground.

Despite prohibitions, the people of the locality appear to have openly continued their ceremonies for in 1678 the church records at Dingwall note how one Hector Mackenzie, his two sons and a grandson were summoned to appear before the presbytery after taking part in pagan rites on the island. These included 'sacrificing a bull in ane heathenish manner . . . for the recovering of health of Cirstane Mackenzie, spouse of the said Hector, who was formerly sick and valetudinaire'.

Loch Maree was not the only place in Scotland where strange ceremonies were performed at holy wells and springs, and the church, which until the seventeenth century had tolerated these practices, then began an attempt to suppress all forms of idolatry associated with them. At the General Assembly of the Church of Scotland in 1638, an attempt was made to discredit all superstitions connected with wells, including persons 'found superstitiously to have passed in pilgrimage to Christ's Well on the Sundays of May to seek their health, that they shall repent in sacco (sackcloth) and linen three several Sabbaths, and pay twenty lib. (Scottish pounds) for ilk fault'.[23]

Thirty years after the General Assembly two outdoorsmen observed quite by accident a strange fertility ritual being performed at a holy well at Kennethmont in the Grampians, one Sunday in May. The account, quoted in J.M. McPherson's book *Primitive Beliefs in the Northeast of Scotland* (1929) describes how the men spied through a fieldglass a group of women gathered around the well. They had their clothes fastened up under their arms and with hands joined, were dancing in a circle round the well. 'An aged crone sat in their midst, and dipping a small vessel in the water, kept sprinkling them,' he writes. 'They were married women who had proved childless and had come to the well to experience its fertilizing virtues. No doubt words had been repeated, but the two observers were too far off to hear.'

Loch Maree begins at the town of Kinlochewe in Wester Ross, and from here visitors can travel north-west along the A832 along the southern shore. There is a visitors' centre, heritage walks and other attractions along the road to Gairloch.

Well of the Heads, Invergarry, Strathclyde

eside the A82 road south-west of Fort Augustus in the Highlands of Scotland stands a strange monument which is a familiar landmark for motorists travelling towards Loch Ness. The stone plinth which stands above Loch Oich at Invergarry, is surmounted by seven carved human heads, and the inscription carved on four sides in English, Gaelic, French and Latin, reads:

> As a memorial of the example and summary vengeance which, in the swift course of feudal justice, inflicted by the order of Lord MacDonell and Aross, overtook the perpetrators of the foul murder of the Keppoch Family, a branch of the powerful and illustrious clan of which his lordship was chief. This monument is erected by Colonel McDonnell of Glengarry, XVII Mac-Mhic-Alaister, his successor and representative, in the year of Our Lord 1812. The heads of the Seven Murderers were presented at the feet of the noble Chief in Glengarry Castle after having been washed in this spring; and ever since that event, which took place in the sixteenth century, it has been known by the name of Tobar-nan-Ceann or the Well of the Heads.

This story is one of the best known of the Highland folk tales and represents two of the most fundamental concepts in pre-Christian belief, that is the combined power of the human head and sacred waters, both symbols of the life force, fertility and often found together at gateways to the Otherworld. In this case the folk-tale is related to a real historical event, namely the treacherous slaying by Alasdair MacDonald of Keppoch of his two young nephews in order to take the chieftainship of the clan, in 1663. He was assisted by six other men, and it was not until two years later that they were all brought to justice and executed, with their severed heads placed in a basket and taken to Inverness. On the way, so the tale goes, because the heads were crashing and grinding against each other, the party stopped by the roadside and washed them in the waters of a spring. The well of spring water, which flows strongly into the loch below, thereafter became known as the Well of the Heads.

Both Dr Anne Ross and Alasdair Alpin MacGregor have noted how this is not an isolated legend, for there are many other wells and springs bearing the name throughout the western Highlands and Islands.[24] All of these are natural springs in remote locations which are connected with some nebulous battle or murder to account for their strange names. For example, on the Island of Mull the story relates to a long-running feud over land between two families, the descendants of brothers born in the fourteenth century. One member of the Duart family was shot and killed by an arrow fired by a Lochbuie man, and his wife exacted her revenge by cutting off the heads of the two children of Lachland Lubanach, of the Lochbuie clan, dropping them down the shaft of a well which became known as the Well of the Heads.

This act led to the feud between the two houses becoming more bitter and deadly, ending in the decapitation of the chieftain of the Lochbuie clan, Ewen of the Little Head, in battle as prophesied to him by a fairy woman. Thereafter he assumed the role of a banshee, appearing as a headless horseman or warning whenever death threatened the Maclaines of Lochbuie.[25]

During her research in the Western Isles in 1956, Dr Ross heard of a similar story told in Gaelic by a woman on the remote island of Vatersay, on the southern coast of Barra. It was a folk-tale handed down in the oral tradition for generations, concerning the murder of three brothers who were decapitated and their heads left in a well, known by the same name as its namesake on the mainland.[26]

In this tale one of the heads spoke, and was able to make prophecies like the stories about magical severed heads found in the old Irish sagas and the head of Bran in the Welsh Mabinogion. The story, told by Nan MacKinnon, tells how the father of the murdered brothers collected their heads in a sack, but as he was returning home to bury them he passed a standing stone where one of the heads came to life, telling him to find a certain woman who was about to give birth to a son of one the dead men who would avenge the murder. In due course, the boy grew and avenged his father's killer, by cutting off the head of the guilty man as he drank from a spring, which became known as Tobar a'Chinn, the Well of the Head.

Five years later, whilst collecting stories on the Isle of Skye, Dr Ross came across the same motif again, writing that 'there are at least seven wells on the island, and a loch and a fish weir at the mouth of a river, which are all called the well, loch or weir of the heads'.[27] None of these stories, which concerned decapitation at wells, had ever been recorded before and were known only by local people who had heard them from childhood.

The symbol of the severed head is found in association with sacred waters both in archaeology, mythology and folk tradition not only in the Celtic lands, but also among the German and Norse tribes, where one of the Prose tales describes how Odin kept the head of Mimir in a sacred well and 'smeared it with herbs to keep it from rotting and sang spells over it ... in this way he gave it the power of being able to speak to him whereby it discovered many secrets to him'.[28]

The symbolic connection between the head and well survived into the Middle Ages, where in the sixteenth century it resurfaces in an English play or ballad known as *The King's Daughter or Princess of Colchester*. In one scene the princess comes upon the Well of Life which disgorges three golden heads which utter prophecies, one of them saying: 'Gently dip but not too deep, for fear you make the golden beard to weep. Fair maiden, white and red, comb me smooth and stroke my head. And every hair a sheaf shall be, and every sheaf a golden tree.'

The well is found on the A82 road linking Fort William with Inverness, a mile and a half south-west of Invergarry.

Wales

Anglesey, Gwynedd
Caerleon, South Glamorgan
Llangynwyd, Mid-Glamorgan
Preseli Mountains, Dyfed
St David's, Dyfed
St Eilian's Well, Clwyd
St Winifred's Well, Clwyd

Anglesey, Gwynedd

Anglesey occupies a special place in the geography of Celtic Britain as a pagan sanctuary of special importance. The island was positioned upon trade routes between the goldmines of the Wicklow Mountains of Ireland and East Anglia, and for that reason seems to have become a centre of economic, religious and political power for the Celtic tribes of North Wales towards the end of the Iron Age. Known to the Romans as Mona, Anglesey was an important stronghold for the druid priesthood who strongly resisted the Empire, and for that reason it seems to have become a target for legionary offensives aimed at crushing their political power.

Tacitus describes Anglesey as being heavily populated and a sanctuary for fugitives. An early campaign in AD 48 was followed thirteen years later by an all-out attack, shortly before the outbreak of the disastrous revolt of the Iceni tribe led by the warrior queen Boudicca distracted their attention to the east. Tacitus writes of the seaborne attack on Anglesey in his *Annals*, which details the campaign of Gaius Suetonius Paulinus, the imperial governor of Britain in AD 61, against the British rebels.

The account of the crossing to Anglesey describes how flat-bottomed boats were built to carry infantry across the shallows. Meanwhile, on the opposite shore waited a dense array of Celtic warriors 'while between the ranks dashed women in black attire like the Furies, with hair dishevelled, waving brands . . . All around were druids, lifting up their hands to heaven and pouring forth dreadful imprecations, scared our soldiers by the unfamiliar sight so that, as if their limbs were paralysed, they stood motionless and exposed to wounds'.

Urged on by their general and bolstered by encouragements not to fail before 'a troop of frenzied women' the Romans advanced 'and wrapped the foe in the flame'. Afterwards the troops destroyed the sacred groves ' devoted to inhuman superstitions' where it was said the druids 'drench their altars in the blood of prisoners and consult their gods by means of human entrails'.[1]

Although the account clearly speaks of the destruction of the sacred groves on Anglesey, it appears the Romans withdrew shortly in order to defend London against Boudicca, and it was left to another governor, Agricola, to subjugate the island. His troops inflicted a crushing defeat upon the tribe known as the Ordovices, who occupied North Wales and Anglesey, in AD 78 and it is clear the Romans saw the island as of great strategic importance, both for grain and mineral wealth. As part of their sea defenses, the legions built a small fort in the third century AD at Caer Gybi, near Holyhead, and a watchtower or signal station on Holyhead Mountain.

What happened to the druidic stronghold which made that fateful last stand on the island remains a mystery, but a chance find of a large hoard of Iron Age metalwork in the 1940s may represent the priesthood's final and desperate invocation to the gods for help before the Roman onslaught. The rich hoard from the sacred lake at Llyn Cerrig Bach (a name meaning 'the lake of the little stones') was discovered in 1942 when the RAF began to clear a bog before the construction of a new runway at Valley, not far from the narrow strait which separates the main island from smaller Holy Island. As it was wartime, a rather hurried excavation of the site was undertaken by Sir Cyril Fox, who organized the movement of the finds for safekeeping in the National Museum of Wales.[2]

His report reveals how Llyn Cerrig Bach was once an area of

standing water as part of a lake, adjacent to an 11-foot high shelf of rock. This seems to have acted as a vantage point from which large numbers of precious military objects had been cast into the water over an extended period. Workmen building the runway first uncovered two huge iron slave gang chains, one of them containing six neck rings joined by heavy links, and in all 138 objects were found all dating from the mid-second century BC to the mid-first century AD. The ritual hoard included many weapons, chariot fittings, long spears, chains, iron-working tools, fragments of cauldrons, trumpets, and pieces of fine bronze work decorated in the insular La Tene art style.

All the metal items recovered during the hurried wartime rescue dig were prestige objects, mainly associated with warfare, and some appear to have been ritually 'killed', the metal bent or broken in dedication to the gods before it was cast into the water. Other finds in the bog included a large quantity of bones – the remains of ox, horse, sheep, pig and dog, possibly sacrifices. It seems the metalwork was either deposited here in small numbers over a long period of time, or represents a huge hoard of material built up over time and deposited in one single ritual act.

It seems Llyn Cerrig Bach was something more than a numinous spot sacred just for local tribes, for experts have identified items within the hoard as having originated in other parts of Britain, for instance some of the chariot fittings seem to have come from Somerset and Dorset, with others seemingly of Brigantian origin (the river Brent in Anglesey may be named after this northern British goddess). Dr Miranda Green sees the presence of a number of different chariot fittings in the hoard as evidence that there was more than a local élite involved, and it seems Celtic chiefs had travelled some distance to take part in the rituals at Llyn Cerrig Bach sanctuary 'which was perhaps sacred to all Britons.' She believes it possible that 'when their sanctuary was threatened, the druids organised the deposition of a precious treasury of hoarded objects, in a desperate act of appeasement to their gods.'[3]

Dr Anne Ross has speculated upon apparent links between Ireland and this part of Anglesey, with the Lleyn peninsula taking its name from settlers who crossed the Irish Sea from Leinster. She sees the island as a depot and trading centre under the control of the druids, and in a recent work suggests the young man sacrificed in a bog at Lindow in Cheshire during the late Iron Age may have been a druid who arrived from Ireland in the aftermath of the disaster which followed the Roman attack on Anglesey and Boudicca's defeat at Mancetter.[4] The presence of fine metalwork in the hoard from the rich areas of southern Britain suggests that there were refugee tribal chiefs and priests on Anglesey at this time, fleeing from the Roman advance and making a final attempt to invoke their war gods before the calamity befell them.

Although the site of Llyn Cerrig Bach is covered by the RAF airbase at Valley, the island of Anglesey and smaller Holy Island are very rich in every kind of prehistoric ritual monuments. A short distance from the Menai Bridge and the A5 is the well known Bryn Celli Ddu burial chamber, a monument which began life in the late Neolithic as a henge with a ring of stand-ing stones and containing examples of megalithic art. Elsewhere in Anglesey, similar carvings are found on stones in the Neolithic burial chamber Barclodiad y Gawres, situated above a spectacular cliffside on the western coastline of the island at Trecastell Bay. The spirals, zigzags and chevron symbols found inside the cruciform passage mound (which appears to be aligned on the midsummer sunset) are similar to those found in other Neolithic passage chambered tombs, most notably New Grange and Loughcrew in Ireland.

Anglesey is reached via the A55 which runs from the Menai Bridge to the ferry at Holyhead. A guide to the prehistoric mon-uments of the island , published by Cadw, the National Museum of Wales, and is available at bookshops and tourist information offices.

Caerleon, South Glamorgan

Geoffrey of Monmouth, writing in his twelfth-century *History of the Kings of Britain*, located the court or round-table of the legendary British king Arthur at Caerleon, now a small town beside the crossing of the River Usk, north of Newport. The ruins here were also mentioned by the traveller Gerald of Wales (Giraldus Cambrensis), and in the fifteenth century the remains were so imposing that French soldiers supporting Owain Glyndwr found time to visit them.

It was not until 1926, when Caerleon was excavated by Sir Mortimer Wheeler, director of the National Museum of Wales, that the true nature of the site was revealed. After 20,000 tons of soil were removed from the knoll the finest example of a Roman ampitheatre – with room for 6,000 spectators and private boxes for the élite – was uncovered. Since then rescue excavations around the fortress town in advance of housing developments have revealed rows of Roman barracks, baths and defences and a complete outline plan of the fortress has been recovered and is on view to the public. Caerleon (Roman Isca) was the base of the Second Augustan Legion, named after the Emperor Augustus. This army of around 5,500 infantry soldiers were stationed at Strasbourg on the Rhine, but were moved to take part in the invasion of Britain AD 43. The legion were stationed at the strategic river crossing in order to suppress the powerful and warlike Celtic tribe of the Silures, whose territory included most of present-day South Wales. From archaeological evidence, it seems troops were stationed here until the end of the third century when the buildings began to fall into decay. Excavations in the ruins of the fortress have revealed an interesting group of triangular roof ornaments made of clay known as antefixa, which were at one time fixed to the gable-ends of military buildings inside the fortress itself. One of the original archaeologists was of the opinion these tiles had a magical purpose, perhaps to deflect evil forces. Similar tiles have been found in Roman York, and we know that within living memory in the Pennine hills, archaic stone heads have been built into the gables of barns and farmhouses for exactly the same purpose.

In her study of the motifs on the antefixes, Dr Miranda Green of University College, Wales isolated two different groups of motifs, both of which featured representations of human heads, some alongside 'wheel' symbols and others alongside what appear to be celestial objects. She interpreted them as 'evidence for the cult of a Celtic solar divinity followed perhaps by the legionaries themselves, who may have been eager to appease not only the traditional deities of classical origin regularly worshipped by Roman forces overseas but also indigenous supernatural powers.'[5]

The cult of the human head is found again at another Roman

fort between Newport and Chepstow, east of Caerleon, where archaeologists have found evidence for a 'deep-seated persistence of Celtic religion into the Christian fourth century'. It was during the excavations of Caerwent (Venta Silurum) in 1901 that a fine Celtic stone head, 9 inches high and 5 inches broad and carved in local sandstone was found standing upon a platform in a chamber of a domestic shrine, east of the Roman house to which it belonged.

The site, christened 'The Shrine of the Head' by George Boon of the National Museum of Wales,[6] was close by an earlier sacred rock-cut pit or pool which contained two human skulls and broken Roman pottery. The carved head itself, now in Newport Museum, has a blank expressionless mask-like quality, with open eyes. There was evidence of tooling on top of the head, perhaps to show hair, and deep indentations for ears which it has been suggested may have been used for the insertion of antlers. It is possible the head represented a dead person or ancestor, the collective spirit of a family or clan living in the house, known to the Romans as a *Lar familiaris*. The shrine where the head was found was in a remote corner of the grounds of the house, well removed from the main dwelling house. Boon thinks it possible the owner of the large house was a Christian, who followed the recommendations of the Council of Elvira (c. 300) which said idols should be prohibited 'as far as possible', but in face of strong opposition could be allowed as long as the Christian kept himself well apart from them.[7] This suggests the shrine was a tolerated place of worship for pagans, whose master kept himself aloof from their activities.

Legend says Christianity first reached Caerwent in the sixth century, when St Tathan, the son of an Irish king, landed there with seven followers after a vision instructed him to set sail for Britain. They were granted land by a Welsh prince who lived in the ruins of the Roman fort, and it is said St Tathan established his first church in the north-east corner of the town. A coffin which contained his bones was dug up in the grounds of the vicarage outside the walls of the fort in 1912 and is now visible inside Caerwent Church, below a slab with a Latin inscription.

Caerleon Roman fort, in the care of English Heritage, is signposted to the north of the M4, between junctions 24 and 25.

There are good car-parking facilities in the town itself, along with visitors' centres and a Roman museum.

Llangynwyd, mid-Glamorgan

L ate in the seventh century AD Theodore of Tarsus arrived in England to become Archbishop of Canterbury, and his *Liber Penitentialis* is the earliest list of ecclesiastic laws to survive. One whole section of the laws relates to paganism, which remained a very strong influence among the common people. After a list of prohibitions, Theodore wrote: 'If anyone at the kalends of January goes about as a stag or a bull; that is, making himself into a wild animal and dressing in the skin of a herd animal, and putting on the heads of beasts; those who in such wise transform themselves into the appearance of a wild animal, penance for three years because this is devilish.'[8]

Yuletime, the Midwinter Solstice, which we know today as Christmas, was a magical time of year when it seems followers of the old religion would disguise themselves as wild animals, the most popular of which were the sheep or ram (in Midlands and North), and the horse in South Wales and Kent. Although written accounts of these curious customs can only be traced back around 150 years, they are clearly of early origin as the laws of Theodore demonstrate.

The carrying of decorated horses in the Celtic lands can perhaps be traced back to earlier cults surrounding horse goddesses, like the Gaulish Epona, known to the Irish as Macca and the Welsh as Rhiannon. In the Welsh valleys, the horse is associated with Christmas Eve and the New Year season, and is known as the Mari Lwyd, a feminine term which appears to mean 'the Grey Mare'. This 'hobby horse' was such a well-known sight in Glamorganshire at one time that the local poet, Dylan Thomas, composed the well-known *Ballad of the Mari Lwyd* in its honour. A very similar tradition was known in Ireland, where the Lair Bhan (White Mare) was paraded through the streets at midwinter evoking the female saint Brigit. This was a kind of hobby horse made from a frame and covered with a white sheet, the jaws worked by a boy.

The earliest account of the ceremony in Wales, written in 1798, describes how on New Year's Day groups of people would visit houses, with one man dressed 'in blankets and other trappings, with a factitious head like a horse, and a party attending him, knocking for admittance, this obtained, he runs about the room with an uncommon frightful noise, which the company quit in real or pretended fright'.[9]

Later accounts make it clear the party with the horse sang a 'cowydd' or special verse where they gave reasons for being admitted, with those inside the house having to give reasons for not allowing them entrance. This contest, always performed in Welsh, could sometimes last for as long as one hour, and if the party gained entrance they would be given food and drink. This could prove expensive if it was a public house, as the landlord might have to provide free drinks for the evening to a good improviser in order to keep out the Mari Lwyd. Once inside, the horse would chase people and some of the performers might dance before singing a farewell song.

The Mari Lwyd itself was made from the skull of a horse mounted on a pole, with a white sheet covering the skull and the man who carried it underneath. The head itself was often covered in brightly coloured ribbons and rosettes, with the bridle consisting of even more ribbons. The skull sometimes had pieces of glass for eyes, and a hinged jaw would make a loud snapping sound with the use of a string or lever.

The Mari Lwyd continues to appear at Christmas and New Year in the village of Llangynwyd, near Maesteg, where the horse is preserved in a back room at the village inn, The Old House, and a film of the custom in progress was filmed for the BBC programme *Chronicle* in 1977. E.C. Cawte, in his study of animal disguise, suggested the Mari Lwyd may have been originally performed by miners in the coal and iron producing areas of the valleys, which seem to match its area of distribution.

Horse disguise is known in many other areas of Britain. In north-east Cheshire around the village of Antrobus, the Old Horse appears at Samhain and features in a Soul Caking Play, and in some villages rival gangs would every year fight for the possession of the head of the horse, which functioned as a bringer of good luck and fertility in the coming year.

At Frodsham in Cheshire the skull used for the horsings is said to have been secretly buried at the end of each season 'possibly to keep it safe, but possibly as part of a ceremony' and there is a clue here suggesting rituals associated with the head of the sacred animal which were separate from the play itself. In Gower, it was recorded in 1879 that the head of the Mari Lwyd was 'buried with mock gravity when the performances were over and dug up for use the next year.'

The hobby horse or 'Hooden Horse' was also known in a number of villages on the east coast of Kent, where the custom of Hoodening has recently been revived by Morris men after a lapse at the turn of the century. Now the Hoodening is enjoying a revival, and in 1956 a country inn at Wickhambreaux near Canterbury was renamed the 'Hooden Horse' in a special ceremony. In Kent the horse appeared both in September, the time of the hop harvest, and again at Christmas, and the earliest written reference appears in 1740 when the vicar of Godmersham described Hoodening as 'a country masquerade'.

At one time it seems many small communities in East Kent had their own horse, with the head on a pole, sometimes lit from the inside by a candle, which was carried in procession from house to house where they received hospitality in return for a song. The Hooden Horse was originally a strange and frightening creature, banned at Broadstairs in 1839 after apparently scaring a woman to death! Writing in 1967, Barnett Field, who helped revive the custom in Kent, said: 'Even with the streets lit by electric light it still has an uncanny air of mystery as its clapping jaws are heard on a winter night. It belongs to the band of sprites, hobgoblins and man-animals who haunt the twelve dark days when nonsense rules.'[10]

The Mari Lwyd is kept at the Old House Inn at Llangynwyd off the A4063 between Maesteg and Bridgend, and appears between 24 December and 6 January. Hooden horses are preserved in the Maritime and Local History Museum at Deal in Kent, while another is exhibited in Folkestone Public Library.

Preseli Mountains, Dyfed

I n *The Fairy Faith in Celtic Countries*, first published in 1911, folklorist W.Y. Evans-Wentz described the ancient and spectacular Mynedd Preseli as a place where he found a real surviving 'Celtic atmosphere'. He wrote 'its centre is the Pentre Evan cromlech, the finest cromlech in Wales if not in

Britain. By this prehistoric monument and in the country round the old Nevern church, three miles away, there is an active belief in the 'fair folk', in ghosts, in death-warnings, in death candles and phantom funerals, and in witchcraft'.

The rugged peaks and 'carns' which make up the Preseli hills, part of the Pembrokeshire Coast National Park, are formed by clusters of igneous rocks which are some of the oldest formations in the world. The archaeologist Sir Mortimer Wheeler believed these mountains were 'an area of special significance' in prehistory for it is clear there was some special magic, which drew the Neolithic people and their ancestors in the ages of Bronze and Iron to these mineral-rich rugged uplands.

They built the enigmatic stone walls and terraces which link the hills, carns and forts and littered the uplands with dozens of burial mounds, cromlechs, stone circles and standing stones, which may have acted as markers for the movements of the sun and moon which were vital to the agricultural calendar. The most spectacular monument in the region is the Pentre Ifan cromlech, which features a huge sixteen-foot-long capstone held eight foot above the ground, allowing (it is said) six people on horseback to shelter underneath!

In 1923 a geologist, Dr H. Thomas may have discovered the reason for the area's 'holiness' for he found it was from Preseli that the famous 'bluestones' of Stonehenge originated. These special stones, the heaviest of which weighs four tons, appear to have been quarried from cairns on the Preseli range before they were transported with great effort and ingenuity along the Bristol Channel on rafts to the River Avon at Bristol. As many as eighty of these bluestones (named from their colour when wet) were brought to Stonehenge for the second phase of construction around 2100 BC, when they were erected in two concentric circles. Later they were dismantled and replaced by the huge sarsen stones with which we are familiar today, the bluestones being reused and repositioned.

Some doubt has been thrown upon this theory in recent years, but if correct then mystery remains about exactly what was so special about these stones to justify such an enormous expenditure of time and energy in their movement. Geoffrey Ashe writes that 'for some reason the Preseli area was sacred, and stones from there embodied a vital magic',[11] and it seems they were regarded as having healing powers until recently. It is possible this may be connected with some magnetic anomaly specific to the location from where they originated, as recent research by Paul Devereux appears to indicate.[12]

In fact, the idea that the stones came from elsewhere 'by magic' actually dates back to the medieval historian Geoffrey of Monmouth, who tells how Merlin used magical arts to bring the stones from Ireland, where they had been taken by giants from Africa – hence the old name for Stonehenge 'the giant's dance'. It is quite possible this disjointed legend actually contains some element of a real tradition which has been passed down from prehistory to the Middle Ages, perhaps via the druid priesthood.

The sacred mountains and hills of Preseli were also special for a sixth century Irish holy man, St Brynach, who came by sea to Milford Haven in west Wales in the time of St David. Like his friend and contemporary, St Brynach lived a very austere life of constant fasting and prayer, wearing rough clothes and travelling around Pembrokeshire helping the poor. It was also said he held discussions with 'angels' on top of Carn Ingli (a name which means 'The Peak of Angels'), overlooking Newport on the Dyfed coast.

St Brynach's *Life* tells how the holy man travelled north on one occasion to visit isolated Gwaun, a deep oak-lined valley which runs from near Newport towards the port of Fishguard. Here he freed the village of Pontfaen from the attacks of evil spirits which had made the area uninhabitable through their 'horried howlings', a legend which may be a memory of battles between Christianity and the native pagan religion. In fact, the Gwaun Valley still retains an archaic atmosphere today, and guidebooks tell how the place 'conceals a lot of Celtic tradition which has vanished elsewhere.'[13]

St Brynach founded several churches during the course of his travels through Pembrokeshire, the most important being the one in the beautiful village of Nevern, north of the Preseli mountains. It was here that tradition says the holy man married the daughter of the local chieftain, and founded a church by a bubbling stream of water after an angel told him to follow a white sow to 'the right place'. The church dedicated to St Brynach, surrounded by an avenue of yew trees, is partly Norman but very probably occupies the site of an earlier pagan temple. The most famous tree in the grove is a 700-year-old 'bleeding yew', which has red resin dripping from a section where a branch has been removed; local legend says the tree will continue to bleed until the overgrown castle in the village is once again inhabited by a Welshman.

In the churchyard is the famous tenth century Great Cross, which stands thirteen foot high and is one of the finest of its kind in Wales. The shaft is carved with curious geometric designs and inscriptions which have defied interpretation. The first cuckoo of spring is said to land upon the cross and sing on the feast day of the saint, 7 April. There are many other very ancient stones both inside and outside the church, including a Sheela-na-gig, fragments of a Roman gravestone and another Celtic stone inscribed with Latin and Ogham characters, an early form of writing using notches cut on the edges of stones. This dates from the fifth century AD and commemorates one Maelgwyn, St Brynach's brother-in-law who died of yellow fever and was buried here by the saint himself.

Nevern is on the B4582, eight miles east of Fishguard, to the north of the main A487 road to Cardigan.

St David's, Dyfed

elsh mythology tells how the birth of St David, the sixth century patron saint of the principality, was foretold by the monk Gildas, and before that St Patrick (himself possibly a Welshman) visited the spot where his cathedral now stands and had a vision telling him this place was reserved for another.

The legend tells how the saint's pregnant mother, St Non, was pursued by an angry chieftain during a terrible thunderstorm, but as she fled she came to a stone circle inside which the weather was 'fine with clear blue skies'. One huge stone upon which she leaned in her agony is said to have split in two at the moment St David was born, leaving the imprint of her hands upon it. The stone was made into an altar table of the church built on this spot, which is thought to be the site of a ruined chapel of St Non, south of the town of St David's. Some writers believe the central stone was a megalith or cromlech, for the story describes how one part of the stone 'remained behind St Non's head and the other stood upright at her feet.'[14]

The Well of the Heads, Invergarry, Scottish Highlands. A stone monument built in 1812 beside Loch Oich to commemorate a place where the heads of seven murderers were washed in the waters of a spring. In Celtic tradition, severed heads are often associated with wells and springs, both gateways to the otherworld

Well dressing in Hope, Derbyshire Peak District. Evidence of the veneration of water has been found in High Peak in the pagan Iron Age at Poole's Cavern and Aquae Arnemetiae (Buxton). Thanksgiving offerings to the nymphs were adopted by Christianity, and today water worship continues in the form of the beautiful summer well dressings in dozens of Peakland villages. The dressings are made from thousands of flower petals and other natural objects collected locally, and pressed into boards of wet clay

The waters of the Stryd, a fast-flowing part of the River Wharfe at Bolton Abbey, North Yorkshire. The goddess of the river would appear here in the form of a spectral white horse on May morning of a year before 'any fatal accident in the river'. The pagan divinities inhabiting many other British rivers were believed to require human offerings – the Dart in Devonshire and the Ure in Yorkshire took one life per year, while the Ribble in Lancashire was happy with an offering every seventh year, but could be appeased by a bird or other small animal

The Major Oak, Sherwood Forest, Nottinghamshire. One of many sacred and venerated trees found throughout the British Isles. Oak trees in particular seem to have been important to the rituals of the pagan druidic priesthood, who are said to have carried out their secret rituals in sacred groves

The Abbey Church and graveyard, island of Iona, Scotland. Holy islands figure prominently as mystical places and burial places for the dead both in Celtic mythology and in the early Christian period. The Irish holy man St Columba founded Celtic Christianity on Iona in the 563 AD, on an island already sacred to paganism, thirty years before the Roman missionary Augustine landed in Kent to bring Christianity to the Anglo-Saxons

The chapel of St Non or Nonna, is probably the oldest Christian building in Wales and was a centre of pilgrimage during the Middle Ages. It contains a large stone of seventh-century AD date which has a cross cut inside a circle, a sun symbol. Close by the chapel are five standing stones which appear to be the remains of a stone circle, and a holy well dedicated to St Non whose water has been used for healing purposes since the time of St David.

Medieval storytellers have described St David as the uncle of the fabled King Arthur, as well as the son of a prince of Ceredigion, and it seems his mother was also of noble birth. His life's work spreading Christianity through the Celtic lands led him to found monasteries far and wide (including Leominster and Glastonbury in England), from where missionaries were sent to convert the pagan countryside. Like his contemporaries, St David lived a very austere life of hard work, prayer and fasting and his life story is filled with the usual tales concerning miraculous cures and triumph over savage secular powers.

St David founded his great cathedral in 'the most secluded and isolated spot he could find', and this seems to have been on top of an important pagan sanctuary which one authority believes was originally the site of a druidic oracle[15]. If this is correct, then the magical reputation of St David's headland had an unbroken continuity as a sacred place from pagan times into the Middle Ages, when the cathedral and St Non's Chapel became a centre of pilgrimage for people from all parts of Europe.

The early literature makes it clear there was strong local opposition to the mission of St David which appears to have been led by the family of a chieftain named Boia who was of Irish descent and whose wife is described as 'a druidess' in one of the lives of the saint. Pagan priests are often portrayed as women, and in this case the druidess tried to prevent the saint from founding his settlement, sending soldiers to kill the monks and, when this failed, dispatching her maids to tempt them by cavorting naked. But the monks held fast, encouraged by their holy father who told them: 'We must stand fast; it is Boia who must give way.'

The tale continues with a most curious episode which has clear overtones of human sacrifice. This tells how the next day, Boia's wife took her stepdaughter into a wood to gather nuts, and as the two sat down the druidess asked the girl to lay her head in her lap so that she could dress her hair. When this was done, the druid decapitated her, whereupon 'a clear fountain arose in the place where her blood flowed to the ground, which abundantly cured many diseases of mankind, which place the common people call the Martyrium of Dunawd to this day.'[16] In one version the chieftain Boia is killed at the hands of an Irish pirate, and in another he is converted to Christianity by St David, but it seems whatever was the truth this event brought the influence of the Welsh druids to an end, allowing St David's Cathedral to be built upon its present site.

Whilst visiting the western coast of Pembrokeshire, you should also see spectacular St Govan's Chapel, perched on a cleft of the limestone cliffs on the very edge of the sea at Bosherton. The present chapel here probably dates from the thirteenth century, but may occupy the site of a Dark Age building. A flight of steps leads to the empty building from the clifftops, and these are said to be uncountable; water from a holy well below the building was used for healing purposes as late as 1812 when a writer saw crutches left behind by people who had been cured. The 'St Govan' to whom the chapel is dedicated is a mystery, but local tradition identifies him as Sir Gawain, one of the knights of Arthur's fabulous retinue, who legend says was buried on the Pembrokeshire coast. He may lie beneath the chapel itself.

St David's is situated north-west of Haverfordwest on a curve in the A487 road. St Non's Well is found a mile to the south at the end of a lane, and is signposted from the city.

St Eilian's Well, Clwyd.

Many of the saints connected with holy wells are associated in some way with the healing powers which the Celts found in spring water. At some sacred springs and wells, wise women or crones acted as guardians or keepers of the mysteries of the water. This was the case at the well of St Eilian (*Ffynnon Eilian*), at Llanelian-yn-Rhos which had a formidable reputation over a century ago, both for its healing properties and its powers to bewitch those who pilgrims

178

wished to curse.

The well was named after a sixth-century Welsh saint and came into being in response to his prayers. At some point in its history the healing well became a 'cursing well', and up until the mid nineteenth century it had a series of keepers, for no one could ask the spirit of the well for help unless approached through its guardian. At the end of the last century a visitor described seeing bushes near the spring covered in bits of rags, and in the well itself floated corks with pins stuck in them.

In Lewis's *Topographical Dictionary of Wales* (1833) it is said the well was annually visited by hundreds of people 'for the reprehensible purpose of invoking curses upon the heads of those who have grievously offended them'. The ceremony was performed by the applicant standing upon a certain spot near the well, whilst the owner or guardian read a few passages from scripture and then 'taking a small quantity of water, gives it to the former to drink, and throws the residue over his head which is repeated three times, the party continuing to mutter imprecations in whatever terms his vengeance may dictate'.

Old accounts of the ceremony refer to a woman residing there who officiated as a 'priestess' of the sacred spring. Evil-minded folk who wished to bring down a curse on an enemy resorted to her and for a small sum she registered the name of the blighted one in a book kept for the purpose. It is recorded that the last 'guardian' of the well in the mid-nineteenth century was a man called John Evans, but previously the owners were female. Describing the well in 1893 Professor John Rhys wrote: 'Here there is, I think, very little doubt that the owner or guardian of the well was the representative of an ancient priesthood of the well. We have however no data in this case to show how the right to the priesthood of a sacred well was acquired, whether by inheritance or otherwise.'[17]

Another holy well associated with a 'guardian' in Wales was found in the Prescelly Mountains of northern Pembrokeshire. This was the location of St Teilo's Well, also known as Ffynnon yr Ychen (the Oxen's Well), still flowing 100 yards to the north-east of a ruined church dedicated to the sixth-century saint at Llandeilo Llwydarth. Here cures for whooping cough, tuberculosis and other ailments were obtained by people who drank out of a human skull, said to be that of the saint, who was the Bishop of Llandaff and the founder of many churches.

This relic was in the possession of a family called by the unusual name of Melchior (pronounced 'melshor'), who lived in a farm beside the well. For the cure to work it was essential for pilgrims to drink the spring water from the skull which must be dispensed by a member of the family born in the house. Unlike the keeper of St Eilian's Well, the Melchiors charged nothing for their service, and it is said they did not believe in the powers of the skull or the well, but still carried on the ceremony. Professor Rhys was of the opinion that there 'seems to be a succession which points to an ancient priesthood of a sacred spring, sacred before the time of St Teilo and one of the reasons why the site was chosen by the Christian missionaries'.[18] However, more recent research has shown the skull has been associated with the well only since the seventeenth century, but the practice has many parallels in early Celtic literature.

One legend tells how St Teilo had a favourite maidservant who attended him on his deathbed. He gave her a strict command that at the end of a year's time from the day of his burial at Llandeilo Fawr she was to take his skull to the other place which bore his name 'and to leave it there to be a blessing to coming generations of men who, when ailing, would have their health restored by drinking water out of it.'[19]

The Revd Sabine Baring-Gould wrote that a surgeon who examined the skull, said it was actually that of a young woman. Whatever the truth is in 1994, the skull of St Teilo was returned to the guardianship of Llandaff Cathedral by a local family who had kept it as an heirloom after emigrating to Australia. The twentieth-century 'guardian', who was shown on TV drinking water from the skull, decided it should be given over to the safekeeping of the cathedral, a ceremony which took place on St Teilo's day, 9 February 1994.[20]

Penglog Teilo was not the only skull used as part of a well ritual in Wales. At Fynnon Llandyfaen in Carmarthen, water was also drunk from a human skull until 1815, and in Dolgelley the skull of a fourteenth-century Welsh prince, Gruffydd ap Adda ap Dafydd, was used for a similar purpose. There are other examples in Scotland, Ireland and Brittany, and it seems the preservation of skulls belonging to kings, saints and ancestors was an archaic tradition in the Celtic lands, with the relics formerly used in a wide range of curative and magical rites.

The remains of St Eilian's Well can be found 600 yards north of the parish church at Llanelian-yn-Rhos, signposted off the B5383 south of Colwyn Bay. St Teilo's Well is 100 yards north-east of the ruined church at Llandeilo Llwydiarth on a minor road east of the B4313 at Maenclochog in Dyfed.

St Winifred's Well, Clwyd

Wales is famous for its holy wells but it was not until 1950 that a comprehensive survey of them was produced by Francis Jones, who identified a total of 1,179 of which less than half were dedicated to a Christian saint. Many wells are said to have healing properties, or could bring luck to people who often travelled hundreds of miles to visit them on pilgrimages.

Jones found a number of wells were associated with prehistoric standing stones and venerated trees, and he wrote: 'there are wells which must have been sacred even in pre-Christian times, wells transformed from pagan to Christian usages, and wells that claim a purely Christian origin. Legends, practices, beliefs and folktales, the accretions of centuries, encrust them, with the result that their original significance has been obscured.'[21]

The best known Welsh holy well is undoubtedly that dedicated to the seventh century AD virgin St Winifred at Holywell, which is today a functioning Catholic shrine visited for cures by pilgrims from all over the world. The waters have been flowing for thirteen hundred years, and have survived all attempts by iconoclastic prelates to suppress the cult during the Reformation, the Civil War and Commonwealth which put an end to many pilgrimages elsewhere.

St Winifred's Well – which disgorges twenty-one tons of water every minute – was certainly the most important well-shrine in medieval Britain, and Francis Jones notes that the prestige of the saint was so high that no other well or church is dedicated to her in the whole of Wales. The power of the healing cult at Holywell was at its height in the fourteenth century when it became one of three main centres of pilgrimage in Britain.

Among the kings who patronized the well was Richard I who

sheltered here after he was attacked by the Welsh in 1189, and Henry V who invoked the saint's aid before the Battle of Agincourt. The mother of Henry VII, Lady Margaret Beaufort, had a fine well chapel built and was influential in the publication of the first printed life of St Winifred. The last monarch to visit was James II in 1686 when the royal couple asked for the help of the saint so that they might be blessed with a son. The king left part of a dress belonging to Mary Queen of Scots at the chapel and his queen gave £30 towards its upkeep. Their son, born two years later, was James Stewart, the Old Pretender.

Since that time dozens of pilgrims, both Catholic and Protestant, and visitors to the shrine are said to have received benefits from its healing water, including a Scotsman who was cured of a chronic spinal disease in 1916. Celia Fiennes, who visited Holywell in 1698, described the bathing scene:

> they walke along the streame to the other end and then came out, but there is nothing to shelter them but are exposed to all the Company that are walking about the Well ... but the Religeuse are not to mind that ... they tell of many lameness's and aches that are cured ... [and] I saw abundance of the devout papists on their knees all around the well.[22]

The legend of St Winifred appears to have been first recorded in the twelfth century by Robert, Prior of Shrewsbury, the custodian of her relics, and some scholars believe the shrine was famous 200 years later when the unknown author of *Sir Gawain and the Green Knight* describes the hero passing by 'the Holy Head' on his way to the Wirral on 3 November, the feast day of the saint.

The story of St Winifred's martyrdom and miraculous recovery contain elements of pagan belief about the severed heads and healing waters. It appears a chieftain from Hawarden named Caradoc attempted to seduce Winifred (known also as Winifrede and earlier as Gwenfrewi), but she escaped his clutches and ran for the sanctuary of the church at Holywell built by her uncle, St Beuno. Caradoc caught the virgin before the door of the church and struck off her head with his sword. Where the head fell a spring of water appeared from the ground. When St Beuno appeared, he picked up the head, placed it back upon her body and then prayed to restore her life. Then, 'a very thin white line like a thread encircled her neck, following the line of the cut; and this, for as long as the virgin lived, remained with her, always unchanged, as a mark of the cutting of the head and as a token of the miracle.'[23]

St Winifred later became the Abbess of Gwytherin near Llanrwst, where she died. Her remains were removed in 1138 and translated to Shrewsbury Abbey, where Robert wrote her early *Life*. Her uncle cursed Caradoc and his descendants, and caused them to bark like dogs, forcing them to bathe in the well as a cure for their affliction! At the bottom of the well today are a group of stones which have red moss growing upon them, and these are said to be the blood and hair of the decapitated saint. The legend also states that for three days after her death, the well gave forth milk, a sacred elixir in pre-Christian times.

The story of St Winifred is not the only one in Wales where the decapitated head of a saint caused a healing spring to appear miraculously. St Lludd was also beheaded on a hill near Brecon, 'her head rowling a little down the hill, a Cleare Spring of Water Issued out of the Rock where it rested', and nearby when St Cynog was beheaded whilst at Sunday prayers his head fell into a well which dried up, whereupon the saint picked it up and walked down the hill![24] Outside Wales, similar stories connecting the martyrdom of saints, holy wells and healing cults are found in the Celtic lands of Brittany and Cornwall.

St Winifred's Well and Shrine is found to the north of the town of Holywell, on the B5121 to Greenfield. It is signposted from the A55, west of Chester.

Ireland

Ballyvourney, County Cork
Boa Island, County Fermanagh
Brugh na Boinne (New Grange), County Meath
Kildare, County Kildare
Loughcrew, County Meath
Navan Fort, County Armagh
Tara, County Meath

Ballyvourney, County Cork

The village of Ballyvourney lies on the road between Macroom and Killarney, on the border between the grasslands of the Lee valley and the hills of beautiful County Kerry in the south-west of Ireland. Here there is evidence of both prehistoric occupation and an early Christian monastic site in and around the village, all linked up in modern times by a traditional round or pattern used by pilgrims.

To the south is a ruined church, the remains of the abbey of St Gobonet, a figure who appears to have become the centre of a mixture of elaborate pagan and Christian rituals. The name Gobonet is similar to that of the Irish smith god Goibhniu, and when in the 1950s an early medieval shrine known as St Gobnet's House or kitchen was excavated it was found to cover a pre-Christian industrial centre, containing more than 137 forges.[1] The use of the site for metalworking appears to have continued into the Christian period, for iron tools, bronze wire, crucibles and whetstones were also found.

However, folk tradition identifies Gobonet as a female saint, a descendant of Conaire the Great, High King of Ireland, who was born near the village and became abbess of the church there in AD 618. Like other female saints and their pagan priestess forebears Gobonet was associated with agriculture and cattle, and like a witch could cast spells on her enemies, and perform wonders and miracle cures.

A wooden image of St Gobonet, of probable fourteenth century date, was at one time kept at her church and exhibited during the pattern to pilgrims who tied rags around the image. It was set up on top of a small stone cross in the churchyard on 11 February (the festival day of the saint) and Whit Sunday 'when the faithful went round it on their knees and tied handkerchiefs about its neck as a preventive of disease', wrote Edith Guest in the *Folklore Journal*, 1937. Like the idols and images of the goddess which were carried around to bring fertility to fields in continental Europe, this figure was brought to sick people, and was said to assist in childbirth. These practices continued until the eighteenth century, despite being forbidden by the Bishop of Cloyne.

The ceremony of 'paying the rounds' often involved offerings to holy wells, trees and stones, and all these elements were present at Ballyvourney. When folklorist Edith Guest visited the church she said pilgrims paused at places known as Stations of the Rounds. The first of these is north-west of the churchyard, a circular enclosure known as St Gobonet's Hut or Cloghan, surrounded by a path worn by the feet of pilgrims. It contains two upright stones between which pilgrims are required to pass. Centuries ago there were three trees within this enclosure, the bark of which was stripped off every year 'for purposes best known to the people'.[2]

Guest said that 'in no case perhaps is the pagan origin of the cult of the Saint so clearly exhibited as at Ballyvourney' with her association with magic water, stones, bushes and rag-offerings, and the connections with cows and other fertility symbols. She also attributed a pagan origin to the ceremony of 'paying the rounds', a practice which priests tried their best to forbid. Sacred places or 'stations' were visited on May Eve, and the great pattern day, Whit Sunday, when up to the end of the seventeenth century at Ballyvourney a large wooden platform was built for dancers at a crossroads near the church. Villagers would then dance for a cake held up on a board at a height of ten feet, around which hung a garland of flowers or fruit, a prize for the best dancers.

Lying among trees to the south-east of the churchyard is St Gobonet's Holy Well, whose water was regarded as sacred on two special festival days associated with the saint. When the writer visited in 1992 the well waters were enclosed in a stone-lined pool covered by a canopy, upon which sat an array of teacups ready for the faithful to drink from. At the ruined church itself, pilgrims slowly encircle the structure, walking sunwise and touching three spots which have 'special virtue'. The first of these was a stone image (actually just a torso) of 'St Gobonet' which is sculptured in low relief above a window on the ruined south wall of the church. This figure is actually that of a Sheila-na-gig, a female fertility symbol of probable pagan origin.

At Ballyvourney, the stone image of the saint has quite clearly become associated with a female fertility figure, of which many dozens of other examples have survived in Ireland, particularly in the ancient province of Munster. These carvings, found in large numbers in central Ireland are known as 'Sheela-na-gigs', a name first recorded in the nineteenth century, when it appears to have been used to describe old women in the Macroom area of County Cork, not far from Ballyvourney (see Introduction).

Some Sheelas are found high up on the walls of tower houses and churches, which usually date from between the fifteenth and seventeenth centuries, but often the stones appear to have arrived there from earlier buildings. Because they were positioned high up on the walls, often overlooking the boundaries of tribal territories, it is probable Sheelas were representations of the local goddess, put there to ward off evil or attack. In folklore they have been known by a number of other names including the Devil Stone, the Idol, The Witch, the Evil Eye Stone and the Hag of the Castle.[3]

Ballyvourney, or Baile Bhuirne, is found in an Irish-speaking region in the Derrynasaggart Mountains beside the N22 road between Killarney and Cork. Travelling south-west from Killarney, the visitor can see two mountain peaks to the north, known as the Paps of Anu named after the mother goddess of Munster.

Boa Island, County Fermanagh

The name of Boa Island is said to be from Badhbha (meaning raven or hooded crow), one of the three early Irish territorial war goddesses. The famous double-faced pagan idol from this island on Lough Erne now stands in the Caldragh graveyard in Dreenan townland. The janiform figure (from the double-faced Roman god Janus) stands just over 28 inches high, and is made up of two human busts set back to back, each with a grossly oversized triangular head and crossed limbs. The two faces are similar, with large staring eyes surrounded by a ridge springing from the long nose. Each face has an upward-curling moustache, and around the disturbed base of the statue is what appears to be the remains of a wide belt.

In her study of the carvings Helen Hickey[4] noted the presence of what looked like a foot at the end of one of the crossed limbs, suggesting they represent crossed legs in the 'squatting Buddhic position' used by the Celts – one of the features associated with Cernunnos, the Horned God. Between the two heads is a deep hollow, thought to be either a socket for the insertion of an additional part of the idol or a receptacle for liquid offerings. The double-faced appearance of this idol is a common feature in Celtic sculpture, reflecting the belief in the power of twins, or the doubling of the power of the deity. Although the idol has been moved into a Christian graveyard at some point, the carving is certainly not an early Christian object as some have suggested.

The Janus figure is only one of a large collection of phallic-shaped stone pillars, 'idol figures' and archaic carved heads found in Ulster, with Lough Erne and the Cathedral Hill at Armagh being the former pagan cult centres which produced them. Standing beside the Janus figure at Dreneen is another carved stone, slightly smaller in height, nicknamed 'The Lusty Man', which was moved here from a graveyard on Lustymore Island where it had been buried, possibly because its powers were still feared. This squatting figure has one circular-cut face and its left eye is incompletely carved, depicting a closed or blind eye. In the Irish tales, Cuchulainn is said to have met divine hags, manifestations of the war goddess, who are described as blind in one eye.

In her survey of the complex sculpture of the geographically isolated Lough Erne basin region (which includes part of County Cavan, in the republic), Hickey writes of the 'remarkable archaism' of the stone carvers, who appear to have retained pagan elements in their tradition into the Early Christian and Romanesque periods and even modern times. It appears Christianity reached this region late, and even then early missionaries were tolerant of native practices. This archaism is reflected in another group of six carved statues which were found built into the walls of a twelfth-century church on White Island at Lower Lough Erne. All these carvings are of fine workmanship, and appear to be no earlier than ninth century AD in date, but have features characteristic of the pagan idols found in the same area. One is a bishop, with a crooked crozier, and another depicts Christ who sits uncomfortably alongside a grinning, lewd Sheela-na-gig type figure.

In the same region, across the border in County Cavan is another centre of pagan Celtic cult significance. It was here that a famous three-faced pagan idol called the 'Corleck God' (on display in the National Museum of Ireland, Dublin) was discovered in the 1850s in a township near Corleck Hill. The striking head is fashioned from a block of sandstone with the features cut in low relief, resembling Iron Age carvings from the Continent. The three faces are distributed around the ball-shaped head, and a hole in the base suggests it may have been attached to a stone pillar or pedestal on which it was exhibited and venerated. One of the heads also has a small hole cut in the centre of the mouth, a puzzling feature found on other heads of the Celtic tradition, and which may have had an oracular function.

In Irish mythology three was a significant number, having many magical and ritual connotations, and the depiction of a tribal god as three-faced greatly increased its power. Local tradition tells how the Corleck head was found along with another janiform stone head now at Corraghy, two miles away, in a place known as the Giant's Grave. This second head was combined back to back with that of a ram, a symbol both of fertility and economic importance to a sheep-farming people. A very similar stone idol, also combined with that of a ram, was discovered in a wall at Mirfield, West Yorkshire, in the 1960s, suggesting a common ancestry of beliefs among the tribes who produced them. Local historian Thomas Barron writes how this group of sculptures from Corleck, along with a third stone head, were once kept as a group and worshipped as a Celtic pantheon.⁵

It is possible these idols were at one time stored in a native sanctuary on Corleck Hill, the site of an annual Lughnasa harvest festival until 1831, with the people gathering at the beginning of August to collect bilberries and visit a 'special' well. The festival was held in honour of Ireland's three most powerful Christian saints, Patrick, Brigid and Columba (Columcille), who were represented by three 'graves or monuments' on the hill, itself a subtle reflection of the Celtic triple deity represented by the Corleck God.

Boa Island is reached via the main A47 road which runs north of Lower Lough Erne between Ballyshannon and Enniskillen.

Brugh na Boinn (New Grange), County Meath

The 5000-year-old passage mound or temple of the sun at New Grange is the finest example of its kind in the British Isles and the most impressive prehistoric monument in Ireland. Built in 3000 BC on the highest part of a ridge overlooking a bend in the River Boyne, New Grange provides the most convincing evidence that megalithic structures were deliberately orientated on astronomical phenomena, in this case the midwinter sunrise.

The brugh (meaning the home of a god, or sidh mound) was a staggering feat of landscape engineering for a farming people who used stone and bone and had no metal tools to help them. From radiocarbon dates taken from inside the mound archaeologists believe work began around 3200 BC. Therefore New Grange predates both Stonehenge, Mycenae and even the Egyptian pyramids, and the true method of its construction and the meaning of the arcane symbols of the 'megalithic art gallery' it enshrines remain a baffling mystery.

Covering an area of more than one acre, the great curving mound was constructed from over 200,000 tons of rock dragged from a nearby riverbank and piled in alternate layers with turf. The mound itself is 36 foot in height and around 300 foot in diameter, and is surrounded by the remains of a great circle of 12 standing stones, the most impressive of which frame the entrance to the passage grave. New Grange was 'discovered' by antiquarians in 1699 and acquired by the Irish state in 1962. Since then Bord Failte have paid for an extensive excavation and renovation of the site, which is now open all year round.

Visitors to New Grange are often stunned by their first sight of this pagan sanctuary which stands in almost perfect condition 5,000 years after its construction; in the Stone Age its appearance would have been even more dazzling, with the surface of the mound covered with glistening white quartz stones. Around the base of the mound, 97 huge kerbstones were revealed by the excavations many of them carved with ancient geometric art – spirals, circles and lozenges, of which some of the finest examples in the world are found in the Boyne Valley ritual landscape.

The decoration is continued inside the spectacular passage leading to the vaulted chamber inside the heart of New Grange. The 62-foot-long entrance passage, entered from the south-east of the mound, is made up of 450 great stones carved so as to channel water away from the chamber, and leads to the roughly round chamber covered by a spectacular corbelled roof. There are three side chambers, containing more richly decorated stones, and each have shallow basins of stone which held burnt human bones and small funerary offerings.

More than a dozen of the stones in the passage are decorated with megalithic art, but the best known example is the magnificent Entrance Stone, which has been described as 'one of the most famous stones in the entire repertory of megalithic art'. The stone is boldly carved with spirals and lozenges, including the triple spiral motif, found twice at New Grange – significantly upon the entrance stone and upon a stone at the end recess of the long chamber itself.

New Grange is actually only one part of the great Neolithic landscape which contains two other huge passage mounds, Knowth to the north-west and Dowth downstream to the northeast, which seem to have been built in a sequence beginning with Dowth. All three are built in commanding positions on the ridge above the river, which was itself regarded as sacred to the goddess Boann in pagan times.

Knowth is the subject of an on-going excavation, but it appears to have had two entrance passages facing east and west to admit the rays of the sun at the spring and autumn equinoxes. Dowth is aligned on the midwinter sunset, and one chamber still admits a beam of light. There are at least twenty other barrows and passage graves in this great ritual complex, with Knowth itself having seventeen satellite mounds all facing towards it. Like the Avebury complex in Wiltshire, all three of the passage mounds in the Boyne landscape are intervisible when an observer stands upon their summits.

The Boyne Valley complex retained its importance from the Neolithic into the Celtic Iron Age, when legend says the pagan kings of Tara were buried at New Grange. In the folk tradition New Grange was not a tomb or grave, but an entrance to the Otherworld, a dwelling place of the Dagda, the sun god, and his son Aonghus, the chief of the Tuatha de Danann (the earth gods). Brugh na Boinne remained a pagan centre into early Christian times and one tale describes how Cormac Mac Airt, one of the later kings of Tara, did not want to be buried here because the Bru was 'a cemetery of idolators'. His servants tried to take his body there but the River Boyne stopped them, 'swelling up thrice so as that they could not come.'[6]

The association of New Grange with the sun god and the illumination of the inner chamber at sunrise at the midwinter solstice survived in the folk tradition and was alluded to by the visionary poet George Russell in 1897, which suggests he had first-hand knowledge of the phenomenon. At around the same time, it appears the caretaker of New Grange and his wife also knew of the arcane secrets of the chamber and its astronomical alignment, but they were ignored by archaeologists who continued to regard New Grange as nothing more than an empty tomb.

The world of archaeology was forced to take the old traditions seriously in the 1960s when Professor Michael O'Kelly of University College, Cork unearthed an odd structure like a rectangular stone window above the main entrance, which was half-closed by a 'shutter' made of crystallized quartz. The slab was marked with scratches which showed it had been slid to open and shut the window in antiquity. He named the window the 'roof box', and its purpose seemed to be to direct the sun's rays into the deepest recesses of the structure, the central chamber.

It soon became clear from the orientation of the passage at New Grange (which opens to the south-east) that if it marked any particular sunrise it must be midwinter. In December 1967 Professor O'Kelly decided to observe the sunrise on 21 December from New Grange, and drove alone from his home in Cork before the break of dawn. As the guidebook to New Grange remarks – 'the result was startling'. When the sun appeared above the ridge formed by the banks of the River Boyne, a distinct shaft of golden light shot through the roofbox and penetrated deep into the heart of the passage grave where he was standing, as far as the basin stone in the end chamber.

Professor O'Kelly has described how the light initially formed as a thin shaft and then increased to a width of approximately 6 inches. He said that he was able to pereceive the roof 20 foot overhead, due to the expanse of light from the chamber floor, and walk around without the aid of a torch and without touching the stones.

'I expected to hear a voice, or perhaps feel a cold hand resting on my shoulder . . . after a few minutes, the shaft of light narrowed as the sun appeared to pass westward across the slit, and total darkness came once more,' he said afterwards.[7]

O'Kelly has returned to witness the spectacle every year since that day, and has concluded the roofbox was deliberately engineered with astounding skill by the Neolithic builders of New Grange.

Jon Patrick of Dublin's College of Technology, who made a detailed survey of O'Kelly's discovery, wrote that the sun has shone down the passage ever since the date of construction and will probably continue to do so for ever, and he concluded 'as the whole monument is so grandiose, it seems likely that its orientation is deliberate.'

After O'Kelly and Patrick's work was published Martin Brennan, an American artist with an interest in megalithic art, made an extensive investigation of the New Grange complex and provided further proof that the sun enters the chamber for around a week before and after the Winter Solstice.[8] Furthermore, Brennan and his team determined that New Grange was also a lunar observatory, with subtle moonlight beams illuminating the inner chamber at certain times of the year.

These discoveries were significant enough, but Brennan's research seems to indicate that the triple spiral carvings on the stone at the end of the chamber, and several in the passageway itself were touched by the solar rays in sequence, and seemed to be intentionally carved at specific points so as to be 'revealed' only at the solstice – implying that arcane knowledge of some kind was being imparted to priests or initiates inside the temple as the sun's rays flickered upon the symbols.

The chamber was perhaps not only intended to be an observatory, but also aimed to 'capture' the essence of the sun itself and bring light into the tomb of the ancestors at a crucial point in the calendar. Perhaps initiates, priests or shamen of the solar cult spent the nights prior to the event in sensory deprivation deep inside the mound, having a 'near death experience' before being reborn when the shaft of light penetrated the mound and brought with it the New Year. Martin Brennan and his team made many observations from sites in the area of New Grange and his research, published in the *Boyne Valley Vision* and the *Stars and the Stones* demonstrate the entire Boyne Valley landscape was built as a complex and sophisticated solar and lunar observatory, with the passage graves aligned to the solstices and equinoxes at a time when religion, art and astronomy were indivisible.

There is direct access to New Grange off the N51 between Drogheda and Navan, north of Dublin. The monument is open daily with guided tours during the summer. A small admission fee is charged, and information can be obtained from the Tourist Office and small display centre at the site.

Kildare, County Kildare

The pagan goddesses play a large and important part in the early Irish stories. Often triple, they are found in many forms, both as local divinities like Aine or Anu, Cleena or Eevill in Munster, or those goddesses with a widespread cult, like Brigid, later St Brigid in Christian mythology. With the advent of Christianity many of these female deities were transformed into saints or nuns, and the story of the goddess Brigit, later St Brigid, is one of the best examples of the way the old religion came to terms with the new.

Brigid or Bride is derived from the very common Celtic root 'brig, meaning 'high' or 'exalted', found in many place or tribal names including those of rivers and holy wells. The Brigantes tribe of Northern Britain were named after the goddess, with dedications to Dea Brigantia a frequent occurrence in their territory during the Roman occupation. The Romans equated her with Victory and Minerva, and throughout the Pennines she was worshipped as a spring or river goddess.

In Ireland she was in pagan mythology the daughter of the all-knowing god, In Dagdae, and the Christian St Brigid was the daughter of Dubhtach, a druid. Her stronghold was the territory of Leinster, where her temple, later a church containing an everlasting fire – was at Kildare, a name which means 'the oak grove'. Historians tend to agree that the story of St Brigit has no historical foundation, and it has long been suspected that her legend, cult and even her great church, where a college of nuns kept her sacred fire burning until the twelfth century, incorporated elements from the worship of the earlier pagan goddess.[9]

Brigid's feast day, 1 February, Candlemas, coincides with the Celtic festival of Imbolc, an important point in the farming calendar, when lambs began to lactate. In the ninth century AD, Cormac mac Cuilennain, king and bishop of Cashel, stated clearly that Brigid was a common name for 'goddess' among the Irish and that a goddess of that name, 'daughter of the Dagdae, was worshipped by poets, that she had two sisters of the same name, who were goddesses of healing, livestock and smithcraft'.

In many tales Brigid appears as the equivalent of Danu/Anu, the mother of the gods and in fact, all the miracles associated with the saint are connected with fertility and livestock. We are told she was born at sunrise neither within nor without a house, was fed from the milk of a white red-eared supernatural cow, hung her wet cloak on the rays of the sun and the house in which she was staying appears to watchers to be all ablaze. It was as such that the cult of this thinly disguised pagan fire goddess ranked second only to that of St Patrick in Early Christian Ireland. Her popularity as a female deity was such that the Brigid cult spread far beyond Leinster, across the Irish Sea to Britain where many early churches, megaliths and holy wells are named after her.

The Welsh historian Giraldus Cambrensis, who visited Brigid's church at Kildare during the twelfth century, described how the nuns there continued to tend her sacred fire before the Norman invasion snuffed it out. As a fire goddess Brigid is at one with the Roman Minerva, for Solinus writing in the third century AD, said her sanctuary in Britain contained 'a perpetual fire'.

In his account Giraldus Cambrensis says the fire of Brigid was 'inextinguishable' and had been carefully guarded by nineteen nuns 'and holy women' since the death of the saint herself. He said that they all took turns, one each night, in guarding the sacred fire and on the final night the nun put wood on the flames and whispered: 'Brigid, guard your fire. This is your night.'

The sacred fire was surrounded by a circular hedge or enclosure which no man was allowed to enter, and Giraldus wrote that only women were allowed to blow on the fire 'and then not with the breath of their mouths, but only with bellows or winnowing forks.'[10]

In all probability, the saint known as St Brigid was actually a priestess of the pagan Brigid who converted to Christianity early in the fifth century, followed by her priestesses who became the first nuns of Kildare. Like the legend of St Patrick, it was then left to the pen of monks to write the mass of historical material and legend which explains her 'life story'.

The Christianization of Brigid went hand-in-hand with the Christianization of the pagan concept of the territorial goddess, 'the sovereignty of the land' with whom the king would symbolically mate at his inauguration ceremony. As a Christian saint, the cult of St Brigit developed strong patriotic flavour in the province of Leinster, where two tribes the Ui Bairrche and the Ui Brigte, traced their descent from her as a divine female ancestor. The goddess functioned as a territorial guardian against tribal enemies in the same manner as the war goddesses Macha, Badb and Morrigan in the Ulster sagas.

The twelfth century cathedral of St Brigid, built upon the site of the earlier monastery, can be visited in the centre of the town of Kildare on the main N7 road between Dublin and Limerick. In the churchyard are a High Cross, a Round Tower and the foundations of St Brigid's 'fire temple', restored in 1988.

Loughcrew, County Meath

Loughcrew lies around twenty miles west of the famous Boyne Valley landscape, and is a peaceful and less well known megalithic ritual complex consisting of around thirty cairns and passage graves built both as a cemetery and a huge astronomical observatory. The Loughcrew Hills consist of a three-mile ridge running east-west, consisting of three summits upon which the cairns cluster, Carnbane East (Slieve na Calliagh), Carnbane West and Patrickstown Hill, half a mile to the east.

The peaks command extensive views over the surrounding land, and the entrance passages to the tombs all seem to have precise astronomical alignments marking the equinoxes and cross-quarter festival dates. The cemetery was first surveyed in the middle of the nineteenth century, when it was found that most of the original thirty cairns had already been robbed or ruined. Today only seven continue to perform their original function as part of the Neolithic landscape calendar, but only one of the cairns has been properly excavated by archaeologists.

The highest and central peak is the 900 foot Carnbane East, or Slieve na Calliagh, a name meaning the Mountain of the Hag or Witch, a term used to describe the whole hill range (known in 1828 as 'the Witch's Hops'). This hill is topped by the largest and most impressive mound, known as 'Cairn T' which is a classic cruciform passage, similar in construction to that of Dowth in the Boyne Valley. It dates from a similar period, around 3200 BC. The passage grave has a diameter of 120 feet and the cairn is surrounded by 37 huge kerbstones.

The chamber inside has side chambers and stones decorated with concentric circles, arcs, 'flower' motifs, zig-zags and spirals, including one particular decorated megalith which is lit up by the rays of the sun on five days before and after the spring equinox (21 March). Martin Brennan notes in *The Stars and the Stones* that on the day of the equinox itself the light beam 'frames a large engraved radial solar disc' on the stone. The chamber is also illuminated on the autum equinox in September, and researcher Michael Dames has discovered Cairn T also stands upon a midsummer sunrise line as seen from 'the stone of divisions' at Uisnech, centre of the mystical fifth province of Ireland in County Westmeath.[11]

In legend Cairn T was the burial place of of the Ollamh Fodla, a high-ranking poet and law giver, with 'fodla' being the sister of the goddess Eriu. The goddess appears in folklore as a giantess or winter hag who 'came from the north to perform a magical feat in this neighbourhood'. She is said to have dropped her apronful of stones upon the Sliab na Caillighe, and today on the north side of the cairn itself is a huge stone ten foot long and six foot high, weighing ten tons, called the Hag's Chair. The Chair is covered with decorations – cups, cup and rings and concentric circles and its top has a cavity hollowed out of the stone where the goddess was said to sit and smoke her pipe! Observers have noted how the hilltop itself, when seen from the entrance of neighbouring cairns on Carnbane West, looks like the breast of the goddess, a landscape 'simulacra' image found elsewhere at sacred sites in the British Isles.

Carnbane West contains Cairn H which is aligned on the Samhain sunrise, and is the only passage grave in the cemetery which has been completely excavated in recent times. Thousands of fragments of bone blades decorated with Iron Age La Tene designs, accompanied by glass beads and burnt bones were found inside the main body of the cairn. This was a startling discovery, for the excavator has dated them to the first century AD, when it seems the passage grave may have been rebuilt, which suggests a remarkable continuity in ritual use of more than 3000 years![12]

Around 11 of the remaining cairns and passage graves in the Loughcrew cemetery contain stones decorated with megalithic art. Cairn H itself has a 24-foot-long cruciform chamber which contains five sculptured stones, one with spirals. The work of Martin Brennan has demonstrated how the passage graves on both Carnbane West and East functioned like a huge landscape clock, and seven of the mounds still admit beams of light at important solar events to this day. Cairn L on Carnbane West has its entrance aligned to receive the rays of the rising sun at Samhain (1 November) and Imbolc (1 February), while Cairn S on Carnbane East is aligned to the sunset on the harvest festival at Lughnasa (1 August) and Beltane (1 May).

The hills are are found beside the R154 road between Crossakeel and Oldcastle, south-west of the main N3 between

Kells and Cavan. A climb is necessary to reach the hilltops, and a key has to be obtained locally to enter Cairns L and T.

Navan Fort, County Armagh

The name of the tribal palace of the Ulster kings is a misnomer because this recently excavated circular earthwork was not a fort but a religious and ceremonial centre. The site lies on the summit of a hill near the city of Armagh, surrounded by a bank with an internal rather than external ditch as would be expected on a fort. Like Tara, it commands an extensive view across the countryside, this time the fertile farmland of Northern Ireland. Navan Fort appears in the early Irish tales and legends as Emain Macha, the capital of the territory of the Iron Age tribe known as Ulaidh, or the men of Ulster. It was here that the most famous of the Ulster epics the *Tain Bo Cuailnge* (The Cattle Raid of Cooley) was based. The legends say Conchobar mac Nessa had his royal court at Emain, with Cuchulainn as his champion, and from here warriors were constantly engaged in battle to defend their territory.

There are two separate legends to account for the name of Emain Macha in the early Irish literature, both of which associate Navan with the goddess of the territory, Macha, and the second element of the name 'emain' connects with the old Irish word for 'twin', a reference to the twins which the goddess is said to have given birth to after mating with a wealthy farmer. Another tale says this great warrior queen ruled over the whole of Ireland, making her enemies slaves who were forced to build Emain Macha. The kings who ruled from here later traced their descent from the goddess, as the Anglo-Saxon kings traced their descent from Woden.

Perhaps with such a rich repository of legend, history and mythology, it is not surprising that when the site was excavated astonishing finds would be made. The late Dudley Waterman of the Ancient Monuments Branch of Northern Ireland's Department of Finance dug the summit of the hill between 1963 and 1971. He found evidence that the site had been occupied in some manner from as far back as the third millenium BC, but the hilltop appears to have only become an important regional centre towards the end of the Iron Age when around 700 BC a large circular wooden house was built on the mound.

This seems to have been a temporary structure as it was rebuilt several times before it was replaced by an enormous round wooden building or sanctuary, 125 foot in diameter. It was made up of five rings of oak posts surrounding a huge central pole which was sunk two metres into the sub-soil. Samples from the axe-trimmed butt of this central pole were sent for tree-ring dating at Queen's University, Belfast, and experts there were able to give an exact date for the felling of the tree – 95 BC. This totem pole would have been as much as 36 foot in height when it was first erected, and had a long corridor leading towards it from the entrance to the 'sanctuary'.

Only a short time after the completion of this building, it appears to have been deliberately destroyed by fire. While the wooden structure was still standing a flat-topped cairn of limestone blocks was placed inside, and the whole structure was burned. Afterwards, the surface of the cairn which remained was covered with a mound of soil and turves.

Interpreting the results of the excavation, Dr Chris Lynn of Belfast University compared its destruction with accounts by Caesar which describe how, less than fifty years after the events at Navan, the druids of Gaul made huge wicker structures, packed human offerings inside them, and burned them. He suggests the wooden building at Navan, rather than being a human sacrifice, was a complex ritual act by the druids who may have been 'symbolically re-enacting myths for religious purposes, perhaps as a foundation sacrifice or in response to military or environmental pressures.'[13]

Dr Lynn has compared the three stages of construction with the traditional belief in magical circular buildings, the sidh mounds, where in the Irish tales heroes are lured by magic into the Otherworld. He sees Navan as 'a druidic tour de force' which demonstrates that philosophy and religion in Iron Age Ireland were more complex and organized than was previously believed – 'the evidence shows large scale ritual architecture and a codified belief system ... [and] it seems reasonable to suggest that, in the beginning of the first century BC, Navan was an otherworld place, the home of the gods and goddesses.'

From other archaeological evidence we know Navan was only one part of a larger ritual landscape, for west of the hill is an artificial lake, the King's Stables, which appears to have been created during the late Bronze Age. Large numbers of animal bones have been dug out of this deep lakelet, including those of dogs and red deer and a part of a human skull fashioned into a mask. On the other side of the fort was another ritual site, Lough na Shade, which contained bronze trumpets and human skulls which appear to have been cast into the bog. On Navan itself, the skull of a barbary ape imported from Spain was one of the most enigmatic finds.

It is certain this part of Ulster was an important sanctuary in the late Iron Age for a highly developed system of pagan beliefs, and it is probable a school of druids was based at Emain Macha or nearby Ard Macha (Armagh). When Christianity arrived in Ireland, this pagan priesthood may have been suffering a decline in its fortunes and some scholars have suggested the wise men of the oak switched allegiance in order to follow the new religion.

St Patrick, the apostle of Ireland, is associated very strongly with the site of the Protestant Cathedral in Armagh, which stands upon Druim-Sailech or 'the hill of sorrows', which has been a cult centre since pagan times. A Christian church was founded here at some point between the fifth and seventh centuries AD, not necessarily by Patrick, who is buried at Downpatrick. Armagh Cathedral contains a number of archaic carved stone heads and idols, including a carving of a sun god, originally from the earlier pagan centre. The church at Armagh quickly adopted St Patrick as its patron and his cult spread rapidly throughout Ireland, so that by AD 640 it had established itself as one of the major ecclesiastical centres of early Christian Ireland.

Navan fort is situated one and a half miles west of the city of Armagh off the A28 Killylea road. A new visitors' centre, Navan at Armagh, opened in the summer of 1993 with interpretative displays and carparking. The centre opens seven days a week – every day except 25 December.

Tara, County Meath

Guidebooks tell visitors to this legendary hilltop which dominates the lush green farming lands of county Meath that Tara has been regarded as the political and spiritual capital of Ireland from a long lost time. It is indeed a 'Celtic Camelot' where archaeology, mythology, folk tradition and fact have become so intertwined they are impossible to unravel.

The pagan sanctuary of Tara, traditionally the seat of 140 Irish kings, lies at the centre of the 4 provinces of Ireland and from the hill both the stone ritual landscapes at Loughcrew and Boyne Valley (ten miles to the south-west) can be seen, a fact which is significant in view of the tradition that the pagan kings of Tara were buried at New Grange. Although we know very little about Tara from archaeology, the royal court here figures prominently in the old Irish literature and was the setting for an important clash between the pagan druids and Christianity in the form of the missionary St Patrick.

The idea of a single High King ruling Ireland from Tara appears to be a myth invented in the Middle Ages, for it is clear the site did not become important as a symbol of Irish sovereignty until it was conquered by the Southern Ui Neill dynasty of Ulster during the sixth century AD. By then the earthworks had been abandoned, but Tara remained an important ritual site strongly associated with the Samhain festival and its archaic names and lore were first recorded around the year AD 1000, in two medieval histories, the *Book of Leinster* and the *Yellow Book of Lecan.*

In pagan times the hill was the site of one of best known Celtic tribal assemblies, the Feis Temhra or Feast of Tara. It is clear from the early literature the druids played a major role in these tribal gatherings, just as 700 years before when Caesar had recorded an annual meeting of the Gaulish druids in the territory of the Carnutes (modern Chartres). The Feis was an initiation rite which involved a ritual 'marriage', for when a new king was inaugurated he had to take part in a symbolic 'mating' with the goddess of the territory. The last Feis was held in the middle of the sixth century AD during the reign of Diarmaid mac Cerbhail, a time of great changes after which Tara was abandoned.

Muirchu's *Life* of St Patrick, written in the late seventh

century AD, tells the story of an epic confrontation between Christianity and paganism which occurred during the reign of King Logaire. He tells how St Patrick set out from his stronghold at Armagh to preach the Christian faith at the royal citadel in AD 433.

It was Beltane and the Druids had extinguished all the fires at the pagan sanctuary, in preparation for a ceremonial relighting of them all from a single sacred flame. St Patrick defied this custom by kindling his 'Paschal Fire' upon the Hill of Slane on Easter Day, so it was clearly visible to the king and his druids at Tara. Patrick seems to have deliberately set out to provoke a confrontation between the new faith and paganism, which in the official story led inevitably to the triumph of Christianity. King Laoghaire, impressed by Patrick's mission but too old himself to change his ways, granted him permission to preach the gospel and set the scene for the destruction of paganism in Ireland.[14]

Historians have pointed out the fact that there is no way in which May Day and Easter could fall upon the same date, which suggests this story is fictitious. However, there was a genuine pagan festival involving the lighting of fires, for an Irish writer in the eighth century AD mentions two huge bonfires lit by the druids at Beltane in honour of the sun god Belenus. When the visitor stands upon the 500-foot-high hill of Tara, he is in the presence not only of a Celtic Iron Age royal palace, but also a sacred place whose sanctity stretches back thousands of years to the Stone Age and encapsulates every era of Irish mythology. Starting at the car park, you will pass through the grounds of St Patrick's Church before reaching the main complex of earthworks. The churchyard itself contains two standing stones. One is a small round block of limestone, with the second and more important being a four-sided pillar known as Adamnan's Cross. Carved in low-relief on the stone is a small cross-legged figure identified as a Sheela-na-gig or a representation of the horned god, Cernunnos. Experts believe these two stones are associated with fertility rites and may have played a part, along with the Stone of Destiny in the inauguration rituals of the High Kings of Tara.

The hilltop is surrounded by a large Iron Age earthwork, of ritual rather than defensive function, known as the Royal Enclosure or Rath na Ri. On the northern edge of the fosse is the oldest feature of the complex, a Neolithic passage grave dating to 2000 BC known as Dumhna na nGiall (the Mound of the Hostages). This is the only part of the site to be excavated, and was found to be made up of a cairn of stones covered by clay containing burials of Bronze Age date, one of them very rich.[15]

Walk south from the mound and the largest structure on the hilltop is reached. These are two linked Iron Age ring forts, Ann Forradh (the legendary Royal Seat of the Kings) and Teach Cormaic (Cormac's House), topped by the remains of a burial mound. In the centre of Ann Forradh is the Lia Fail or Stone of Destiny, a phallic standing stone which is said to scream or cry out when it comes into contact with a man destined to be king. The word Fal is also used as a poetic synonym for Ireland, and demonstrates the importance of this myth to the concept of the Irish High King. The standing stone was moved 400 feet in 1798 from its original position near the Mound of the Hostages to the centre of the Tara earthworks in honour of men who died during a rebellion here in 1798.

Also of interest are the twin parallel earthen banks in a hollow immediately north of the church, known as An Teach Miodhchuarta or 'the Banqueting Hall'. The parallel banks are over 750 foot long and 75 foot wide and researcher Martin Brennan has noted the hall's north-south alignment with the Mound of the Hostages, marking the position of the midday sun.[16]

Early accounts tell of a huge aisled wooden hall, the interior partitioned elaborately by status, where up to one thousand people gathered for the great Feis at Samhain. Some historians have dismissed these stories, and suggest it is more likely the earthworks formed part of an elaborate ceremonial roadway or avenue leading to the sanctuary itself. Next to the churchyard are earthworks known as Rath na Seanad, the Rath of the Synods, which appears to have been used from the first to third centuries AD from finds of glass, pottery and a Roman lead seal. Two beautiful gold Iron Age torcs (ritual neck ornaments) were discovered here in 1810. They date from around 1000 BC and show the importance of Tara as a place of assembly and the inauguration of the pagan High Kings of Ireland before the arrival of Christianity

Tara is signposted from the N3 road between Dublin and Navan, and there are car parking facilities and a shop at the site.

Select Bibliography

Bede, *A History of the English Church and People* (trans. Leo
  Sherley-Price; Penguin, 1955)
Bord, Janet and Colin, *Mysterious Britain* (Garnstone Press, 1972)
  Earth Rites (Granada, 1982)
  Sacred Waters (Granada, 1985)
Branston, Brian, *The Lost Gods of England* (Thames & Hudson, 1974)
Dames, Michael, *The Silbury Treasure* (Thames & Hudson, 1976)
  Archaic Ireland (Thames & Hudson, 1992)
Devereux, Paul, *Places of Power* (Blandford, 1990)
  Symbolic Landscapes (Gothic Image, 1992)
  Secrets of Ancient and Sacred Places (Blandford, 1992)
Ellis-Davidson, H.R., *Myths and Symbols in Pagan Europe*
  (Manchester University Press, 1988)
  The Lost Beliefs of Northern Europe (Routledge, 1993)
Green, Miranda J., *The Gods of Roman Britain* (Shire, 1983)
  The Gods of the Celts (Alan Sutton, 1986)
  Dictionary of Celtic Myth and Legend (Thames Hudson, 1992)
Hutton, Ronald, *The Pagan Religions of the Ancient British Isles*
  (Blackwell,1991)
McCana, Proinsias, *Celtic Mythology* (Hamlyn, 1970)
Merrifield, Ralph, *The Archaeology of Ritual and Magic* (Batsford,
  1987)
Parker Pearson, M., *Bronze Age Britain* (English Heritage/Batsford
  1993)
Phillips, Guy Ragland, *Brigantia: A Mysteriography* (RKP, 1976)
Powell, T.G.E., *The Celts* (Thames & Hudson 1953)
Reader's Digest, *Folklore, Myths and Legends of Britain* (Reader's
  Digest Association Ltd 1973)
Ross, Anne, *Pagan Celtic Britain* (Routledge & Kegan Paul 1967)
  A Traveller's Guide to Celtic Britain (Routledge & Kegan Paul
  1985)
  The Pagan Celts (Batsford 1970)
Westwood, Jennifer, *Albion* (Paladin/Grafton 1985 and 1987)

Exploring Further

If you have enjoyed this book and wish to find out more about Earth Mysteries, folklore, alternative archaeology and recent developments in the world of archaeology, you can explore further by writing to some of the organizations and magazines in the following list. Some of them specialize in covering one particular area of the British Isles you might visit using this guidebook:

The Ley Hunter, PO Box 92, Penzance, Cornwall TR18 2XL. International Journal of Earth Mysteries and Geomancy.

Fortean Times, The Journal of Strange Phenomena. 20 Paul Street, Frome BA11 IDX. Also publishes *Fortean Studies*, annually, available from editor Steve Moore, 7 Hillend, Shooters Hill, London.

Folklore Journal (publication of the Folklore Society). Membership details from University College London, Gower Street, London WC1E 6BT.

Current Archaeology. Published six times per year. Subscription details available from 9 Nassington Road, London NW3 2TX.

The Centre For English Cultural Tradition And Language (CECTAL). Sheffield University, 9 Shearwood Road, Sheffield S10 2TD. Began life as the Survey of Language and Folklore in 1964 and is now the principal repository for material on all aspects of English Language, folklore and cultural tradition.

Northern Earth. John Billingsley, 10 Jubilee Street, Mytholmroyd, West Yorkshire HX7 5NP. Bi-monthly journal of the Northern Earth Mysteries Group.

Mercian Mysteries. Bob Trubshaw, 2 Cross Hill, Wymeswold, Loughborough LE12 6UJ. Earth Mysteries research in the Midlands.

Meyn Mamvro. Ancient stones and sacred sites in Cornwall, 51 Carn Bosavern, St Just, Penzance TR19 7QX.

References

Introduction

1 Bede, *A History of the English Church and People* (ed. Leo Sherley-Price), Penguin edition, 1986 p. 68 ff.
2 Op. cit., pp. 130-31.
3 Angela Care Evans, *The Sutton Hoo Ship Burial* (British Museum Publications, 1989); *Current Archaeology*, no. 128 (1992).
4 William Chaney. 'Paganism to Christianity in Anglo-Saxon England' (*Harvard Theological Review*, vol. 53, 1960).
5 Prof B. Dickens, 'English Names and Old English Heathenism' (*Essays and Studies of the English Association*, vol. XIX, 1933).
6 Wilfred Bonser, 'Survivals of Paganism in Anglo-Saxon England' (*Transactions of the Birmingham Archaeological Society*, vol. 56, 1932).
7 Miranda Green, *The Gods of Roman Britain* (Shire Publications, 1983).
8 See Christina Hole, *Saints in Folklore* (G. Bell & Sons, 1965), Chapter 3.
9 Stuart Piggott, 'The Sources of Geoffrey of Monmouth' (*Antiquity*, 60, December 1941).
10 D.A. Binchy, 'The Background of Early Irish Literature' (*Studia Hibernica*, 1, 1961).
11 *Historical Memoirs of the City of Armagh* (undated), courtesy of Armagh Cathedral.
12 Bede, op. cit., pp. 126-7.
13 P. Lambrechts, *L'Exaltation de la Tete dans Pensee et dans l'art des Celtes* (Bruges, 1954).
14 T.G.E. Powell, *The Celts* (Thames & Hudson 1983).
15 Hugh H. Franklin, Signposts in Nemetland' (*Wisht Maen Devon Earth Mysteries* magazine, 2, Spring 1994).
16 Bede, op. cit., p. 119.

17 See Anne Ross, *Pagan Celtic Britain* (Routledge & Kegan Paul, 1967), chapter 2 'The Cult of the Head'.
18 David Key, 'Heads of Stone cast new light on Celtic Cult' (*The Independent*, 30 May, 1988).
19 Bonser, op. cit.
20 Ibid.
21 *Antiquity* (December 1968), pp. 167-8.
22 Brian Branston, *The Lost Gods of England* (Thames & Hudson, 1957), p. 77.
23 Eleanor Hull, *Folklore Journal* (September 1927), p. 224.
24 Anne Ross, 'The Divine Hag of the Pagan Celts' in *The Witch Figure*, ed. V. Newall, (Routledge & Kegan Paul, 1973).
25 Anthony Weir and James Jerman, *Images of Lust – Sexual Carvings on Medieval Churches* (Batsford, 1986).
26 Etienne Rynne, 'A Pagan Celtic background for Sheela-na-Gigs' in *Figures from the Past: Studies in Figurative Art in Christian Ireland in Honour of Helen M. Roe* (Glendale Press, 1987).
27 Branston, op. cit., p. 155.
28 Bede, op. cit., pp. 86-7.
29 Barry Cunliffe, *The Celtic World* (McGraw Hill, 1979).
30 Anne Ross, 'The Horned God of the Brigantes' (*Archaeologia Aeliana* , vol. 4/39, 1961).
31 Anne Ross and Ronald Sheridan, *Grotesques and Gargoyles* (David & Charles, 1975).
32 William Anderson, *The Green Man* (HarperCollins, 1990).
33 Kathleen Basford, *The Green Man* (Ipswich, 1978).
34 Kathleen Basford, in *Folklore* (1991, 2, p. 237).
35 R.O.M. & H.M. Carver, 'The Foliate Head in England' (*Folklore*, vol. 78, 1967).
36 See David Clarke, *Strange South Yorkshire* (Sigma Press, 1994).

Northern England

1 David Clarke, 'Screaming Skulls' (*Northern Earth Magazine*, 52, Winter, 1992); Christina Hole, *Haunted England* (Batsford, 1940), Chapter 4; Kathleen Briggs, *A Dictionary of British Folktales*. Part B (Folk Legends), vol. 1, p. 475. (RKP, 1971).
2 J.G. Lockhart, *Curses, Lucks and Talismen* (Geoffrey Bles, 1938).
3 Gerald Findler, *Legends of the Lake Countries* (Dalesman Publishing, 1970).
4 *The English Heritage Guide to Hadrian's Wall* (London, 1987) text by David Breeze; Anne Ross, *Pagan Celtic Britain* (Routledge & Kegan Paul, 1967), Chapter 8.

5   Lindsay Allason-Jones and Bruce McKay, *Coventina's Well: A Shrine on Hadrian's Wall* (Oxford, 1985).
6   C. Coulston and E. J. Phillips, 'Hadrian's Wall West of the Tyne and Carlisle' (CSIR , vol.1, fasc. 6, *Open University Press* 1988).
7   Brian Ashmore, *Senhouse Roman Museum Guide* (Carlisle, 1991); Ross, op. cit.
8   Sidney Jackson, 'Tricephalic Heads from Greetland' (*Antiquity*, December, 1968); *Celtic and other Stone Heads* (Bradford, 1973).
9   John Billingsley, 'Archaic Head Carving in West Yorkshire and Beyond' (Unpublished MA thesis, Centre for English Cultural Tradition and Language, Sheffield University, 1992).
10 Peter Brears, *North Country Folk Art* (Edinburgh, 1989).
11 Edward Armitage, 'Halifax Gibbet Law' (*Halifax Antiquarian Society Transactions*, 1948).
12 T.W. Hanson, *The Story of Old Halifax* (S.R. Publishing, 1968).
13 Andy Roberts, *Ghosts and Legends of Yorkshire* (Jarrold, 1992); Parkingson, *Legends and Traditions of Yorkshire* (1889).
14 M. Barber, *The Trial of the Templars* (Cambridge, 1978).
15 Thomas Middleton, *Legends of Longdendale* (Manchester, 1906).
16 Bede, *Ecclesiastical History*, pp. 180-1.
17 *The Ancient Crypt Church of St Mary Lastingham* (Lastingham 1982).
18 Guy Ragland Phillips, *The Unpolluted God* (Northern Lights, 1987).
19 Janet & Colin Bord, *Earth Rites* (Granada, 1982).
20 Ian Taylor, 'The Burning of Bartle' (*Northern Earth Mysteries*, 30, Spring 1986); Julia Smith, *Fairs, Feasts and Frolics* (Smith Settle, 1989).
21 Ian Taylor, *The Giant of Penhill* (Northern Lights, 1987).
22 Taylor, op. cit.
23 John Billingsley, 'The Lady of the Dark Waters' (*Northern Earth*, 54, Summer 1993).
24 David Joy, *Yorkshire Legends* (Dalesman, 1993).
25 M. Agatha Turner in *Folklore* (vol. 15, 1904).

Central England including East Anglia

1   Francis Pryor, *Flag Fen Bronze Age Excavations*. site guide book obtainable from Fenland Archaeological Trust, Fourth Drove, Fengate, Peterborough PE1 5UR.
2   Francis Pryor, 'Flag Fen' (*Current Archaeology* 137, February/March 1994).

3   Mike Parker Pearson, *Bronze Age Britain* (English
      Heritage/Batsford, 1993).
4   Jacqueline Simpson, ' "Waendel" and the Long Man of
      Wilmington' (*Folklore*, vol. 90, 1979).
5   Jennifer Westwood, *Albion: A Guide to Legendary Britain*
      (Grafton/Paladin, 1987).
6   T.C. Lethbridge, 'The Wandlebury Giants' (*Folklore*,
      December 1956).
7   Ibid.
8   T.A. Ryder, in *The Countryman* (1956), p. 169.
9   *Daily News (London)*, 26 April 1929, quoted in *Folklore
      Society News*, 1993.
10   Bob Trubshaw, 'Hallaton' (*Northern Earth Mysteries*, 41,
      Spring 1990)
11   J.R. Magilton, *The Doncaster District; An Archaeological
      Survey* (Doncaster, 1977).
12   W. Peck, *Topographical Account of the Isle of Axholme* (1815);
      Revd W.B. Stonehouse. *History of the Isle of Axholme* (1839).
13   Ibid.
14   R.C. Turner & C.S. Briggs, 'The Bog Burials of Britain and
      Ireland' in I.M. Stead, J.B. Bourke and D. Brothwell (eds),
      Lindow Man: The Body in the Bog (British Museum, 1986).
15   E.O. James, *Prehistoric Religion* (Thames & Hudson, 1957).
16   Jim White, 'Not so much a mudbath, more a way of life'
      (*The Independent*, 8 January, 1993).
17   Anne Ross and Don Robins, *The Life and Death of a Druid
      Prince* (Rider, 1989).
18   P.V. Glob, *The Bog People* (Faber, 1969).
19   Head of Worsley Man displayed at the Lindow Man exhibition,
      Manchester Museum, 1991.
20   F.B. Pyatt, E.H. Beaumont, D. Lacy, J.R. Magilton & P.C.
      Buckland, 'Non isatis sed Vitrum or, the colour of Lindow Man'
      (*Oxford Journal of Archaeology* 10 (1), 1991).
21   Dr Robert Plot, *The Natural History of Staffordshire* (1686).
22   Doug Pickford, *Myths and Legends of East Cheshire and the
      Moorlands* (Sigma, 1992).
23   *Sir Gawain and the Green Knight*, trans. Brian Stone (Penguin,
      1959); see also John Speirs, *Medieval English Poetry* (Faber,
      1957), Chapter 4.
24   Ibid.
25   Ralph W.V. Elliott, 'Sir Gawain in Staffordshire: A
      Detective Essay in Literary Geography' (*The Times*, 21 May
      1958).
26   John Matthews, *Gawain: Knight of the Goddess* (Aquarian,
      1990), Appendix 3.

27 Quoted in Sir Frank Stenton, 'The Historical Bearing of Place-name Studies: Anglo-Saxon Heathenism' in *Transactions of the Royal Historical Society* (4th series, 23, 1941).
28 Merlin Price, *Folktales and Legends of Warwickshire* (Minimax Books, 1982).
29 Margaret Gelling, Placenames and Anglo-Saxon Paganism' (*University of Birmingham Historical Journal*, vol.8, 1961).

Southern England and Wessex including Guernsey

1 Quoted in Michael Pitts, *Footprints through Avebury* (Stones Print, 1985).
2 Aubrey Burl, *Prehistoric Avebury* (Yale University Press, 1979).
3 Michael Dames, *The Silbury Treasure* (Thames & Hudson, 1976).
4 Paul Devereux, *Symbolic Landscapes* (Gothic Image, 1992).
5 David Keys, 'Godmanchester's Temple of the Sun' (*New Scientist*, 23 March 1991).
6 Ralph Merrifield, *The Archaeology of Ritual and Magic* (Batsford, 1987).
7 Quoted in Anne Ross and Richard Feachem, 'Heads Baleful and Benign', in Miket & Burgess (eds) *Between and Beyond the Walls* (Edinburgh, 1984).
8 Bede, *Ecclesiastical History*, op. cit., p. 87.
9 Gwyn Jones and Thomas Jones (trans.), *The Mabinogion* (Everyman, 1949).
10 Keith Parfitt, 'Excavations at Mill Hill, Deal' (*Kent Archaeological Review*, 101, Autumn 1990); Dr Ian Stead, 'Iron Age Burial in Deal' (*British Museum* magazine, Summer 1990).
11 Anne Ross, *Pagan Celtic Britain* (Routledge & Kegan Paul, 1967).
12 Anne Ross, talk on *Celtic Landscapes*, Ley Hunter Moot, Wales, September 1991.
13 Keith Parfitt, 'The Deal Man' (*Current Archaeology*, vol. 9, 1986).
14 T. D. Kendrick, *The Archaeology of the Channel Islands* (1928).
15 Barbara Mannox, St Andrew's, *Hornchurch; A Guide* (undated).
16 S. Palmer, 'Uffington: White Horse Hill Project' (*Archaeological News* (newsletters of the Oxford Archaeological Unit), vol. 18, 1990).
17 *The Ley Hunter* (120, Midwinter 1993-4).
18 William Chaney, *The Cult of Kingship in Anglo-Saxon* England (Manchester University Press, 1957).

19 Sir Frank Stenton, op. cit.
20 Jacqueline Simpson, ' "Waendel" and the Long Man of Wilmington' in *Folklore* (vol. 90, 1979).
21 Peter Underwood, The Ghost Hunters (Hale, 1988).
22 Jennifer Westwood, Albion (Paladin/Grafton, 1987); *Folklore, Myths and Legends of Britain* (Reader's Digest, 1971).
23 Peter Underwood, *A Gazetteer of British Ghosts* (Souvenir Press, 1971).
24 Ibid.
25 A. & C. Cowley and Alan Cleaver (eds), *Strange Berkshire* (Strange Folklore Society, 1986).

South-west England

1   James Campbell (ed), *The Anglo-Saxons* (Phaidon, 1982).
2   Barry Cunliffe and M.G. Fulford, 'Bath and the Rest of Wessex' (CSIR , vol. 2, Open University Press, 1982); Ian Richmond and J.M.C. Toynbee, 'The Temple of Sulis-Minerva at Bath' (*Journal of Roman Studies*, 1955).
3   A.T. Fear, 'Bladud: The Flying King of Bath' (*Folklore*, vol. 103, 1993).
4   John S. Udal, *Notes and Queries* (4th Series, 1872).
5   Frank Smyth, 'The Skulls that Screamed' (T*he Unexplained*, vol. 8, issue 85, 1982).
6   'Strange Stories & Amazing Facts' (*Readers Digest*, 1975).
7   J. H. Bettey, 'The Cerne Abbas Giant: The Documentary Evidence (*Antiquity*, LV, 1982)
8   Ibid.
9   Jeremy Harte, *Cuckoo Pounds and Singing Barrows* (Dorset Natural History and Historical Society, 1986).
10 Stuart Piggott, 'The Cerne Abbas Giant' (*Antiquity*, vol. 12, 1938 and vol. 15, 1940).
11 Harte, op. cit.
12 M. & L. Quiller-Couch, *Ancient and Holy Wells of Cornwall* (London. 1894).
13 Quiller-Couch, op. cit.
14 Paul Devereux, *Places of Power* (Blandford, 1990).
15 See Janet & Colin Bord, *Earth Rites* (Granada, 1982).
16 Homer Sykes, *Once A Year: Some Traditional British Customs* (Gordon Fraser, 1977).
17 'Wistman's Wood' in 'Wisht Maen' (*Devon Earth Mysteries* magazine, 1, Winter, 1993).
18 Theo Brown, 'The Black Dog in Devon' (*Report of Transactions of the Devonshire Asociation*, vol. xci, 1959).

19   Ruth St Leger-Gordon, *The Witchcraft and Folklore of Dartmoor* (Bell, 1975).
20   Sabine Baring-Gould, *A Book of Dartmoor* (Wildwood House, 1982).
21   Ibid.
22   *Folklore*, vol. 61 1950, p. 153.
23   Baring-Gould, op. cit.
24   *Wookey Hole Caves & Mill Guidebook* (undated).
25   Hawkes, et al., 'Romano-British Cemetery in the fourth chamber of Wookey Hole Cave' (*Proceedings of the University of Bristol Speleological Society*, vol. 15, 1978).
26   Ibid.

Scotland including the Isle of Man

1   Duncan Fraser, *Highland Perthshire* (Montrose 1958).
2   David Clarke, 'The Hag's House' (*The Ley Hunter*, 120, Midwinter 1993/1994); Anne Ross, *Celtic Landscapes* talk at the Ley Hunter Moot, North Wales, September 1991.
3   Julia Smith, 'A Walk around Killin' (*Northern Earth*, 58, Summer 1994); Fraser, op. cit.
4   Marc Alexander, *Enchanted Britain* (Arthur Baker, 1971).
5   Ian Findlay, *Columba* (Richard Drew, 1979).
6   Bede, *Ecclesiastical History*, op. cit., pp. 146-7.
7   A.O. & M.O. Anderson, *The Life of St Columba* (Thomas Nelson, 1961).
8   Guy Ragland Phillips, *The Unpolluted God* (Northern Lights, 1989).
9   Aubrey Burl, *The Stone Circles of the British Isles* (Yale University Press, 1981, p. 148-9).
10   *Folklore Journal* (vol 6, 1895) p. 164.
11   Ibid, p. 152.
12   Margaret Killip, *The Folklore of the Isle of Man* (Batsford, 1975).
13   A.W. Moore, *The Folklore of the Isle of Man* (S.R. Publishing, 1971).
14   Moore, op. cit.
15   Ibid.
16   Killip, op. cit.
17   Ian Richmond and O.G.S. Crawford, 'The British Section of the Ravenna Cosmography' (*Archaeologia*, 1949) pp. 1-50.
18   C.A. Ralegh-Radford, Locus Maponi (*Transactions of the Dumfries and Galloway Natural History Society*, 31, 1953-4).

19 Ian Richmond, 'Two Celtic Heads in Stone from Corbridge, Northumberland' in D.B. Harden (ed.), *Dark Age Britain* (London 1955).

20 Lewis Spence, *The Minor Traditions of British Mythology* (Benjamin Bloom, 1972), Chapter 1; Gertrude Godden, 'The Sanctuary of Mourie' (*Folklore*, 1891).

21 Ibid.

22 Ross, op. cit; Ronald Hutton, *The Pagan Religions of the Ancient British Isles* (Blackwell, 1992).

23 Alasdair Alpin McGregor, *The Peat Fire Flame* (Ettrick Press, 1937).

24 McGregor, op. cit; Anne Ross, 'Gently Dip, But Not Too Deep' (*The Listener*, 30 August, 1962.

25 Gerald Warner, *Tales of the Scottish Highlands* (Shepheard-Walwyn, 1982).

26 Anne Ross, 'A Story from Vatersay' (*Scottish Studies*, 5, 1961).

27 Anne Ross, 'Severed Heads in Wells: An Aspect of the Well Cult' (*Scottish Studies*, 6, 1962).

28 Brian Branston, *Gods of the North* (Thames & Hudson, 1990).

Wales

1   Quoted in Anne Ross, *The Pagan Celts* (Batsford, 1986); and Lesley Macinnes, *Anglesey: A Guide to Ancient and Historic Sites on the Isle of Anglesey* (Cadw Welsh Historic Monuments, 1989).

2   Sir Cyril Fox, *A Find of the Early Iron Age from Llyn Cerrig Bach* (Anglesey, Cardiff 1946).

3   Miranda Green, *A Dictionary of Celtic Myth and Legend* (Thames & Hudson, 1992).

4   Anne Ross and Don Robins, *The Life and Death of a Druid Prince* (Rider, 1989).

5   Miranda Green, 'Celtic Symbolism at Roman Caerleon' (*The Bulletin of the Board of Celtic Studies*, vol. 31, November 1984).

6   George Boon, 'The Shrine of the Head, Caerwent' in George Boon and M.J. Lewis (eds), *Welsh Antiquity* (National Museum of Wales 1976).

7   Miranda Green, *The Gods of the Celts* (Alan Sutton, 1986).

8   Wilfrid Bonser, 'Survivals of Paganism in Anglo-Saxon England' (*Transactions of the Birmingham Historical Society*, vol. 56, 1932).

9   E.C. Cawte, *Ritual Animal Disguise* (Folklore Society/Brewer & Co., 1978).

10 Barnett Field, 'The Hooden Horse of East Kent' (*Folklore* 78, 1967).

11 Geoffrey Ashe, *The Mythology of the British Isles* (Methuen, 1990).
12 Paul Devereux, *Places of Power* (Blandford, 1990).
13 Roger Worsley, *The Pembrokeshire Explorer*; Coastal Cottages of Pembrokeshire (1988).
14 Francis Jones, *The Holy Wells of Wales* (University of Wales Press, 1954).
15 W.Y. Evans-Wentz, *The Fairy Faith in Celtic Countries* (Colin Smythe 1977).
16 Jones, op. cit.
17 Lewis Spence, *The Minor Traditions of British Mythology* (Benjamin Bloom, 1972).
18 Joan P. Alcock, 'Celtic Water Cults in Roman Britain' (*Archaeological Journal*, vol. 122, 1965).
19 John Rhys, 'Sacred Wells in Wales' (*Folklore Journal*, 1893).
20 *The Llandaff Monthly* (magazine of Llandaff Cathedral), March 1994, personal communication.
21 Jones, op. cit.
22 Jones, op. cit.
23 R. C. Turner, 'Boggarts, Bogles and Sir Gawain and the Green Knight: Lindow Man and the Oral Tradition', in I.M. Stead, J.B. Bourke and D. Brothwell (eds), *Lindow Man: The Body in the Bog* (British Museum, 1986).
24 Anne Ross, 'Severed Heads in Wells: An Aspect of the Well Cult' (*Scottish Studies*, 6 1962).

Ireland

1 See Ronald Hutton, *The Pagan Religions of the Ancient British Isles* (Blackwell, 1991); and Proinsias McCana, *Celtic Mythology* (Hamlyn, 1970).
2 Edith M. Guest, 'Ballyvourney and its Sheela-na-Gig' (*Folklore*, vol. 48, 1937).
3 Stella Cherry, *A Guide to Sheela-na-Gigs* (National Museum of Ireland, 1992).
4 Helen Hickey, *Images of Stone* (Blackstaff Press, 1976).
5 Historian Thomas Barron, quoted in Hickey, op. cit.
6 Claire O'Kelly, *Concise Guide to New Grange* (Cork 1991).
7 Quoted in Simon Welfare and John Fairley, *Arthur C. Clarke's Mysterious World* (Fontana/Collins, 1980); see also Jon Patrick, 'Midwinter Sunrise at New Grange' (*Nature*, vol. 249, June 1974) and M.J. Kelly, *New Grange* (London, 1982).
8 Martin Brennan, *The Stars and the Stones* (Thames & Hudson, 1983).

9   Michael Dames, *Archaic Ireland* (Thames & Hudson, 1992);
    McCana, op. cit.
10 Proinsias McCana, *Celtic Mythology* (Hamlyn, 1970); *Gerald of*
    Wales, The History and Topography of Ireland (Penguin, 1982).
11 Dames, op. cit.
12 Peter Harbinson, *Guide to the National Monuments in the*
    Republic of Ireland (Gill and McMillan, 1970).
13 Chris Lynn, 'Navan Fort - Home of Gods and Goddesses?'
    (*Archaeology Ireland*, 23, 1993).
14 Elizabeth Hickey, *The Legend of Tara* (Dundalgan Press, 1988).
15 Harbinson, op. cit.
16 Brennan, op. cit.

Index